T0250027

Information System Audit

The digitalization of companies is a recurrent topic of conversation for managers. Companies are forced to evolve at least as fast as their competitors. They have to review their organization, their processes, and their way of working. This also concerns auditors in terms of their audit strategy and working methods.

Digitalization is the tip of the iceberg that represents the increasing reliance on information technology of the company's information system. Companies have seen new competitors succeed with a digital approach, competitors that have opened new markets or new ways of interacting with their customers, and all business processes can be digitalized.

In this new paradigm, auditors have to renew themselves too. Long gone are the days of auditors specializing in one technique, like financial auditors or IT auditors. This makes it a phenomenal opportunity for auditing to renew itself, embracing the vision of the company's information system: long live the information system auditors!

This book proposes you to go step by step from a common understanding of our history of auditing to gradually defining and justifying the impacts of digitalization on the audit strategy and the preparation of audits.

Security, Audit and Leadership Series

Series Editor: Dan Swanson, Dan Swanson and Associates, Ltd., *Winnipeg, Manitoba, Canada.*

The *Security, Audit and Leadership Series* publishes leading-edge books on critical subjects facing security and audit executives as well as business leaders. Key topics addressed include Leadership, Cybersecurity, Security Leadership, Privacy, Strategic Risk Management, Auditing IT, Audit Management and Leadership

Say What!? Communicate with Tact and Impact: What to say to get results at any point in an audit
Ann M. Butera

Auditing Information and Cyber Security Governance:
A Controls-Based Approach
Robert E. Davis

The Security Leader's Communication Playbook: Bridging the Gap between Security and the Business
Jeffrey W. Brown

Modern Management and Leadership: Best Practice Essentials with CISO/CSO Applications
Mark Tarallo

Rising from the Mailroom to the Boardroom: Unique Insights for Governance, Risk, Compliance and Audit Leaders
Bruce Turner

Operational Auditing: Principles and Techniques for a Changing World (Second Edition)
Hernan Murdock

CyRM^SM: Mastering the Management of Cybersecurity
David X Martin

For more information about this series, please visit: https://www.routledge.com/Internal-Audit-and-IT-Audit/book-series/CRCINTAUDITA

Information System Audit

How to Control the Digital Disruption

Philippe Peret

CRC Press
Taylor & Francis Group
Boca Raton London New York

CRC Press is an imprint of the
Taylor & Francis Group, an **informa** business

First Edition published 2023
by CRC Press
6000 Broken Sound Parkway NW, Suite 300, Boca Raton, FL 33487-2742

and by CRC Press
4 Park Square, Milton Park, Abingdon, Oxon, OX14 4RN

CRC Press is an imprint of Taylor & Francis Group, LLC

© 2023 Philippe Peret

Library of Congress Cataloging-in-Publication Data
Names: Peret, Philippe, author.
Title: Information system audit : how to control the digital disruption / Philippe Peret.
Identifiers: LCCN 2022001328 (print) | LCCN 2022001329 (ebook) | ISBN 9781032136165 (hardback) | ISBN 9781032136172 (paperback) | ISBN 9781003230137 (ebook)
Subjects: LCSH: Information technology--Auditing. | Management information systems--Auditing.
Classification: LCC HD30.2 .P466 2022 (print) | LCC HD30.2 (ebook) | DDC 657/.458--dc23/eng/20220113
LC record available at https://lccn.loc.gov/2022001328
LC ebook record available at https://lccn.loc.gov/2022001329

ISBN: 978-1-032-13616-5 (hbk)
ISBN: 978-1-032-13617-2 (pbk)
ISBN: 978-1-003-23013-7 (ebk)

DOI: 10.1201/9781003230137

Typeset in Sabon
by KnowledgeWorks Global Ltd.

Dedication

To my son, I love you so much.

Contents

About the Author

Philippe Peret received his Master's Degree in Business Administration from Toulouse School of Management in France. He is an Information Systems Engineer with a major in Information Systems Audit from the CNAM University in Paris, France.

His career has allowed him to develop a vision at the crossroads of the financial/accounting world and the IT world. He is co-author of the SDMS21™ information system management methodology and developed CIMCO, a computer-aided software engineering platform. CISA certified, he has worked as an external and corporate auditor and performed financial, IT, legal and forensic engagements (e.g., KPMG, Avon Cosmetics, Tyco International).

Other book (French and English):

- *More Haste? Less Speed!—Effective IT Project Management—* ISBN 978-2-9557622-0-2

Preface

> Nature in the whole universe had only one aspect, called chaos. It was a coarse and confused mass.
>
> Ovid, Metamorphoses (Book I—Origin of the World)

Once upon a time, Enron was an enterprise renowned for its strategy and financial results. Enron had a new, modern vision of energy management at the end of the 20th century. From its core business of gas trading, the company became the world's largest broker of gas and electricity in the 1990s. Enron denigrates its competitors, because they are stuck with an obsolete and backward vision of the energy market.

Enron announces billions of dollars in profits but pays almost no dividends. Yet dividends are the usual primary evidence that reported profits are real. Enron and its auditing firm share an enthusiasm for an accounting technique called mark-to-market. It allows future revenues to be recognized before they materialize in the bank. Its accounting is extremely complex and therefore difficult to understand. It uses various techniques to hide losses or turn them into profits. But at the end of 2001, Enron exploded in a few months.

His fall brought about the fall of his auditing firm, Arthur Andersen. No one in the profession imagined that this audit firm could be dragged down by the fall of Enron and collapse with it. At the time, it was one of the five largest auditing firms in the world, with 85,000 employees and a history of over 90 years. A scandal due to a problem of mastery of the figures in the financial reports by the leaders, incompetence of the analysts, greed of the investors, and negligence of the auditors.

Once upon a time, an enterprise was renowned for its strategy and financial results. It had a new, modern, and conquering vision of the market. Tyco International Ltd. is a very large conglomerate, which in the 1990s and early 2000s compulsively buys companies. It transforms low-margin companies into profit-generating companies. Tyco is present in very different sectors, such as valves or security, with more than 240,000 employees in December 2001. Its sales increased from $95 million to over $4.5 billion in less than ten years, from 1992 to 2001.

This winning strategy is appreciated by investors, despite warning signs of a future disaster such as higher than expected dividends paid despite revenues falling more than 20% short of expectations.

In June 2001, Tyco's president was indicted on more than 30 counts, including falsification of accounts and tax evasion. It is a scandal due to a problem of fraud of the company's management, incompetence of the analysts, naivety of the investors and negligence of the auditors.

All this suggested that the functioning of the business world was flawed and needed to be cleaned up. So, in response to these scandals, as in previous scandals of the 20th century, reforms are requested, particularly in the world of finance and auditing. It is with a very simplistic vision that these reforms are requested because they mainly concern financial documents, their annexes, and the related flows.

This vision is oriented toward financial techniques, as if the figures appeared ex nihilo without any correlation with the reality of the activities. The external auditors who certify the accounts, under pressure from the media and investors, announce that the scandal is unique and that an internal investigation has been carried out, which has enabled them to modify their working methods and thus avoid the recurrence of such errors. Internal auditors are also reorganizing. They are changing their working methods to reassure investors and to reduce the costs of external auditors' services. Here are many problems of the perversion of the modern financial world! Really? Do we have a short memory or are we too naive to believe that these scandals are specific to the 20th and 21st centuries?

Let's travel quickly through time and stop at the 17th century. Why the 17th century because there are also representative examples from antiquity to the 19th century? Simply because we have an example that includes most of the protagonists of the examples mentioned above: Investors, businessmen, control authorities, and a stock exchange.

Once upon a time, there was a company, also renowned for its strategy and financial results. It had a clear vision of conquering exotic products for the European market. It had the capacity to supply these products at lower prices and in greater quantities. It is the Dutch East India Company.

Since the first known commercial relations of antiquity, merchants met in person with the sovereigns and negotiated advantages to trade from the country, such as privileged customs duties, low taxes, equal rights with the locals, or the free practice of their religion. India, which abounds in products that Africa, Asia Minor, and Europe do not have, is another perfect example. The installation of trading posts in India made the fortune of the Arabs, the Portuguese, and then the Dutch.

If we take India's trading posts, companies are usually allowed to trade subject to paying, among other things, taxes on the goods exported. Some rulers, more "professional" than others, reserve the right to control that the company actually and accurately pays the taxes due on the exports made.

To do this, they inspect, or audit as we would say today, the trade statements and warehouses of exporting companies. Knowing the loading capacity by type of vessel, it is easy to verify the consistency of the figures between the purchases of goods and the vessels that have been loaded in the port for a given period. It is then enough to calculate the amount due and check whether it has been paid. (We will not discuss here the fraud techniques associated with the loading of vessels, i.e., the means of thwarting these checks.)

Even if financial statements are available, it is still necessary to physically check the reality of these figures. The further away from the parent company, the greater the risk that the information is false.

The States General of The Hague, which nowadays would correspond geographically to Holland, invited the various companies trading with the Indies to join in a single company. This company received extensive immunities and privileges. The Dutch East India Company, "Verenigde Oost Indische Compagnie," was created with a capital of 6,300,000 florins. It began operations on March 20, 1602.

India's trade was thus centralized, expressly declared a state affair, and placed under the supervision and protection of the government, without interfering with private investors. Although it was endowed with substantial capital at the time of its creation, it faced the Spanish-Portuguese power that had been established for more than a century in a remote region that was little known to the Dutch.

To evaluate the risk of lack of controls, it should be remembered that the establishment of direct relations between Europe and India considerably lowers the purchase prices of goods from that region, almost by half. In addition, the cargo of a single ship of Indian products in the port of Amsterdam exceeds in value and quantity what the largest caravans from Asia can carry, all the while being much faster.

A first charter is thus signed. It granted the privilege of trade with India for 21 years to the Dutch East India Company. Later charters also limited it to short periods. This certainly reminded the Company of its dependence and responsibility toward the government, but above all, the renewal of these charters cost the Company considerable sums each time. Moreover, in times of war or other difficult times, the state often borrowed from the company.

The administration of the company is in the hands of 60 directors in the metropolis. They are elected by the shareholders and divided into six chambers which sit in Amsterdam and five other cities. The care of the general affairs is entrusted to a committee of 17 persons, chosen among the directors. This committee of directors determines, in particular, the number of ships to be shipped, the schedule of departures, and the destinations. The chambers apply these general instructions. The company is operated in the name of the States General of The Hague.

As communications with India took time, authority locally was exercised by a council presided over by a governor general in Batavia (present-day Jakarta), the Raad van Indië, but for the most important matters, the agreement of the directors of the Netherlands was necessary. In India, the company organized itself with an army, strongholds, a cartographic and hydrographic service, and an administration.

This administration, a kind of financial department, manages all the financial information of the company. Its budget is larger than that of the States General in The Hague. An accounting is done locally in India and financial information is sent to Europe.

However, the term accounting should not mislead us. It is an exaggeration of our current modes of operation because the financial organization is limited. Its objective is to be able to provide financial results that are presented annually to the General Assembly in The Hague. Moreover, these results only include the company's assets and debts in Europe and ignore those in the Indies.

The company therefore has the characteristics of a multinational corporation as we know them today. It issues shares and bonds and is in countries that are, for it, on the other side of the world.

The company accomplished a great deal during the first 21 years of its first charter. The dividends paid to shareholders give a good idea of the financial amounts involved. Until 1720, profits never fell below 15%. On average, they were 20% over the period. In some years, they reached up to 50%.

The price of the 2,100 shares increases by 600% to 18,000 guilders from their nominal value of 3,000 guilders. It succeeded in enriching its shareholders. The Amsterdam stock exchange is more concerned with the company than the States General itself. It was interested not only in transactions in the company's shares, but also in all transactions in the exotic products carried by its ships.

All commanders of squadrons or isolated ships are required to provide the government of the States General with a report on their voyage and on the situation in India. The government may, at any time, take cognizance of the company's budget. However, the supervision of the States General in The Hague over the company's possessions was not regular. It is all the less so because business is going well, and fortunes are being made in Holland.

Bad habits are taken, and more particularly three:

1. The keeping of disjointed accounts between the metropolis and India,
2. The non-representativeness of the figures regarding the business done, and
3. The lack of on-site controls and of follow-up of the figures reported.

The company's management has the possibility to hide the real profits or losses from the shareholders.

With more than a century of activity behind it, the company had an immense reputation thanks to the regularity of its very good results. But the business deteriorated for various reasons, such as competition with the English, corruption of the local management, and the greed of investors, but more particularly because of the lack of control by the States General.

The first signs of decadence are visible after the peace of Utrecht in 1713. From 1780 onward, the deficit increased every year. It could no longer be hidden. When the difficulties are known, when the company no longer pays dividends, only then do the flaws of the organization come to light. Despite the company's efforts to keep its management secret, the affair breaks out. Increased competition, inadequate financial policy, and international politics led to its downfall in 1799.

Alex Berenson's point about recent scandals in his book *The Number* applies to all scandals, like the Dutch East India Company:

> the most important question now is not what happened at WorldCom or Enron or Arthur Andersen or any individual company or accounting firm. It is why the system as a whole failed, why accounting and financial reporting at so many companies became criminally shoddy.

We could simply refer to human nature and we would be right. Many studies on criminality are regularly conducted. We will mention, if necessary, the risks of errors, including voluntary ones. We will rather dwell on the non-human causes, such as the imperfections of work methods or processes, the rigidity of procedures, or the technical capacities of the means used.

In the previous examples, the actors react according to numerical information. The figures allow them to appreciate the use of the funds. The context makes it easier for them to understand the figures and to understand the forecasts or projections of these figures. Since the company's management provides them with strong arguments, they seem reliable.

It is all about information and it is the whole of this information that interests us as much as its perimeter and its validity, as well as its transformations or its suppression. Some of this information concerns either the internal functioning of the company such as productivity or commercial policy, or the consolidation of information for communication to third parties such as investors.

The information communicated may be correct or incorrect and may or may not accurately represent the company's operations. If it is incorrect, it may be because of incorrect internal information or because of incorrect transcription of this data before dissemination. We will mainly deal with the internal data of the company and if it is useful, we will make the link with the communicated data, which consolidate and synthesize the internal data.

Which actors within the company exchange information and how do they process it? Companies are organized around departments. Each department has a function, a mission, and working methods.

Humanly speaking, everyone tends to privilege his or her own square. Feudalities appear with their software, their data, and their good practices without which, they could not function. To produce more, such as more resumes processed during recruitment, or to reduce the costs of a workstation, information technology (IT) is put to good use. Software and hardware are becoming more and more flexible. They adapt to the needs of management.

This concern for financial efficiency leads to quite siloed operation of these departments. They develop communication habits to ensure their continuity. Knowledge and information are associated with the notion of power. The difficulty in getting software from different departments to communicate is only a reflection of the quality of communication between these same departments. It is amusing to note that even if the company does not solve its organizational problems, IT nevertheless offers solutions.

The first solution proposed to share information starts with the notion of data warehouse. Schematically, the data warehouse consists in putting all the company's data in the same place and looking for answers to questions and even sometimes without knowing the questions.

This approach assumes that the data used by the different departments are identical, because they would have the same name. In practice, this is not possible for three main reasons:

1. Data have the same name, but do not describe the same thing,
2. Data have the same name, refer to the same thing, but do not describe it in the same way, and
3. Data have the same name, refer to the same thing, describe it in broadly the same way, but manage it differently.

The holy grail of making the data from different departments consistent is a real headache, bordering on a financial abyss. Faced with this real difficulty of implementation, the idea has changed. There are two possible solutions: The first is to reduce the number of applications in the application portfolio and the second is to restrict the scope of the analysis.

Reducing the portfolio of applications can be easily achieved with the implementation of an Enterprise Resource Planning (ERP) system for instance. The objective of this is to replace one, or more software applications used in the various business processes. Indirectly, this allows the transfer of data used by the different software packages to the new software.

Reducing the application portfolio is also done by consolidating applications within the same group. Instead of using different applications that provide equivalent services, only one is selected to replace all others.

For example, your company is a multinational which, through acquisitions of other companies, finds itself with several ERP packages such as a mixture of JDEdwards, SAP, Oracle for main applications. The IT department then studies the opportunity to retain only one software package for all regions or sites, or only one software package per size of sites, for example.

International companies are the result of mergers and acquisitions. In addition to the management software packages, other software is added within the company. The larger the number of applications, the larger the maintenance budget and the greater the risk not only of diverging application developments but also of losing expertise. Consolidating the portfolio indirectly consolidates the data.

The second solution consists in reducing the scope of the data analysis. This solution consists of working on data from one or possibly two directions and is called "Datamart." The job of data analysts is to find nuggets. After discovering easily accessible veins (gold is very often found by gold panning), they turn to more difficult veins and then dig mines. For this, the technique must evolve.

Just as gold miners and miners work with methods and tools, data analysts also use methods and techniques to identify information in data. They use statistics, models, algorithms, and artificial intelligence, with all the risks that this can entail.

Computer data are also a subject of interest for auditors. They support or confirm facts, it can be evidence, and their analysis can identify errors, trends, and ultimately potential or proven risks. However, auditors face, on the one hand, the same problems as gold diggers, the data are not structured, potentially inconsistent, and not necessarily reliable, and on the other hand, the same risks of making incorrect analyses.

But auditors have an advantage over gold diggers: They know what they are looking for! They can go back upstream to the elements that make up or contribute to the figures in the financial results. Auditing covers the notions of inspection, verification, and control, which can be found in the earliest traces of writing, particularly those of economic exchanges.

Today, with the increasing complexity of identifying and verifying these numbers, audit firms are using IT to form an opinion on financial results and their production. Their two main concerns are general IT controls and segregation of duties. General IT controls ensure that the production or operation part of the IT system complies with the state of the art. Separation of functions provides a complementary view to the analyses performed in the case of manual processes.

The IT audit was designed to meet the needs of accounting professionals and enable them to fulfill their legal obligations, such as the few IT controls present in the initial version of Section 404 of the Sarbanes-Oxley Act of July 30, 2002. All subsequent efforts to change this situation without calling it into question are temporary solutions, such as adding additional IT controls, which do not call into question the control of financial auditors over these new tools. This position is hardly tenable with the digitalization of business processes, including the generation of new revenues from the recovered data.

Let's look at the situation in reverse. To do this, we will firstly look at the different approaches used to develop IT auditing and, secondly, given the limits of these approaches, analyze the needs at the beginning of the 21st century to identify new ones.

What are the main options in this book for the evolution of IT auditing?

At first glance, we can classify them into three categories:

- Moving from the notion of IT to the notion of information systems,
- Linking IT risks to business risks, and
- Creating services around the company's operational functions.

Since the mid-80s, audit firms have been renaming their IT audit services and using the terms "information systems" or "IT risks" for example. New services are offered in relation to security. They include the information security policy or the adequacy between the company's strategy and the IT strategy.

Major communication and change management efforts are being made to promote these new services both to companies and within the audit firms themselves. And yes, this change is also a change for the technicians of the figure. Directors and managers know little or nothing about IT, they do not see the relevance of these new services unless they have had a bad experience with IT investments. Investments cannot support the turnover or the changes in activity (expansion or reduction of activities) as it was planned.

Another approach is to link the various aspects of IT to the impact on the company. Even if from a technical point of view the audit identifies problems, it is still difficult to make non-IT professionals aware of the importance of an IT problem without having made the link with its financial consequences for the company. IT auditors have a hard time assessing the impact of poor IT control on the business. By reflex, they quantify the risk of the control deficiency from a technical point of view and stop there. This difficulty is due, on the one hand, to the fact that IT auditors are trained purely in IT, without any distance from the business, and, on the other hand, to the fact that financial auditors are trained purely in finance, without any distance from the IT business.

A final approach is to propose operational audits. These operational audits are similar in spirit to "financial" audits. Their objective is also to analyze an operational process, other than the financial one, but using the fact that all or part of the operational processes are supported by applications and IT systems and thus to audit the computerized/automated controls. In the example of an ERP system such as SAP or Oracle, the operational audit is the only one that offers a complete approach of a process from the initiating events to the results in the financial module.

Renewing the audit. A new approach that has recently emerged is to focus first on risks, both business and IT risks. This approach presents the same constraints as the previous ones. How can IT risks exist ex nihilo, i.e., without any link to a risk for the company?

This approach is inherently biased. IT is perceived as a necessity, not to say an inevitability, by non-computer experts. Identifying the specificities of IT allows these non-computer experts not to worry about IT, to leave it to the specialists. If IT people can make the connection between a problem labeled "IT" and a risk to the company, then these non-IT people will argue to minimize the impact to reduce the issue. How is it still possible in the 2000s to ask whether IT is a cost center or a profit center as it was done in the previous century? Who will either think not using any IT to run their business nowadays?

It is time to think differently, that is to say neither as a financial auditor, nor as an IT auditor. To think like a financial auditor is to focus on the regulatory part necessary for investors, therefore like a number cruncher. To think like an IT auditor is to see the world through IT technology for the sake IT technology. But between these two visions, we have all the company's management, which also look at the company's operations differently.

Thinking differently means thinking about information and its processing, i.e., the information system. Information and processing may or may not be computerized. To think about auditing information systems, we must first recall the fundamentals of auditing. Then, we need to clarify the difference between IT and information systems. From there, we will have a common understanding of the similarities and differences between auditing, IT auditing and, of course, the audit of information systems. This is the subject of the first chapters.

The information system is complex and evolves at the pace of the company. However, just because the company's information system is modified does not mean that the types of risks are also modified. In the following chapters, we will focus on the risks that impact the information system, independently of the company's strategy, which will vary the probability of their occurrence. We therefore have a complex information system, many risks, and various controls to check. How can we make it simple to have a reasonable assurance of the reliability of the information and therefore a reasonable assurance? The definition of controls, their selection, implementation, and monitoring are a necessary, but not sufficient condition for success. For these controls to remain relevant, their definition, implementation, and monitoring must be verified at regular intervals. Controls must adapt to changes in the company's processes. Dedicated chapters propose an approach for grouping controls by confidence level and for understanding their interactions. It also discusses how the tools and techniques proposed by professional auditing organizations can be used.

It is not appropriate to treat all controls with equal attention. Checking all the controls is not feasible in a short period of time and is neither relevant nor productive. The more checks that need to be done, the greater the cost of auditing. The deficiency of some controls is more serious for the company than others. These should be audited first. The last chapters explain how to implement the associated audit strategy.

Therefore, in the next chapter, we will discuss the need for regulation of marketplaces for their proper functioning as well as the main characteristics and obligations of the audit, both with respect to accountants and to other company departments. We will not consider, except to mention them, the actors outside the company who profit from a large financial literature and standards. We will focus on best practices and their evolution to better benefit from them in the audit of information systems.

We then will have a closer look at all the information required to audit, in the second chapter. If we reduce this information to financial management, the audit will be financial. If we focus on operational information, the audit will be operational and so on. Departments communicate with each other and information is exchanged, so before deciding what to audit, it is necessary to define the information system and the areas at risk. We will show that the computerization of the company's information system influences the historical methods of financial auditing and risk management, including financial risks.

The COSO Framework, in 2003, defines the information system by:

> the set of activities, involving people, processes, data and/or technology, which enable the organization to obtain, generate, use and communicate transactions and information to maintain accountability and measure and review the entity's performance or progress towards achievement of objectives.

It is now common practice during mergers or acquisitions to audit the IT processes and infrastructure, and if done well with an information system vision. Regardless of the sector of activity, the costs of integrating IT systems, on the one hand, and the risks of changes in working methods and processes, on the other hand, can justify stopping an acquisition or merger project.

Based on the presentations of audit and information systems in these two introductory chapters, the third one describes the audit of information systems. When applied to a company, it will be called an information system audit or IS audit. What is the relationship between the information systems audit and the other audits we are used to, such as financial audits, operational audits, or IT audits? How to use the information systems audit and for what results?

Chapter 1

Audit

If one knows the reasons why things are as they are, he can better fore-see how they are likely to be in the years ahead.

John L. Carey, "History of Public Accounting"
foreword from James Don Edwards

1.1 LEGACY

John L. Carey's quote above summarizes the route used to understand the business of a company and assume or expect what it would be in the following years. The only piece missing in this smart sentence is about the understanding of the current technological trends and their impacts, for us the current information technology (IT) trends. Before focusing on IT trends and the need for an information system audit strategy, let's all agree on our past, our audit past.

Information about commercial transactions has been recorded, annotated, controlled, and tracked since ancient times. Merchants record amounts, quantities, and types of products and with whom. They can find information they would otherwise have forgotten or check that a delivery corresponds to an order. Control has always been present, but it is the transformation of exchanges that brought the need to formalize the way of controlling. Products against products, then products against gold or silver (mainly), then products against bills of exchange, then exchanges of shares and bonds: Fairs have changed to become financial marketplaces.

Richard Brown goes back to 4500 BC to indicate that the Babylonian Empire was the first to have bookkeeping [RBR]. Since this period of book-keeping, time has passed to arrive at the notion of accounting we refer to now-adays. The term accounting appeared in the 16th century and was defined in 1753 in the encyclopedia. The techniques of bookkeeping also evolved in parallel, with the first known book describing double entry bookkeeping by the Italian Lucas Pacioli in 1494. It was during the 19th century, as compa-nies were structured differently with companies organized in different ways that accounting services appeared. The term bookkeeping was reduced to its technical aspect.

DOI: 10.1201/9781003230137-1

Even today, all this continues to change. The terms used by accounting standard bodies are significant. The International Accounting Standards Committee (IASC), established in 1973, was replaced by the International Financial Reporting Standards (IFRS) foundation with the International Accounting Standards Board in 2001. The focus shifts from International Accounting Standards (IAS) to International Financial Reporting Standards (IFRS). With this change, the emphasis is on the shift from an accounting view to a financial view of information in international accounting standard setting.

Auditing has had to adapt to these changes, on the one hand, to take into account changes in working methods and obligations of accountants, and, on the other hand, to extend its scope of information analysis, largely out of obligation, because of the computerization of all company processes. A company is the sum of these components and the internal and external interactions. We can't separate finance from information system. Pure financial indicators are not enough, the auditor must analyze a company as an all and not in parts.

As in medicine a company cannot be reduced to 3 silos, finance, operations, and information system. This is why occidental medicine practice realized again that human nature cannot be reduced to the duality of Oromaze and Ahrimane, or matter and spirit. A purely physiological vision is not sufficient, Jo Marchant proposes as an example the research of Noakes:

> The dogma was that athletes get tired when their bodies hit physical limits-their muscles run out of oxygen, fuel or become damaged by the accumulation of toxic byproducts such as lactic acid. This in turn triggers pain and fatigue, forcing us to stop exercising until we recover. Noakes proved that "In other words, fatigue isn't a physical event, but a sensation or emotion, invented by the brain to prevent catastrophic harm."
>
> [JMA]

Audit must avoid this caveat. It has long been understood without misunderstanding as auditing finance or accounting. However, nowadays we are getting more and more familiar having the term used with other words such as with operational audit, quality audit, and social audit. Financial audit is now being used to differentiate it.

Audit is used so frequently, in so many different contexts, that defining it is an exercise in style. Its usage is so common that the temptation is great to analyze management practices since antiquity with our modern understanding of the word audit. To avoid this pitfall and to put things into perspective, it is necessary to note some remarkable points in the history of business and then to specify the context of the current use of the word audit. History will explain why audit used to be a financial audit as we now still think about it.

All this is mainly induced by Anglo-Saxon audit firms and large regional firms that apply equivalent working methods. The combined revenue of the largest audit firms, such as E&Y, PWC, KPMG, and Deloitte, increased steadily in the last decade, exceeding 157 billion U.S. dollars in 2020. This amount shows the importance of auditing for the proper functioning of financial markets. These firms work mainly with listed companies. These companies are required to have their accounts certified. This obligation is the result of an evolution of the financial regulations that govern the official stock exchanges, more particularly since the 19th century.

The use of the stock exchange as a trading place originated in the Netherlands. Some trace it to a Van der Beurse family from Bruges, because in the 13th century, traders met in their house. Others state it to be originating from the three purses carved above the door of the house that brought buyers and sellers together in Amsterdam, as purses as an object were used by traders at international fairs and marketplaces in Europe long before the Middle Ages.

The insurrection of Flanders against the House of Austria in 1488 made the commercial place of Bruges decline. The international trade then moved to Antwerp. Its trade was very dependent on its relations with the Spanish Empire. The war between the Spanish Empire and the North Sea provinces brought about the ruin of Antwerp. Businesses migrated from this place to Amsterdam. It was already flourishing because it had been a part of the Hanseatic League, before leaving it.

At that time, Lisbon was the only port that directly received products from India thanks to the traffic set up by the Portuguese and Amsterdam trade with Lisbon to supply products to northern and central European countries in particular. In 1580, Portugal came under Spanish rule and Philip II confiscated 50 Dutch ships.

Amsterdam was forced to review its strategy. It noticed the dependence of its trade with the Spanish Empire and thought about how to maintain its commercial activity on the products coming from India. Amsterdam was no longer thinking only of keeping the profits from trade with India, but also of increasing them. It cared little for the papal decision that divided the world and its discoveries between the Spanish and the Portuguese. She decided to follow the Portuguese example and go to India to trade with her own ships by direct routes. Amsterdam quickly became the center of world trade which did not yet include the American continent.

Its stock exchange allowed the development of all the wheels of commerce, with banks and insurance companies. Various scandals enameled the Amsterdam stock exchange like those of the East India Company or the tulip bulb bubble. The effects of the abuse of futures trading on the Amsterdam stock exchange are still fresh in our minds. These purchases were mainly for the shares of the East India Company. One buys and sells without having the goods, and one pays the difference up or down on the day of delivery of the ships.

The famous trade in tulip bulbs is of the same nature. From 1634 to 1637, all classes of the population engaged in what looked more like gambling. People speculated on the rise or fall of the price of tulip bulbs. People bid and paid large sums of money for bulbs that they did not have and did not plan to deliver. On the day of delivery, the flowers are not even delivered, and the price is not even paid, but just the difference.

In absolute terms, this is not different from what happens nowadays on the London International Financial Futures and Options Exchange (LIFFE) for Robusta coffee and the New York International Commodity Exchange (ICE) for Arabica coffee.

> Trading in options (the option, not the obligation, to make or take delivery of a futures contract at a certain price threshold or expiration period) began in 1986 in New York. It has brought many speculators into the market, to the point that in 2015 the volume of contracts traded was 27 times that of world Arabica production.
>
> [JMO]

Certainly, these speculations damaged the reputation of the Amsterdam Stock Exchange, but it was the decline of Holland's maritime and commercial power that led to the decline of its stock exchange. The English statesman Oliver Cromwell promulgated a Navigation Act on October 9, 1651, which was one of the main triggers for this decline. This act favored the development of the English navy. It detailed the terms of international trade with England. Its expansion and the regulation on insurance, already published a few years before in 1600, led merchants to deal with increasingly large volumes.

The rise of the English maritime trade is, there also, encouraged by the Spaniards, as it had been the case with the Dutch. Philip II closes the port of Lisbon to the English, and thus indirectly forces them to go themselves in India to trade. The English navy becomes the most important and the most essential navy. It went to India by direct route and organized the recent discovery of the New World.

In the 16th century, Thomas Grasham, the richest merchant in London at the time, officially opened the first stock exchange in England, the Royal Exchange, in 1571. He had worked as an agent in Antwerp and knew its exchange well; he took it as a model. The location of the building is not insignificant, it is in the district of London where merchants already meet to negotiate the prices of products, but without having a particular place. They are not accepted at the Royal Exchange because of their manners, their education. The London Stock Exchange was then created in 1801 to consider the importance of world trade of the first maritime power of the time.

In the 16th century in France, things were also moving. At the end of the 16th century in particular, the operations that gave rise to successive government loans were important and justified the creation of eight security brokers, the ancestors of stockbrokers. They were increased to 30 by Louis XIII and an edict of 1638 ordered them to pool a quarter of the profits. This is the origin of the reserve fund.

At that time, there was already a kind of stock exchange in Paris. This word with the meaning of the meeting of financiers to sell and buy securities is in use since the reign of Henri III. The meeting was first held in the northern part of the Pont au Change downtown Paris (letter of Louis VII in

1141, confirmed by an order of Philippe le Bel in 1304), then moved to several places not far away. Under the Regency of the Duke of Orleans, the money changers moved to rue Quincampoix, in the vicinity of rue des Lombards, where foreign banks and a tradition of financial business had long existed. The ordinance of September 21, 1724, organized the Bourse (the Exchange), which moved to the eastern part of the Hôtel Mazarin, overlooking the rue Vivienne. It remained there until the Revolution, with discount offices, a cash office, a dividend office, and a stock office for duly authorized persons.

But why the need to create exchanges when exchanges were already taking place without them? The difference between these exchanges and the Italian Loggias of the 12th century or the English salons of the 16th century, for example, is that they are regular, regulated, and in controlled places.

Exchanges are places of exchange with regular days and hours of operation. It is much more convenient and interesting to sell or buy if there are more people involved, so knowing where and when to meet is necessary. To avoid having your goods stolen and to organize to bring them, the place must be well identified and protected.

In Paris, for example,

> In the Quincampoix street, such a crowd was pressed that horses and carriages had to be banned and guards had to be placed at both ends of the street, drums and bell-ringers had to be placed there to warn, at 7 o'clock in the morning, of the opening of the operations and to clear the place at night. Never had such madness reigned, and it was with great difficulty that the entrance to the narrow alley was forbidden on Sundays and holidays.
>
> [CST]

Given the inconveniences such as noise for the neighborhood or the risk of theft, exchanges were transferred to more and more enclosed and secured places. Thus, at the beginning of the 18th century, the rue Quincampoix was a vast free market in the middle of the street, anyone could come to buy or sell anything. This includes snuffboxes through canes and watches.

1.2 REGULATION, CONTROLS, AND AUDITS

The concerns of the authorities, whether in Paris, London, Chicago, or New York, have always been to designate a specific and fixed location, to the exclusion of all others, to serve as a framework for the trading of goods or securities. More particularly for stock market exchanges, which evolve and concern not so many goods as financial securities, the centralization of these exchanges in a single place is a necessary, but not sufficient condition for their sincerity and regularity.

The regulation of these marketplaces is the next step in the formalization of stock market exchanges. Apart from the fact that the marketplaces are covered, regulation is the main difference with the fairs and markets of the

Middle Ages, which were used for exchanges until then. Exchanges on marketplaces and fairs are made on products that are physically present on the place of exchange. But for these products to be there, they must have undergone the vicissitudes of caravan journeys from the East to the West or the risks of the sea with ships in the Mediterranean Sea and then on the oceans. It is therefore tempting to sell loads of goods still in transit before their arrival (provided that the ship is still afloat). In the stock exchanges, we only trade on the values that represent them. Moreover, speculation on capital increases.

The regulation of the exchange market requires the establishment of regulations enforced by identified and authorized actors. To continue our example of the rue Quincampoix, the street, initially free to enter, was forbidden to "non-professionals," such as artisans, workers, and peddlers, in an attempt to curb excesses. These same concerns led to the denial of access to money changers at the Royal Exchange.

In addition to identifying the players, the rules govern not only the terms of the exchanges, but also the ability to participate in the exchanges and under what conditions. The historical marketplaces such as Amsterdam, London, Paris, and New York have all defined and implemented regulations to guarantee their proper functioning.

These regulations, of course, have more "civilized" provisions for dealing with bad debtors than the erring ways that took place until the Middle Ages. Shakespeare mocks these practices in The Merchant of Venice:

> Shylock—And I want to have this kindness; come with me to a notary's office, sign a simple bill to me, and for our amusement, we will stipulate that in case you do not return to me, at such day and place designated, the sum or sums expressed in the deed, you will be condemned to pay me a fair pound of your beautiful flesh, cut on the part of the body that I will be pleased to choose.

and further

> Shylock—In that case, go and wait for me at the notary's; give him your instructions about this buffoonish bill.

Antiquity knew only the trade of goods. The Middle Ages invented bills of exchange and later, with the establishment of banks, created the money trade. The Italian republics, the cities of Upper Germany, and the Netherlands had bankers especially occupied with money business, who discounted bills of exchange, made advances on goods, and sometimes also lent to great lords or governments, usually their own. Florence, and after her, Antwerp mainly, will surprise their contemporaries by the importance of these transactions. It goes without saying that these transactions, like all others, follow the movement of trade and exchanges. At the time of the fall of the Hanseatic League, merchants, manufacturers, and bankers emigrated from the banks of the Scheldt to those of the Amstel. They brought their capital and their credit. The silver trade followed that of goods, and it increased its activity by the increase in the availability of precious metals.

By the end of the 16th century, no other country had money as readily available or as cheaply priced as Amsterdam. This was enough to ensure the preponderance of Dutch trade, thanks to the aggressive commercial policy of the bankers. They lowered their prices, reduced their margins, granted longer payment terms, and speculated more than in other European markets. Foreign exchange in Amsterdam is preferred to other markets. Many important trading cities can only make their discounts in Amsterdam. Indeed, if a paper is quoted on other places, comparatively it gives loss.

At the beginning of the 18th century, the Dutch circulated two-thirds of the value of Europe, which amounted to three or four billion guilders. This amount was renewed every two months. Amsterdam maintained relations with all countries and gradually received such a mass of altered, worn, and trimmed currency that the currency in circulation or current currency fell to 6% and even 9% below the value of the newly minted Dutch currency. Traders were unable to obtain enough quality currency to pay their exchange losses without loss. Added to this inconvenience was the embarrassment and loss of time that the payment of large sums of money generated, as well as the risks involved in keeping money at home. So, in 1609, the merchants of Amsterdam founded, with the guarantee of the city, an establishment where any merchant, whose business required large sums, could deposit most of his funds, and make his payments as well as his receipts, with simple entries.

This establishment, the Bank of Amsterdam, accepts not only foreign currency, but also the worn-out currencies of the country for their real value, minus the costs of coinage and custody. To put an end to the uncertainty about the value of commercial bills, all bills of exchange of 600 florins, drawn on Amsterdam or subscribed in this city, were paid in bank money. The Bank of Amsterdam was indeed a simple bank of deposit and transfer, but it favored the commercial and stock exchanges. The trade in these bills of exchange was very buoyant on the Amsterdam stock exchange.

The Middle Ages also saw borrowing. Emperor Charles V borrowed from the Fruggers, Pope Alexander from the Medici, but securities became objects of commerce circulating like goods. They too were listed on the Amsterdam stock exchange. For the first time, then, the debts of a state were raised to the level of an economic system, and speculation took hold of them.

So, we have an identified place, authorized actors, and defined operations. One last element is missing to finalize all this, third parties to guarantee not the proper functioning of the exchange, but the quality of the financial information necessary for trading. With the London Stock Exchange, the participants and the products come from all over the world. Past mistakes or scandals require that the information be reliable. Regulation is evolving and intervening on the functioning of companies. It is the modernization of the bookkeeping profession to the accounting profession.

In France, the term "commissaire" appeared in the law of May 23, 1863. This law recognizes a supervisory function already present in companies. The law of July 24, 1867, repealed the law of 1863, without, however, specifying the notions of independence, competence, or respect of professional secrecy. No accounting skills, no particular requirements are required to be appointed as statutory auditors. The decree law of August 8, 1935, prohibits the auditor from interfering in the management or passing judgment on the company, whose accounts he verifies as providing a true and fair view of its activity. This change in French regulations followed the Stavisky affair of January 1934.

The Stavisky affair is a Ponzi scheme, and we remember the scandal of the world's largest Ponzi scheme created by Bernard Madoff. Bernard Madoff's stock and securities Ponzi scheme was discovered in 2008. In response, the Securities and Exchange Commission (SEC) changed its regulations two years later in 2010 with the Dodd–Frank Wall Street Reform and Consumer Protection Act. Since its inception, the evolution of Anglo-Saxon regulation has also been the result of various scandals. It was a scandal that gave us the first known audit report in North America with the case of the Sawbridge Company subsidiary of the South Sea Company.

> It was in 1720 that the first major recognition of a public accountant was given to Charles Snell, one of the outstanding English accountants of the eighteenth century, who had written "Observations Made Upon Examining the Books of Sawbridge and Company"...The South Sea Bubble in December 1720 was the collapse of a series of financial projects which originated within the incorporation of the South Sea Company in 1711 and ended nine years later in general disaster.
>
> [JDE]

England, through the Company Clause Consolidation Act of 1845, as amended in 1868, has made provision for the auditing of the accounts of listed companies. At least once a year, companies' accounts must be audited, and their balance sheets be checked by auditors. As in France, because of the incompetence of some stakeholders since there is no requirement for professionals to have a particular qualification, a bill was proposed to create the Institute of Chartered Accountants of England and Wales. In 1880, the Institute was founded and merged with the various existing Institutes. Its charter required members to pass an examination of auditing competence.

Nevertheless, it is to Scotland that we owe the first efforts to define the accounting and auditing profession. The first work on the creation in 1854 of the charter of the Society of Accountants in Edinburgh had been started a year earlier by a group of 14 accountants: The professionalization of accountants and auditors began. The work of the auditors could not be limited to ensuring the arithmetical logic used. They must also ensure themselves that the accounting entries really reflect the company's operations.

Let's use an example to explain what this change means:

> The first important English court case on the duties of an auditor was the Leeds Estate Building and Investment Company vs. Shepherd, rendered by Justice Sterling in 1887. This case extended the auditor's duties to inquiry into the soundness, not merely the mathematical accuracy, of the figures included on the balance sheet.
>
> [JDE]

Operations, at that time, were not computerized—20th century meaning—at all of course, but were traced by different documents throughout the processes. It should also be noted that the auditors' opinion is admissible in court. If this opinion does not synthesize the facts correctly, it can lead them to court through the action of shareholders as in 1895 for a report of 1891 on the accounts of the London and General Bank.

> It is readily apparent that the profession in the United States has a rich inheritance of European tradition. The profession in these countries received its beginning in the field of auditing. By the middle of the nineteenth century provisions had been made for the audit of companies regulated by Parliament.
>
> [JDE]

The American Association of Public Accountants, founded in 1886, became the first professional organization of accountants in the United States. Its purpose was to promote the reputation and professionalism of "public accountants" following the example of developments in Great Britain. The first official recognition of the profession dates from 1896 with the first certified public accountant law in New York. Indeed, it is necessary, because in the United States,

> the modern era of derivatives trading began when the Chicago Board of Trade was established in 1849, allowing for the buying and selling of futures and options on agricultural commodities.
>
> [GTE]

Before the 1920s,

> brokerage firms were even making bets on the outcome of the presidential elections!
>
> [BGD]

In 1920, prudent investors still considered the New York Stock Exchange little better than a casino. Federal regulation and transparency laws for the market were almost non-existent. The exchange did not even require listed companies to produce their results to investors, other than an annual balance sheet with assets and liabilities. Most players on the New York Stock Exchange saw themselves more as speculators than as investors.

Following the speculative bubble of 1929, the US Senate hearings produced three laws. The first is the Securities Act of 1933 on securities. The second is the Glass–Steagall Act of 1933 to force financial institutions to choose between investment banking and deposit banking. The third is the Securities and Exchange Act of 1934, which created a federal agency, the SEC, to supervise stock exchanges. The SEC requires all publicly traded companies to file periodic financial reports endorsed by members of the accounting industry. The American Institute of Certified Public Accountants (AICPA) established accounting standards until 1973, when the Financial Accounting Standards Board (FASB) was launched to set standards for private companies.

Moreover, still in 2009, James Grant notes that even these elements and the precautions taken are not sufficient to form an opinion as an investor:

> Not all elements affecting value are captured in a company's financial statements—inventories can grow obsolete and receivables uncollectible; liabilities are sometimes unrecorded and property values over- or underestimated.

> [BGD]

Large American companies are going international and are bringing with them in Europe the Anglo-Saxon audit firms that already advise them on the American continent. They specialize in contractual audits, organization, and consolidation missions, as in France, at the very beginning of their installation. The term consolidation, moreover, was absent from the French Chart of Accounts in 1957. In France, Anglo-Saxon firms took off in the early 1970s for various reasons, such as the highly qualified profiles of their recruits and auditing work methods that had a different aura from those of public accountants.

The evolution of the regulations confirms the need to transpose international requirements into France. The law of July 24, 1966, defined the status and role of the company auditor, who became a statutory auditor, then the decree of August 12, 1969, organized the profession of statutory auditors, and finally the Commission des Opérations de Bourse (COB) was founded by order of September 28, 1967, based on the example of the SEC. For French groups with international ambitions, it is also important to have an internationally recognized signature.

This is a glimpse of the ups and downs of the financial markets. Stakeholders trade on the confidence they have in their interlocutors, on the one hand, and the relationship between risks and expected gains on the other. Confidence concerns, first of all, the feasibility of the project, whether it is plausible or not, who is leading it and the organization chosen. Confidence therefore concerns the ability of the partner to carry out a project, but also the assurance of being paid. At present, balance sheets, profit and loss accounts, and annexes provide information to form an opinion.

The relationship between risks and expected gains shows the complexity of projecting past results over the short, medium, and long term and of analyzing the possibility of future benefits. To compensate, minimize, or cancel these risks, insurance was created. Marine insurance naturally preceded fire or life insurance. It is claimed that it was first introduced by the Romans, when several emperors, to encourage the import of grain, promised indemnities to importers in the event of shipwrecks or accidents at sea. But this insurance does not constitute an insurance as such, because it does not result from a contract. It is nothing more than a guarantee given by the emperor, in his capacity as the purchaser of grain, to those who supply it to him, to take on the risks of transport by sea.

Certainly, the Romans, like the Greeks, practiced contracts such as the "contrat à la grosse" which are an implicit way of practicing insurance. It is a loan granted at a very high rate by an individual to finance a long-distance journey without establishing a long-term association between the parties. It has essentially an insurance function. The origin of maritime insurance can be found in Genoa and Florence from the beginning of the 14th century. The provisions were separated from the bill of sale and became their own documents, which preceded the Barcelona ordinances. In the 14th century, Barcelona was distinguished by a significant navigation in a stable environment, unlike Genoa and Venice. The ordinances of Barcelona were of great importance, as they formalized maritime insurance.

Moreover, already in 1255 in the church of Saint Sophia in Constantinople, the Venetians wished to establish the maritime law on a fixed basis. This one was so "limited" that it was rather the arbitrary one and the violence which had force of law. To regulate navigation, they used a collection of navigation customs, prepared shortly before in Catalonia, to make this document accepted as law in all the ports of the Mediterranean Sea.

The insurance industry developed rapidly and significantly when navigation reached the oceans and the transport of goods by sea became more and more important. Without it, it can be said, there would never have been transatlantic trade.

Insurance turns uncertainty into security. The capital of the trader who floats on the high seas and is threatened by storms and privateers is just as protected, perhaps even more so than that of the farmer. The merchant can conceive projects and prepare operations without worrying too much about the risks. It was in England that they took the most extension.

Faced with the importance of the capital needed, the quantity of chartered ships, and the number of goods transported, the division of labor was established in the trade with specialties that were even more separated from each other. The division of labor was established well before the early 20th century, distinguishing the exporter from the importer, the commission agent from the shipper, the shipowner from the charterer, and the brokers who served as intermediaries for all of them.

On the stock exchanges in the 21st century, the participants to the exchange from start to end are specialized too. The number of transactions evolves upward over time and the participants are spread all over the globe. The quality of financial information and quarterly meetings between companies and their investors and shareholders is paramount. Investors are expected to have the same level of information at the same time.

Certainly, stock market malfunctions always make headlines. In March 2017, the chairman of the China Banking Regulatory Authority, Guo Shuqing, says that in China,

> Banks, investment funds, brokers and insurers manage comparable assets, but are subject to separate rules and different regulators. It's the Wild West!

> [AFP]

How can such dysfunctions and scandals occur knowing the context and the obligations of certification of accounts via financial audits? The expected benefits are the provision of reliable and controlled information to third parties. Reliable implies the implementation of regulations in the organization and the correct consolidation of financial information. Controlled means that a third party ensures that the regulations have been implemented and that the information reflects the reality of the company's operations. It should be noted that the audit is based on controls but that controls do not need the audit to justify themselves.

Third-party control is all the easier as the operating methods between the actors are formalized and the rules and vocabulary defined. These efforts are made in the same country, thanks to a common language and legal legislation. But for companies with an international presence, it is not so simple. Bilateral agreements are put in place between clearly identified players, between a company and a country or between two countries. When the country is part of a larger legal entity, it is more practical to approach this entity directly to make the effort to reach an agreement more cost-effective and to increase the size of the potential market. If this is not the case, multilateral agreements can be negotiated, usually in the form of an economic power or a grouping of economic powers. This context influences the legal risks incurred by companies trading in such environments.

The ability to audit is the best way to obtain the most reliable audit opinion possible. The control is "a rule or law that sets a limit on something" (Cambridge dictionary). To control the finances of a company, the auditor relies on the books of accounts. The keeping of books of account was rapidly organized, particularly in Italy. This technique appeared and developed simultaneously in several Italian commercial centers during the 14th century: Genoa, Florence, Venice, not to mention Siena, Milan, or Lucca, and then its use gradually spread to the whole of merchant Europe during the following centuries. But it was not until 1494 that the mathematician monk Luca Pacioli published his treatise "De Computis et scripturis" which described double-entry accounting. Pacioli does not pretend to invent double accounting. For this he credited Benedict Cotrugli (Benedict Kotruljevic of Dubrovnik, Croatia), who according to these writings reportedly treated double-entry bookkeeping in his book "of trading and the perfect trader" in 1458, but this book was not published more than a 100 years later.

> Within a few years the chapter was published separately as an instructional pamphlet, translated into English, German, French and Dutch. As late as the nineteenth century, Russian and American editions were still commercially viable.
>
> [JFL]

Double-entry accounting is a powerful control, in that sense already the beginning of the audit. This method has two advantages. The first is the possibility of having two books kept by two different clerks, which reduces the risk of fraud. The second, more effective or more important, is that the two books can be regularly balanced with each other. If a clerk makes an error, intentional or not, it is identified by the person reconciling the books. In 1795, in France, the invention of the journal ledger and the theory of the five accounts defined and presented by Degrange the father, further improved working methods. The theory of the five accounts is that every merchant uses five general accounts in connection with his activity, the accounts of goods, money, bills receivable, bills payable, profits, and losses.

The word audit as we understand it today has been used since the early 15th century in English. The Cambridge dictionary defines it as "an official examination of the quality or condition of something" and in the context of accounting as "an examination of the accounts of a business, usually by experts from outside the business." Given the evolution of financial regulations, the obligations of auditors have largely evolved since then, thanks to professional bodies. The audit is not a preventive measure but facilitates analysis, promotes improvement, and allows lawyers to take legal action if necessary.

For the International Federation of Accountants (IFAC),

> the purpose of an audit is to enhance the degree of confidence of intended users in the financial statements. This is achieved by the expression of an opinion by the auditor on whether the financial statements are prepared, in all material respects, in accordance with an applicable financial reporting framework. In the case of most general-purpose frameworks, that opinion is on whether the financial statements are presented fairly, in all material respects, or give a true and fair view in accordance with the framework. An audit conducted in accordance with the International Standards on Auditing (ISA) and relevant ethical requirements enables the auditor to form that opinion.

In the US, audits of publicly traded companies are governed by rules laid down by the Public Company Accounting Oversight Board (PCAOB), which was established by Section 404 of the Sarbanes–Oxley Act of 2002. Such an audit is called an integrated audit, where auditors, in addition to an opinion on the financial statements, must also express an opinion on the effectiveness of a company's internal control over financial reporting, in accordance with PCAOB Auditing Standard No. 5. Worth reminding that a motto from the PCAOB is "Protecting Investors through Audit Oversight."

To protect investors, they must be confident on how the audit work is performed. The AICPA takes care of that in its Statements of Auditing Standards (SAS), about the auditor's responsibility to detect and report errors and irregularities. However, it distinguishes between unintentional (errors) and intentional misstatements (irregularities). The importance of errors and irregularities in the audit process is emphasized. Assessing the risk that errors and irregularities have caused material misstatements in the financial statements requires that auditors understand the characteristics of errors and irregularities and the links between those characteristics. To achieve that understanding, auditors design and perform appropriate audit procedures and can evaluate the results.

Controls therefore help to identify errors and irregularities. The implementation of controls affects the work of people. The workflow can be changed because controls are implemented much earlier in the workflow or because the responsibility for controls changes from one person or department to another.

On the other hand, controls may be more or less practical or blocking the purpose of the workflow, such as delivering an order in less than two hours or releasing an order in less than a few minutes. Stakeholders will then work to ensure the goals of the process at the expense of controls if necessary. This starts with a one-time self-derogation, if you will, duly argued or justified by the importance of the order or the customer. This deviation can be due to a problem and generate a risk—the same method is used in the implementation and maintenance of IT security.

The need for a derogation is induced by the inadequacy of the control. It is either poorly designed or obsolete because it has not kept pace with changes in the company's practices. The lack of control design is a classic example of the implementation of an internal control policy. The challenge is to find the minimum number of controls to implement relative to the level of risk in the workflow. In addition, the controls chosen must be relevant and appropriate. Relevant in terms of risk management and sensible in terms of the least possible interaction with the purpose of the workflow.

As far as the relevance of controls is concerned, we can draw a parallel with what is called lean management. Lean management aims to streamline and purify a process—originally designed for industrial automobile production processes. This approach, initiated by Taiichi Ohno [TOH], simplifies a person's workstation and facilitates relations with other workstations. The simplification of the workstation's design allows the person to focus more easily on the work to be done, minimizing the risk of accidents for the person and the losses, loss of time, loss of materials or intermediate products. The fluidity of the relations with the other workstations allows to consider the good progress of the workflow as a whole and not only at the workstation.

What does this have to do with our controls? The relevance of controls is more important when the workflow is simplified and fluid. It's impossible to keep controls simple if the workflow is cumbersome, such as constantly going back and forth between one workstation and another. It is impossible to keep it simple in terms of both the quantity of controls to be implemented and their simplicity. The implementation of controls that satisfy the proper regulation of workflows should not be done without considering the simplicity and fluidity of these workflows.

About the least possible interaction with the workflow, we can link it with the fluidity of the process and make the analogy with the implementation of metrics. When a physicist measures a phenomenon, he makes sure that his measurement method does not modify the phenomenon to be measured. For nuclear physics, the measurement and analysis of phenomena is becoming more and more complex due to the difficulty of having measurement and analysis tools that do not influence the phenomenon being studied. In sociology, it is very difficult not to observe without influencing who or what is observed. The mere presence of an observer in the school class disrupts the behavior of that class.

Companies invest in setting up smooth operations and in maintaining and improving that smoothness. It is counterproductive for the company to invest in controls that are cumbersome in both design and implementation. As soon as controls interfere too much with the fluidity of workflows, stakeholders will gradually tend to make sure that they no longer block the flow. Ideally, by correctly applying the guidelines, but in practice by diverting them. The most symptomatic example is the increase in cases of "social engineering."

The goal of "social engineering" theft is to circumvent existing controls by requesting or helping someone in the company. To succeed, the perpetrator usually poses as either a supervisor, preferably a position that intimidates the caller, or as an IT support technician. With all the investments companies have made in securing hardware and software to prevent external computer attacks, thieves get in touch with an internal person directly by phone to get what they want, instead of wasting time once the level of computer security is too high.

One of the most famous cases of "social engineering" is that of Kevin Mitnick. In the early 1990s, he became the world's most wanted hacker after breaking into the computer systems of 40 major corporations, stealing corporate secrets and jamming telephone networks. He was also suspected of hacking into the National Defense Warning System and wiretapping the Federal Bureau of Investigation. He testified before the US Congress in 2000:

> "I was so successful in that line of attack I rarely had to resort to a technical attack." He added: "Companies can spend millions of dollars toward technological protections and that's wasted if somebody can basically call

someone on the telephone and either convince them to do something on the computers that lowers the computer's defenses or reveals the information they were seeking."

As Bruce Schneier writes:

> The mathematics are impeccable, the computers are vincible, the networks are lousy, and the people are abysmal.

[BSC]

This basic approach is very simply reflected in the studies on armored doors. Armored doors secure the entrance to your apartment, but they also encourage the thief to look elsewhere, because he has two enemies, noise and time. If the level of security is too high, he will try to find another less secure entrance and if there is none, he will visit another apartment.

Another reason for the misuse of controls is internal fraud. Very classically, an internal person will recklessly trust his colleagues with whom he has worked for many years or he will not respect basic security rules. Let's take the case of a treasurer who goes on leave and, in order not to block the workflow following the implementation of a new Enterprise Resource Planning (ERP) system, leaves her password in the desk drawer with the CFO. It turns out that the CFO is going through a bad patch in his personal life (divorce), has gambled, and has many debts. He can then bypass the safeguards in place for the separation of duties and make transfers to pay off his debts. The forensic team only takes over the case when there is a suspicion of fraud.

Here we are with a trilogy that cannot be ignored for the rest of our discussion: Regulation, controls, and audit. These three very old themes are still valid with the computerization of information systems. They just need to be understood in the new context, not as such, i.e., in relation to their definition or their objectives, but in relation to their implementation.

1.3 AUDIT AND DIGITAL TRANSFORMATION

We've been through history to confirm that ensuring thrust has always been a challenge and financial audit used to be the most used solution. What's happening for auditing in the 21st century? How digital transformation has impacted both companies and auditing firms? If history tells us that nothing has changed for the needs for audit and if we say that it is just a matter of integrating IT controls into our workplans, why does it look so complex and why it is not fully done yet? Well, because IT is an evolving foundation on which all the companies are relying on. Any new technology may either modify or disrupt part or all of the business processes, if not the entire company.

For auditors relying on the results of the 2013 paper from Carl Benedikt Frey and Michael A. Osborne [BFO], there are more reasons to be scary.

They examined how jobs would be subject to computerization, the higher percentage the riskier it is. Two groups were defined and related to our subject "Accountants and Auditors" and "Bookkeeping, Accounting, and Auditing Clerks" and they achieve respectively a probability of 0.94 and 0.98: Accountants and auditors being replaced by artificial intelligence, and clerks being replaced by robots. Don't be surprised by these results, when digging into the inputs they use, o∗net, an online service developed for the US Department of Labor. The profession already knows and already is since a few decades moving forward embracing their clients' evolution and the new tools improving the quality of their work or their productivity.

Moving forward when speaking with the transformation of paper-based information into an electronic format of 0 and 1, we may use the word digitalization. We use digital transformation when more than data is involved, such as the processes. Digital transformation applies to data, processes whatever the way as whatever it modifies the operations and quite often the business model. The verb digitalized might be used for practicality and within the idea of digital transformation, i.e., moving from analog to digital.

Digital transformation impacts:

- Organizations,
- Processes, and
- People.

We can simplify the impact of digitalization saying that there is a shift left trend and a move to more or new services provided by the audit companies. Shift left is a recent IT buzzword re-packaging an old IT practice, that with time passing by, had been misunderstood and misapplied, reason of the lifting. Let's enjoy the explanation of buzzword by Paul A. Strassmann: "A new word that masquerade as the solution to an old problem. The repackaging of old buzzwords is a major source of new revenue for consultants and computer vendors" [PAS]. In a non-IT world, it means that you have data-related work performed upfront in a process. What does that mean? Well, think about the work you do when filling electronic forms before reaching out to the customer service or chatting with a bot, without any human being answering. Within a company think about the data entry workload moved upstream in the processes when implementing an ERP. This is happening too between a company and its external auditors. The more the processes are automated, the more the manual entries disappear from the accountant's duties. Therefore, the auditors workplan must change, as they don't have to dive into papers but into digitalized information in different formats, text, pictures (scan), digital approvals, to name a few. The following need is to simplify manual entries, simplify meaning more efficiently (less time and less human errors) or in a more cost-effective manner. But other IT trends impact companies. These days, companies' organization must adapt to the new 21st consulting trend of being agile. Processes must become workflows, getting rid of disturbances creating delays.

People must assimilate the new paradigm, accept, and adapt to the changes. People means every layer of the organization. The current SARS-CoV-2, aka COVID-19, pandemic shows that the resources adapted to the need to work from home and management was obliged to accept it. As soon as the risks were lower, top management decided that it was mandatory to come back to the office. Companies can be split between brick-and-mortar companies and fully digital companies, and more specifically audit companies. Current companies and their processes are evolving due to IT, new companies provide digital services while being fully digital, and auditors must adapt their approach and the techniques and tools they use to remain pertinent or efficient to these different situations. For current companies, IT has digitalized business processes and underlying data some faster than others, and if it is not the case for some of them, they will definitely be. It's only a matter of time. In addition to brick-and-mortar companies going through the challenges of the digital transformation, since a few decades, fully digital companies have been created and selling fully digital services, such as Weibo, Facebook, Twitter to name a few of them. The difficulty to apprehend their strategies and provide a relevant analysis of their business models reached a climax during what has been called the dotcom or Internet bubble in the late 1990s. Internet-based start-ups were highly praised and companies delivering physical goods not fully embracing the Internet wave/trend saw their valuations decrease down to 86%.

Today, this bubble looks more like an irrational rash. Irrational because only the ones in the know were able to compensate losses from different start-ups with gains from at least a successful one. Rash as it was a frenzy atmosphere for everyone, either professionals or non-professionals; the professionals quite often lacking IT knowledge and non-professionals lacking professional's information. It used to be called the new far-west for a reason.

As a legacy of this period, the idealization of failure is still vivid along with the moto "move fast and break things." In the 2020s, all things have more or less settled down. Companies' strategies and businesses evolve at the IT pace since IT is available for them. It started in the 1960s when IT invaded companies' premises. It was the time when finance people were wondering if an IT department was a cost center or a profit center. Some still do. Nowadays, IT is no more an add-on or a tool facilitating tedious manual, time-consuming work for the finance or accounting departments for instance. IT is now consubstantial with the companies processes and businesses such as with the Internet-based companies. Digital transformation underlies that IT is critical for business survival. To audit a company, it is mandatory to have an expertise in IT management, contract management, and project management. IT management and contract management relate to all the work to keep the lights on, starting with the administration of the IT department. Project management relates to the delivery of new assets or enhancing them to reduce operating expenses or to support new services.

To fully benefit from IT hardware and software, processes must be designed with IT tools in mind. As a result, the reliance on IT is greater, current risks become riskier and new risks appear. For instance, due to the scarce availability of IT experts and good expertise, HR risks become important. That's a way to look at the current trend on subcontracting software, platform or infrastructure management and ownership, being rebranded/called "as a service." The other way is financial, you reduce capital expenditures and expect better control over operational expenditures. Auditing this increased reliance on IT and its extensive externalization requires thorough IT and legal knowledge. Thorough IT knowledge as the main technical argument is that the challenge of following the IT pace is managed by the suppliers. One must understand what the services provided will be and agree on the contractual content particularly all the "details" dealing with operational excellence.

Internally, managers were late realizing the importance of this on-going challenge. It's a challenge because the world is no more split in silos finance on one side, operations on the other side, and IT because it is said that IT must be audited. IT pervades every activity and it is difficult to realize that even when your minor is Information System Management.

Externally, the auditing firms must evolve to respectively improve their understanding of the adequacy of the controls at their clients' organization and ensure that they know enough to identify the IT root causes of errors.

But auditing companies are companies too, impacted by the digital transformation. They are concerned by it internally with their own processes and the ones of their clients. This makes sense, as regulation and control are impacted by the digital transformation; therefore, companies and audit companies also get impacted. It's obvious for everything else anyway, organizational changes in companies, the increase in the number of suppliers and customers, and the increase in the complexity of products and services sold or purchased force auditors to re-align their work methods to be as relevant as possible to audit the company's processes. In addition, legislative and regulatory changes also need to consider updating the controls. The auditing firms are the first ones concerned. Only very large companies can invest in-house to keep up to date, otherwise the majority of companies rely on external firms. To satisfy their internal needs and services, audit firms consolidate. They reach sufficient size to offer services wherever their clients operate, to train their staff, to develop new services, and to improve their expertise on standards.

Where are the risks greater? With fully digital companies, with "brick-and-mortar" companies moving to digital or even with digital companies adding "brick-and-mortar" services? Of course, pure "brick-and-mortar" companies such as mom-and-dad establishments are out of our scope. Ranking high would be "brick-and-mortar" companies, medium digital companies moving to brick and mortars, and ranking low would be the digital companies.

Digital companies (and mom-and-dad shops too by the way) are quite stable in their functioning. As an auditor you know what to expect, as all businesses and operations are consistent. When planning an audit, time will be spent on IT controls, change management, etc.; in fact, all the standard IT general controls plus focus on key areas are identified as riskier. The context is different for "brick-and-mortar" companies moving to some digitalization or for digital companies moving to "brick-and-mortar" activities. For both, the main reasons are people and processes. People will have the expertise of their current business and lack it in new operations. Processes will have to be consistent/coherent with both types of operations.

The main impact for audit and as such the main risk for auditors is the risk of inadequacy between auditor's IT skillset and IT evaluation pace. IT understanding is critical to perform our audit duties since the 90s a lot of studies and thesis have been written on the impact of digitalization on audit practices. They take often for granted the magic around the new buzzwords created by the IT specialists, such as artificial intelligence or the blockchain, an IT technique we will speak about later on in the following chapter. Usually at least three of them are selected at least and they assume that they are stable, i.e., won't evolve or change, and that the touted benefits are actual and future proof. Then, as for other business activities, the conclusion is that the work done the way it is now will be done differently later on. A consequence might be job losses. This is quite a risky affirmation, as more and more complexity is embedded into our information systems due to the evolution in IT technologies, the tasks performed will change for sure.

Being positive, if we agree on that assurance is required on financial figures and future forecast enablers, auditors are needed. How this trust will be achieved is one aspect of this book diving in the next and following chapters in the information system.

BIBLIOGRAPHY

BFO: Carl Benedikt Frey and Michael Osborne, *"The Future of Employment,"* 2013, Working paper, University of Oxford

BGD: Benjamin Graham and David L. Dodd, *"Security Analysis,"* 6th Edition, 2008, McGraw Hill, 978-0-07159-253-6

BSC: Bruce Schneier, *"Secrets and Lies. Digital Security in a Networked World,"* 2000, John Wiley & Sons, Ltd., 0-471-25311-1

CST: Casimir Stryienski, *"Le XVIIIe siècle,"* 1912, 2e édition, Hachette et Cie

GTE: Gillian Tett, *"Fool's Gold,"* 2009, Hachette Digital, 978-0-7481-1221-0

JDE: James Don Edwards, *"History of Public Accounting in the United States,"* 1960, MSU Business Studies

JFL: Judith Flanders, *"A Place for Everything,"* 2020, Picador, 978-1-5098-8159-8

JMA: Jo Marchant, *"Cure: A Journey into the Science of Mind Over Body,"* 2016, Canongate Books, 978-0-85786-884-8

JMO: Jonathan Morris, *"Coffee: A Global History,"* 2019, Reaktion Books Ltd, 978-1-789-14026-2

PAS: Paul A. Strassmann, *"The Politics of Information Management – Policy Guidelines,"* 1995, The Information Economics Press, 0-920413-4-3

RBR: Richard Brown, *"A History of Accounting and Accountants,"* 1905, T. C. and E. C. Jack

TOH: Taiichi Ohno, *"Workplace Management,"* 1982, JMA Management Center, 978-1-257-30107-2

Chapter 2

Information system

> Like long echoes that from afar merge
> In a deep and dark unity
> Vast as night and as light,
> Scents, colors and sounds answer each other.
>
> Charles Baudelaire, "The Flowers of Evil"

2.1 INFORMATION

Well, all looks fine in audit history. Progress has been made, new methods implemented, expertise improved, standards developed, and profession eventually got organized. However, in the early 20th century, all was not so ideal:

> Standard Oil had tons of cash but didn't know what to do with it, because the company didn't know how much it had. It hadn't standardized its accounting practices over its long existence; none of the books matched up.
>
> [NSA]

One of the reasons is that the businesses were going bigger and bigger, wider, and wider geographically. To help them sustain their growth, new office furniture, new building options, and new organization were designed. These changes along with scientific progress in information technology, theoretical then practical shifted how society look at the world. And this starts with words.

Nowadays we are taking for granted the significance of the word "information" for instance. Let's have a look at Google Ngram [GNG] in Figure 2.1. The appearances of the words "data," "information," and "knowledge" correlate with the organizational shift in the companies. The data retrieval is based on English (American and British) from 1900 to nowadays. The knowledge word usage (top line in 1900) is quite flat during all this period. Instead the information and data words (respectively second line and third lines in 1900) have seen a stable usage trend up to the mid-60s. A huge increased

DOI: 10.1201/9781003230137-2

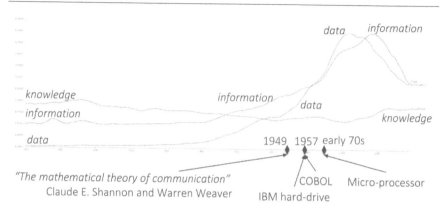

Figure 2.1 Data, information, and knowledge words appearances since 1900.

usage starts when practical implementations of the seminal book of Claude E. Shannon and Warren Weaver take place.

The scientists followed the path shown to them and the scientific literature grew bigger and bigger enabling major innovations. To cite a few of them, we have IBM introducing the hard drive in 1957, the specification of a common business languages to reduce programming costs, for instance COBOL, issued in January 1960, and the first micro-processors produced in the early 70s.

In addition,

> in the 1960s, management theorists began to imagine new kinds of office workers who, aided by technological advances in computing, would become "knowledge workers"—highly educated, creative white-collars professionals who would be paid to think. Office design theorists tried to house this new kind of worker with a bewildering number of designs.
>
> [NSA]

Alongside these architectural changes, the workplace changed too, starting with the evolution of the desk design. Up to the end of the 19th century, desks were not a flat surface. They were a stand-alone place of work, with plenty of drawers underneath and above, with specific pigeon-holes and other specificities to fit different type of documents (e.g. the multiple patents granted to Wooton Desks). The clerks were people of knowledge.

The 20th century confirmed the trend to document sharing seen as information as they were useful to more than one clerk. The filling cabinet invented in the 1890s gained popularity when loose leaf were accepted for accounting:

> No improvement in financial accounting since the introduction of double-entry bookkeeping has been of such importance as the introduction of removable-leaf systems to accounting books.
>
> [CAS]

Book-keeping used to be performed writing down transactions in books. Having leaves, or pieces of paper bounded added a security layer.

For example, the well-known explicit ruling of the case 23998 in 1935 in Oklahoma *Maney v. Cherry* states:

> The defendants' objection that the sales tickets are not "books" within the meaning of the statute is without merit. Under modern bookkeeping practices, loose-card and loose-leaf systems have largely supplanted the earlier use of bound volumes. Entries on such loose leaves or cards are just as truly "entries in books of account," within the meaning of the statute, as though the leaves were bound into a volume. This view is supported in 22 C. J. 870, which states: "In view of the growth in modern times of the system of using 'loose-leaf' books of account, it would seem clear that leaves from such books should be competent, and they are held to be so."
>
> (https://law.justia.com/cases/oklahoma/supreme-court/1935/23756.html)

There is no surprise as, *"a number of scholars have argued that a distinctly modern conception of information became comprehensible in part through a connection to the properties of paper documents, 'separate and separable, bounded and distinct'"* [CRO]. How we use the word information nowadays is the result of these decades of information technology studies with the shifting of Weaver's point of view. Donald Ray distinguishes three information ages in his analysis of the invention of information:

> European documentation before and soon after World War II, United States information theory and cybernetics soon after World War II, and the "virtual" age that is proclaimed today.
>
> [DRA]

What information technology tells us is that information is the result of information processes. They use data as an input and provide information as a result. But during the first age of information, information was everywhere available for everyone without the need of computers.

Alexander Von Humboldt for instance (1769–1859) performed tremendous trips in the world with the amazing one in South America, traveling where no Europeans traveled before. He prepared them in such a way to both enjoying being part of nature and writing down a lot of information on the nature around him:

> Obsessed with scientific observation, the thirty-two-year-old had brought a vast array of the best instruments from Europe. For the accent of Chimborazo, he had left most of the baggage behind, but had packed a barometer, a thermometer, a sextant, an artificial horizon and a so-called

"cyanometer" with which he could measure the "blueness" of the sky. As they climbed, Humboldt fumbled out his instruments with numb fingers, setting them upon precariously narrow ledges to measure altitude, gravity, and humidity. He meticulously listed any species encountered—here a butterfly, there a tiny flower. Everything was recorded in his notebook.

[AWU]

Latour also was looking at nature as full of information:

Latour begins his essay with a self-portrait by Pierre Sonnerat in 1776, "Voyage à la Nouvelle Guinée," in which Sonnerat is depicted as seated in a tropical environment drawing natural objects while he is surrounded by specimens destined for, among other places, the laboratory and, like Briet's antelope, the Jardin des Plantes. For Latour, this self-portrait demonstrates several things. First, as in Briet's book, Latour's analysis doesn't focus on books or other paper materials as documents but on natural objects. This is important because Latour argues that information should not be characterized in terms of a representational fact; rather, it is a relation between two places, a peripheral and a center. This relationship is a practical relationship between what Latour terms a "center of calculation" or "center of measure" ("centre de calcul") and the objects which that center organizes.

[DRA]

Fast forward in today's environment, information technology is not the single source of information. It's a source of data, quite often grouped or structured in different ways, there acquiring some meaning such as financial data, inventory data.

2.2 INFORMATION SYSTEMS

Information systems include all personnel, facilities and services associated with the creation, processing and distribution of information following a prescribed procedure, without necessarily applying any computers.

[PAS]

Information System is a word whose usage started growing following scientific and technical evolutions like the word information. In Figure 2.2, the Google Ngram [GNG] shows "information system" from 1900 to nowadays.

Expressions with the word system were used of course, such as scientific system, information system notion is highly dependent on the results of the computing environment, called information technology. As auditors we know that remote audit can only be applied to specific narrow focused

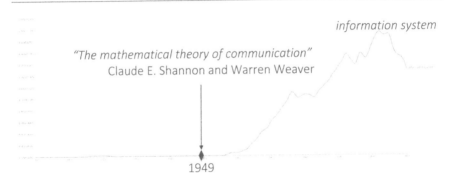

"The mathematical theory of communication"
Claude E. Shannon and Warren Weaver

information system

1949

Figure 2.2 "Information system" appearances since 1900.

audits. Remote audit is not a panacea and it is needed to go on site to gather additional information. Information from the context, environment where the processes are taking place. How can you know with data in the computerized information system that a flowerpot or a green plant is standing above computers in a data room on a specific site without going there? This book is titled *Information System Audit*, we focus on the changes implied by the digitalization of the information system, how this impacts, and how it should be audited. Regulation, Controls, and Audit are based on information. They ensure that this information is available and reliable. But what information are we talking about? In the previous chapters, we talked mainly about financial and accounting information. But there is a lot of other information that is necessary for the operations of the company, such as when checking the cargo of a ship and reconciling it with its load sheet. To be as generic as possible and not to reduce us to a sector of activity, we will retain the main common departments found in listed companies:

- Finance,
- Human Resource,
- IT,
- Marketing,
- Operations management,
- Purchasing, and
- Sales.

All these departments use information to achieve their objectives. This information comes from other departments or from the company's environment. Each department produces new information for internal use or for third parties. This information has borrowed other media than the voice for reasons of memorization, communication, and control. This goes from fixed supports like the part of the wall dedicated to writing down a shopping list still visible in a house in Ephesus to mobile supports like the clay tablets with a wax coating used by the Romans to temporarily note down information with their wooden stylus (iron styluses used for writing were banned in Rome following the murder of Caesar). This technique continued until the Middle Ages. Fixed or mobile, these supports can be for multiple use as in the two previous examples or for single use. The flexibility of multiple use has a disadvantage, the information can be deleted or altered making the deletion or alteration almost impossible to identify depending on the medium and the technique used. The single-use medium, on the other hand, makes it possible to show whether the initial information has been altered, such as a stone or a leaf.

In ancient times, important information was recorded on metal plates. In Rome, the laws of the Twelve Tables are so called because they are engraved on 12 bronze plates. The bronze plates are used for public and private acts, such as certificates of military leave or civil status. The debris of pottery is also of very widespread use among the Greeks and Egyptians: One inscribes there, contracts of sale, particular acts, letters, and accounts of kitchen. The leaves, even if perishable, but easily available and therefore inexpensive, are used in different parts of the world, the leaf of makarekau in the Maldives, of talipot in Ceylon, of the olive tree for the votes of the inhabitants of Syracuse (and of oyster scales for the vote of the Athenians). With a more elaborate technique, the Chinese produce silk or rice paper. As exchanges developed and the number of transactions became more and more important, easy technical solutions to transport information were constantly invented. From the use of leaves and tree bark, we move to the manufacture of Egyptian paper or papyrus. A flourishing industry was created around the cultivation and processing of this plant which grows easily and naturally only in the Nile Valley. All the parts of this plant have a utility for the Egyptians. They made ropes, fabrics, sails, for example, and, of course, paper. The Egyptologist Jean-François Champollion found dated contracts on papyrus that date back to 1700 BC. Papyrus became an important export product for the Egyptians when they decided from the 7th century BC to sell the paper they made. They will always keep the product for themselves and will only sell what they do not use. In 450 BC, Hieron of Syracuse, gets papyrus plants. He planted them in Sicily, but the plants vegetated and gave only poor-quality leaves. Moreover, like any agricultural crop, papyrus is subject to the vagaries of the climate both during its cultivation and in its transport on the Mediterranean Sea. This results in periods of shortages. These shortages of papyrus paper paralyze the good functioning of the societies of this time. They block, for example, the functioning of the Roman administration and the trade until provoking riots under Tiberius as told by Pliny.

This reminds us a lot of the floods in Thailand in 2011, which affected the world production of hard drives. Indeed, Thailand is then the second-largest exporter of hard drives in the world after China, with approximately 25% of world production. The shortage is estimated to last six months and costs have increased by 20–40% depending on the model.

These problems of shortages of papyrus and dependence toward Egypt incite the king of Pergamon, Attalus II to organize or support the competition in Asia Minor, toward the 3rd century before Jesus Christ. Industrialists of Pergamon perfected the treatment of animal skins to use them as a medium of information. The "paper" of Pergamon or parchment becomes a product competing with papyrus paper both by its price and its technical qualities. The range of products is smaller than that of papyrus; it is limited to two categories. The first one uses goat or sheep skins. The second uses calf, lamb, and stillborn goat skins for a superior quality, called vellum. This new product line has two competitive advantages. The first competitive advantage is that the manufacturing is industrialized with clearly defined steps to produce papers of the same quality. The second competitive advantage is that the production of raw material is not random. But the decline of papyrus paper will not be due to this competition but to the invasion of Egypt by the Muslims in the 9th century. Papyrus paper is not of one quality. In fact, several grades are available at different prices. Techniques are also evolving to ensure that the written information does not disappear because the ink does not hold on the support or the support is too thin to facilitate its reading.

As Pliny explains, adding a little vinegar to the most common black ink, which is a mixture of lampblack, gum, and water, is enough to make it indelible. He says that by infusing wormwood into the ink, manuscripts are preserved from mice. The mice, a danger for the information systems well before the "bugs" for the computer systems! This ink will be replaced only in the 12th century by new inks composed mainly of iron sulfate, gallnut, gum, and water. Papyrus paper is made of more or less narrow strips. They are wound in rolls or volumes in Latin, around a cylindrical wooden rod whose end ends in a button. To this button is attached a label that gives the title of the work. They are stored horizontally on shelves in repositories or libraries. The filing is essential to find the information easily.

In computing, filing is also essential. It is one of the characteristics of computer processing. This is found in the way of storing data in databases, different methods of database management systems have been created, to find the data as easily and quickly as possible.

The storage of volumes also requires important precautions against fire and flooding, as is the case for our modern data centers. Famous libraries have suffered these perils. The libraries of Carthage, of the palace of Tiberius, of the Capitol, or of Alexandria at different periods were destroyed by fire. The backup at that time is the other libraries. They have the advantage of being geographically distant and under different climates. But these "backups" are imperfect because they do not contain exactly the same books. There is therefore a loss of information and significant delays in reconstituting the lost library. Copyists must travel to other libraries to copy the volumes.

If we compare with the ease of saving information nowadays, the associated audit control becomes fully justified, because the cost of saving is extremely low and fast compared to the difficulties of antiquity and the Middle Ages. This information is so important that Evergetes II, successor of Ptolemy Soter at the head of the library of Alexandria, industrialized a method now well known in computer science to increase the quantity of books in the library: A kind of downloading.

The digital transformation of information, in this case digitalization, simplifies the saving, copying or use of information by an increasingly large population. This practice is no longer limited to the physical loan of a book or DVD to friends.

Copying at that time is an inconvenient and time-consuming process and is therefore "ad hoc." Evergetes II uses this in a simple but organized way: He had all the books that entered his lands seized and sent to Alexandria. There, if the book is not already present, copyists recopy it. The original remains on site and the copy is given to the owner. In the computer world, this would also involve both the interception of information on the computer network and the downloading of files.

Bookstores, these old warehouses, or data centers, must also consider other risks for the preservation of information media. First, the premises must be ventilated and be at a stable temperature, protected from light and free from insects (bugs) or rodents. Computers are not the only ones that require a protected environment.

The risks are all the greater because copying the information itself creates risks. Copying a volume takes time, because not all copyists are competent. They are more or less fast in execution and do not necessarily understand what they are copying, hence the copying errors in addition to the involuntary errors. The major drawback is that these errors accumulate to result in legible but incorrect or illegible copies. In the 4th century, the tragedies of Aeschylus, Sophocles and Euripides were so full of inaccuracies that the orator Lycurgus had corrected copies made from the available volumes [PLU].

These "originals" or "master copies" are stored in the Acropolis. Ptolemy, king of Egypt, borrowed these "originals" on a pledge from the Athenians to make copies for his library in Alexandria. But he would rather lose his pledge than return them. The texts that remain to us from Greek or Roman antiquity are distanced from the original texts by at least 20 consecutive copies. The copyists are themselves aware of their mistakes. In the Middle Ages, for example, they put on the last page an apology to the reader for the errors they might have let pass. This type of error also affects computer copies of data. These errors concern either the information or the medium, which may be defective. In both cases, mathematical work has made it possible to compensate, detect, and correct these errors. If the creation of a copy uses a network, we have in addition the errors attributable to the network.

From the 10th century, the East provides paper of which cotton is the principal material at the time when the paper of papyrus disappears, and the parchment remains at a high price. The high cost of the raw material has two consequences, the first is the modification of the writing of information and the second is the reuse of the raw material. The writing of information tends to become finer and finer and to tighten to put more information on the same surface.

The other trend to optimize the use of paper was the use of abbreviations, called Tironian notes in this period and shorthand in the 20th century. Tullius Tiron, a freedman who became a friend of Cicero, invented the first system of signs dedicated specifically to the speed of writing information and optimizing the use of raw material. These tachographs (from their Greek name, fast writers) formed an important service within the imperial chancelleries of Rome and Constantinople.

We can draw a parallel with the initial maximum capacity of 160 characters for text messages or Short Message Service (SMS) or 140 characters for messages on Twitter. In the manner of what is called a "telegraphic style" with the use of the telegraph, abbreviations are widely used when communicating by SMS or tweets as in the time of Tiron.

But writing information with abbreviations is also very useful for students. The rhetorician and teacher Quintilian complained that students were selling his lessons to the public. This risk of "intellectual property" is sufficiently well known that the abbreviator of Pliny the Elder, Solinus, points out in the preface of his book "Polyhistor" that a copy, which is, moreover, incorrect, is published under a different title Collectania. To counteract this fraud he revises his book, i.e., writes a new revised edition, so that the publications, the "originals" and the "copies," with an earlier date become obsolete.

With the scarcity and high cost of blank parchment in the Middle Ages, the idea came up to wash and scrape old parchments that had already been written on, to resell them. Of course, this idea was applied to any parchment, no matter what information was written on it. This is how many writings were lost. So much so that in the 12th century, there were more washed and scraped parchments (palimpsests) than new ones. This work is done for the sake of profit, not to recover quality parchment that could be mistaken for new parchment. To ensure productivity, the parchments are poorly washed and scraped. As a result, it is still possible to read the old writings if not in full then at least in part. During the Renaissance, it became important to recover historical texts to take advantage of the benefits of printing. To recover the original text, chemical treatments were applied, but this damaged the palimpsest. With the evolution of analysis techniques, it was possible to find more information on the parchments without damaging the information written over them.

In computing, to delete your file you drag it into the trash can, then you empty it. There you go, the confidential document has disappeared on your screen. Only on your screen. Indeed, the medium keeps, like parchment, more or less complete traces of the data that have been stored there. Various computer techniques have been developed to remove this data from magnetic media. In practice, they try to rewrite on the whole medium or to make an equivalent. The magnetic medium is preserved and can be reused like a palimpsest. But the best way to ensure that the old information can no longer be read is to physically destroy the magnetic medium. The NSA/CSS makes very pragmatic recommendations to ensure that data deletion is effective.

The technique of paper evolves and from the end of the 13th century, beginning of the 14th century, the paper of linen or rag, i.e., containing rags reduced in paste is invented. This linen paper should not be confused with the linen prepared to be used as a support of information which was used punctually since centuries. This invention makes it possible to support, on the one hand, the diffusion of the books by lowering the costs of production by a less expensive raw material and, on the other hand, the evolution of the techniques of storage of information. Let us note in passing that the paper of papyrus is too fragile to be printed under press and for the parchment it is the opposite, this invention was necessary so that the printing industry can be industrialized. Paper remains the technique with the best quality-price ratio for the storage of information for several centuries. Its production technique has evolved widely, to satisfy needs, to reduce production costs, to increase the range of products, to guarantee the independence of production from climatic constraints, and to improve the security of information.

Before the spread of printing in Europe, handwritten books were extremely expensive due to the cost and time of production. The printing press changed all that. During the first period of printing, between 1467 and 1500, 14,750 editions were printed by the 212 cities in Europe that had printing houses. During the second period, from 1501 to 1536, the printing houses are consolidated from 212 to 184. They produce 17,779 editions, an increase of 20% with 3029 additional editions. This increase, already very important in itself, is even more so when one knows that the printers limited the number of copies produced in the first period to keep up with the prices of the manuscripts. But with the help of competition and the desire to increase sales by increasing volume and lowering prices, the average number of copies produced per edition increased from 435 to 1000, an increase of 230% [PRA]. The information medium of paper became an industry in its own right. The information spreads more and more, starting with schoolchildren and students. The quantity of different subjects available in these editions amounted to more than 32,000 from 1467 to 1536. The printing industry needed new uses and new texts to develop. Just as computerization improved the speed of information preparation in the 20th century, printers and ink work increased production. This information on paper concerns, of course, the commercial information, the keeping of accounts and progressively all the functions of the company. Industrialization in the 20th century favored an increase in the size of companies and the amount of information they processed.

> Industrialization in Britain and America was producing more and more administrative work, and alongside it a need for a rational approach to managing accounts, bills, ledgers: in short, paperwork.
>
> [NSA]

More or less ingenious processes are put in place to store this information, already by separating what is necessary to continue the activity from what can be archived. This work is even more difficult if it has not been prepared in advance with relevant storage and classification. An initial sorting must be done, which is therefore more or less rapid depending on the organization in place. This sorting also makes it possible to delete documents considered to be of no use to the company's future activity and to limit the quantity of documents to be stored. Archiving used to be done annually, based on the fiscal year. The amount of information has increased so much that annual archiving blocks the personnel for too long a period and archiving at a faster frequency is preferred.

Companies are physically structured to set up spaces dedicated to this paper production: Offices. Either the company separates its production sites from the offices by having the production inside or not far from the city, or the company separates the production and the offices with the production on the first floor and the offices on the second floor or if it is on the same level with two separate entrances.

In the same way, permanent inventories facilitate annual inventories, which then become (theoretically) a simple formality. It is interesting to draw a parallel between the management of the stocks necessary for production and the management of the information used, transformed, and created for this production, its management and monitoring. There are four kinds of information stocks:

- Raw materials and components ready to be used in production,
- Products in the process of production,
- Finished products available for sale, and
- Consumables, such as ink, stationery, energy.

The raw materials and components ready to be used in production are, for example, regulatory texts, standards, methodologies, and information provided by another department of the company or by the external environment of the company. The function of a documentalist in a law firm will provide information on demand thanks to the storage, archiving of the documentary fund, and the indexing of reference texts. Audit and accounting firms have the same need.

Products in production are, for example, e-mail exchanges, test results, and intermediate versions of documents that will benefit from various reviews. Properly defined business processes identify the intermediate stages of product progress. At these intermediate stages, the information to be communicated to the next one is identified, and the other information is reprocessed by archiving or deletion. Ideally, work-in-progress should be eliminated, as it only produces finished goods, which are the only things the company can sell for money. Poor management of work-in-progress is a significant risk for the company. This is an operational risk that we will discuss in a following chapter. The end products are all the documents validated and approved by the appropriate managers, such as quarterly results by the financial management and the company's executive, internal, institutional, commercial communications, or packaging. Validated and approved information is vital information for the company, as it is "sold" directly or indirectly. It is the tangible result of the company's investments, culture, and work methods.

The consumables are mainly the ideas, work, and efforts provided by the company's personnel. The transformation of information into new information is the result of the reflection and analysis of those involved. Nowadays, artificial intelligence is already a part of this transformation. This work is already often delegated to computer programs, called bots, apheresis of robots. The best known are the chatbots that greet you on the page of the website you are visiting. They are an improved version of the software that handles incoming phone calls. The logistics of the first three types of information inventories, raw materials and components, work-in-progress, and finished goods, quickly becomes problematic as information is produced and not managed. The undeniable advantage of having the information on paper is that the problem is obvious to all management. Their involvement in solving the problem is extremely easy to obtain. Necessary investments are approved. Usually, solutions that are more of a flight to quality are adopted, such as larger offices, better office furniture or more budgets for archiving. Changing the medium of information with computerization will not solve the problem. The main reason is that computer storage media take up much less space than paper-stored information. This makes it much more difficult to involve and explain the situation to management. For them the problem does not exist, because it is no longer visible.

The techniques used to protect information evolve at the same time as the technical supports. When it's paper, it's not a big problem to understand. There are:

- Medium,
- The means of recording or storing the information, and
- The coding of the information.

By working on each of these three elements, a security strategy can be defined. As an auditor, if a security strategy has been defined, it is possible to audit its implementation and effectiveness.

Aulu-Gelle, a 2nd century Roman, explains different methods of securing information in his book "Attic Nights." For point 1, the support, he reports the following story:

> An illustrious personage of Carthage resorted to the following expedient to conceal a correspondence on important secrets: he took new tablets, which were not yet coated with wax; he wrote on the wood, then spread the wax over them according to the custom, and sent the tablets, where nothing seemed to be written, to his correspondent, who, warned, scratched off the coating, and read the letter easily on the wood.

For point 2, the means of recording information, he gives this example:

> Histiaeus, established among the Persians at the court of Darius, wanted to secretly send important news to a certain Aristagoras. Here is the curious means of correspondence to which he had recourse: one of his slaves had suffered for a long time from the eyes; under the pretext of curing him, he shaved his whole head, and traced characters by pricks on the exposed skin. He wrote whatever he wanted. He kept the man at home until his hair had grown back; then he sent him to Aristagoras: "When you have arrived," he said to him, "recommend him well, in my name, to shave your head, as I have done myself." The slave obeyed, went to Aristagoras, and conveyed to him the recommendation of his master.

For point 3, the coding of information, there is already the language and the associated writing conventions. But as this coding is too well known, to make the information less visible at first sight, different techniques have been developed. Some are less well known than others, such as the time it took to understand Egyptian hieroglyphs. Aulu-Gelle quotes,

> a collection of letters from C. Caesar to C. Oppius and Balbus Cornelius, charged with the care of his affairs in his absence. In these letters, one finds, in certain places, fragments of syllables without connection, isolated characters, which one would believe thrown at random: it is impossible not to form any word of it. It was a stratagem they had agreed upon among themselves: on the paper one letter took the place and the name of another.

In an unusual way, the code of Caesar was reused in particular at the beginning of the Internet and forums, through the ROT-13. The ROT-13 is simply the code of Caesar, where a ROTation of 13 letters (A->N) is chosen. The idea is not to broadcast encrypted messages, but to make sure that the message is not read involuntarily, for example, if it reveals the plot of a movie or gives the answer to a riddle.

More recently, point 3 has been used for romantic correspondence. Marie-Antoinette, not yet queen, met Count Hans Axel von Fersen at the Opera ball in 1774. They were then 18 years old. Hans Axel von Fersen participated in the American War of Independence. He entered into a secret correspondence with the Queen in 1792. They exchanged love letters coded with a polyalphabetic cipher system, called Vigenère cipher (Blaise de Vigenère "Traité des chiffres ou des manières secrètes d'écrire," 1586).

It is necessary to have the table and the decryption key to read the correspondence. A very reliable encryption, broken only after three centuries by Charles Babbage in 1854. Their epistolary exchanges took place in the middle of the French Revolution, Marie-Antoinette was locked up in the Tuileries.

The coding also protects Alex de Fersen. However, we do not yet know how the decoding key was transmitted.

Aulu-Gelle gives another example which combines at the same time point 1, the support, and point 2, the way of noting the information:

> Formerly in Lacedemonia, when the State addressed to its generals secret dispatches which were to remain unintelligible with the enemy in the event of their being intercepted, one resorted to this stratagem. One had two round sticks, elongated, of the same thickness and length, polished and prepared in the same way; one was given to the general at his departure for the army, the other remained entrusted to the magistrates, with the Tables of the law and the public seal. When one had to write to the general something secret, one rolled on this cylinder a strip of mediocre width and of sufficient length, in the manner of a spiral. The rings of the band, thus rolled, had to be exactly applied and joined to each other. Then the characters were drawn transversely, the lines going from top to bottom. The band, thus loaded with writing, was raised of the cylinder, and sent to the general with the knowledge of the stratagem. After the separation, it offered only truncated and mutilated letters, bodies, and heads of letters, divided, and scattered: also, the dispatch could fall to the power of the enemy without it being possible for him to guess its contents.

Aeneas the Tactician (Aeneus Tacticus), a Greek writer of the 4th century B.C., specialized in the art of war, also analyzed the options for securing messages. Some of them are like those quoted by Allu-Gelle. All these options are known today with different names due to the use of computer techniques. He also proposes twice to work on the ink and to make it invisible, i.e., to erase it from the support to be made visible by the recipient. The work on the invisible ink is, moreover, an axis of preponderant security during the 1st and 2nd World Wars and the Cold War. The examples presented above do not guarantee that the sender or receiver is who he or she claims to be. Histiée prevents the slave from suspecting the original intention and thus from being betrayed voluntarily or not. As for the wax-covered tablet and the coding of the information, the sender and receiver have agreed on the method beforehand. But if a third party intercepts the medium and knows the method, the information is perfectly readable. This is the risk cited in advance by Aeneas The Tactician (Aeneus Tacticus):

> as regards secret messages, there are all sorts of ways of sending them: a private arrangement should be made beforehand between the sender and the recipient.

[ATA]

Paper has been a medium of information for thousands of years. We have become accustomed to evaluating and thinking about information according to the medium and the techniques used. These habits have penalized us during the progressive digitalization of information and information systems. We are considering all the people who did not work in IT such as the overall company's management.

2.3 IT IMPACT ON INFORMATION SYSTEMS

The habit of paper had accustomed us to see the world in the following way as shown in Figure 2.3.

So, we thought that computerization simply changed this vision into what we have shown in Figure 2.4.

What could be more convenient than to consider that the paper medium is simply replaced by a screen that provides information at will? But this apparent simplicity is deceptive. Let's take a recent example of what this move from media to information technology means. TietoEVRY, a Finnish IT software and service company, launched a typographic initiative against cyberbullying, enter the multi awarded The Polite Type. It is an open-source font created by a diverse team and in collaboration with teenagers from different schools. It has been taught to recognize and rewrite cyberbullying and hate speech. With the help of machine learning, it will be taught to understand broader contexts.

From 1980s onward, the spread of microcomputers in companies and a decade later among individuals followed by widespread access to the Internet, then in the 2010s' with mobile phones, has spread the culture of computing

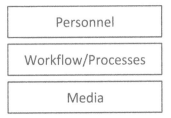

Figure 2.3 Paper based understanding.

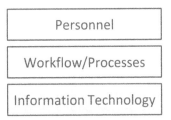

Figure 2.4 Information technology current shift.

and the provision of digitalized information. The understanding of digital technology is improving, on the one hand, because it is a fundamental movement that concerns all people, and, on the other hand, because in 40 years employees have changed, with retirements and new training for students. But so many new applications, such as the font The Polite Type, and new hardware are developed that of course it is difficult to stay tuned.

Shoshana Zuboff sees this as the foundation of surveillance capitalism and calls it "the problem of the two texts":

> The specific mechanisms of surveillance capitalism compel the production of "two electronic texts," not just one. When it comes to the first text, we are the authors and the readers... Everything that we contribute to the first text, no matter how trivial or fleeting, becomes a target for surplus extraction.
>
> [SZU]

When you read a paper book, it is you, the novel, and the book. When you read an e-book, it is you, the novel and all the technology behind. Replace book by a website and here we are. These traces are found also in the company's information system.

This global ignorance of digital technology was clearly visible during the Internet bubble of the 1990s. The lack of knowledge of investors and the lack of knowledge of the financial analysts on whom investors relied. Financial analysts specialized in Internet stocks had become the new "gurus":

> In 1996, only a year after the Netscape IPO, few institutional investors had a firm grasp of the various businesses that made up the Web, and even fewer Wall Street executives had a clue to what was going on.
>
> [CGA]

What are the main differences brought by the digitalization of information? First, it has multiplied the quantity of information produced, stored, and deleted, far more that what happened with the printing in Europe. The digitalization of information has also modified the three points mentioned above for paper: The medium, the way of recording information, and the information.

The amount of digitalized information produced, stored, and deleted has become phenomenal. Seneca was already quite critical in his time about the libraries that are becoming fashionable and about the indiscriminate accumulation of books:

> What do these thousands of books, these innumerable libraries, do to me, whose titles, in order to read them, would hardly suffice the whole life of their owners? This multiplicity of books is rather an overload than a

nourishment for the mind; and it is better to be attached to a few authors than to lose one's capricious attention on a hundred works.

[SEN]

A concern shared by Descartes several centuries later.

Louis von Ahn, founder of reCaptcha, has worked on this issue of books and their digitalization:

> With reCaptcha we had to become really efficient. The problem we had with reCaptcha's, they are a hundred million books that needed to be digitized. That was the total number of books that has ever been written before the digital era was one hundred million. at the pace we were going, we were able to digitize about two to three million books a year.
>
> [LVA]

Seneca's use of the word "book" does not designate the same object as Louis von Ahn's use of the word "book." Since the 1960s, the continuous decline in the price of computer media has encouraged this accumulation of digitized information. In about 50 years, digital information has been stored on various media, some of which have become obsolete, such as punched cards, magnetic tapes, 5 ¼" floppy disks and 3 ½" disks. Each time it is a desire for simplification, performance and lower storage cost that justifies these technological changes. Most of the digital information at the beginning of the 21st century is on hard disks.

This information is stored using 0 and 1, it is a binary coding. Each piece of information is called a byte, because the coding requires eight positions of 0 and 1 to code a letter or a number, for example. Their storage capacities in megabytes have increased since the first hard disks were made by IBM in 1956 by an order of magnitude of more than 800,000 times. Conversely, the price of information storage, i.e., the price per megabyte of storage, has decreased during these years by an order of magnitude of several billion.

So far from public libraries like Alexandria or Pergamon, and the personal libraries of the rich owners of antiquity to store information, we have data centers in or outside our companies' sites and networked or portable hard drives on each of our companies' sites with increasingly large storage capacities. Let's not forget the memory sticks used to be called USB keys, whose storage capacities are steadily increasing to carry documents with you, are being replaced by storage accessible by telephone network or in the cloud. A definite change for auditing purposes.

Digitalization therefore increases phenomenally the amount of information to be managed by a company and to manage a company. At the same time, it also affects the medium with changes during technical developments. All types of media can be used such as paper (e.g. cards and punched tapes), magnetic media (e.g. magnetic tapes and hard disks), and optical storage (e.g.

CD and DVD). Depending on the medium it is possible to "hide" information, such as having a non-visible space, or a protected space or invisible files. It affects the way information is recorded by encoding it. It has become a very important area of application of mathematical research. But the riskiest element, because it has become the most complex due to the digitalization of information, is its transport. It has become almost totally electronic whether it be with telephones, wired or wireless networks such as Wi-Fi. The medium that carries a message or information from the sender to the recipient is very understandable when it is paper. With the interconnection of computers in all countries of the world, knowing where the information is sent has become very technical and complex. It is so important that we must take stock of it.

The first case is the messenger who memorizes a news or carries an information. The carrier pigeon is a particular messenger who knows only the return to his loft and has the advantage of maintaining the anonymity of his sender. It knows only one destination. The human messenger can know the sender or the receiver or only follow delivery indications. This simplicity exists by definition in a computer network. A computer network delivers a reliable message to the right destination as quickly as possible.

The whole job of anonymizing or securing information transfers is to provide functionality in addition to the information transfer function. These concerns have grown with the importance of digitalization of exchanges.

As the Cold War was winding down, the Crypto Wars were about to begin.

[AGR]

In this book, we will not cover all the technical possibilities for limiting, securing, and auditing these traces.

Why this interest in securing these digital exchanges? For several reasons that you can already see by using the Internet. Without going into detail about the information that the sites you connect to can retrieve, the site knows the location of your computer if you connect with a computer (called IP address), the server of your access provider, the operating system of the device used and the type of browser used as well as the web page that allowed you to access a site and other details (http://www.anonymat.org/vostraces/index.php).

Whether you are accessing a network from your company or from home, you leave traces. If you transfer files, they will pass from machine to machine on the network until they reach the recipient. If you don't control these machines, the transmitted information can be intercepted.

Let's take the example of a company with an R&D center on a single site in Australia. You decide to use your group's expertise in India and split the research between two sites, the one already in Australia and the other one in India. Thanks to telecommunications, computer networks and the reduction in their costs, it is very easy for researchers to collaborate.

Regardless of where the intellectual property is created and the possible taxes associated with document transfers, if you use the Internet, for

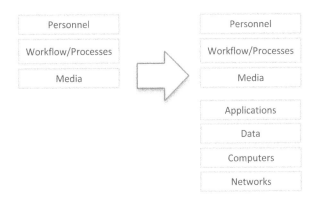

Figure 2.5 The underlying complexity for the media.

example, without special precautions, the controls set up in each of the two sites become useless: You have no control over what happens between them, on the network. The organizational decision to move from one R&D site to two R&D sites changes your information system.

Our simple vision by just replacing the medium by the computer is wrong. The medium is always present, it is more often the screens of all kinds. These screens mask the underlying computer complexity, as shown in Figure 2.5.

The first difficulty is that the medium (the screen) only presents information at a point in time "t." A person can look at an inventory on a screen and form an opinion at that moment. But if he comes back a day later, the information displayed may be different. The easiest solution for him is to print this inventory with the date and time of printing on paper.

The second difficulty comes from the additional technical elements that have been added: Applications, Data, Computers, and Networks. As users, we forget this technical complexity of the information system and only see the medium. An auditor must ensure that the technical elements that transform this data into information are reliable, at least as reliable as paper. Yves Jeanneret also analyzes the difference between the medium and the information in his book "Is there (really) information technology?"

But how do you define the information system in a practical way? Paul A. Strassmann proposes the following definition: "Information systems encompass all information processes that depend on a formal procedure for completion" [PAS]. This definition is interesting for two reasons. The first one is that there is no mention of information technology, the second one is that the information considered is that which is used for the activities of the company, which have a purpose for it.

What is the scope of this information system? It depends on your organization and the management of this organization. The whole can be all or part of a company, from the company itself to the expertise of the personnel, passing by the directions, or the various sites of a company. This set of information is necessary for the management of the company, for the manufacture, the sale, the repair of the products and services, for the control of all these activities.

An auditor will quickly identify the asynchronization between the company's strategy and its technical IT architecture. Asynchronization means that the company's strategic vision is contradicted by the IT infrastructure chosen. Where are the data, what are the flows, where do these flows go through, reflect the reality of the company's operations, which can be very far from the will of the management and the strategy presented in the annual report?

Such a company manager will explain at the financial statements meeting that the company has fully integrated the recently acquired company. This company already represents more than 30% of the turnover in the consolidated accounts. The presentation will be filled with figures and graphics of the group's activities under one banner. The communication and marketing departments have worked fast and hard to refine the language and symbolism with words like "new," "integration," "global," and "synergy."

On the ground, the staff will go at their own human pace to appropriate this new context. The IT specialists, on the other hand, will quickly try to connect the information system of the acquired entity to that of the group. They need several years to finalize the merger or the integration of the information systems. But the group will not give them the time, either the IT people are not available for these projects, because other companies have still been acquired, or quite simply, the graft did not take and the acquired company is resold; they must then untie the links that they had taken care with professionalism to weave as well as possible.

This example explains the difference between two expressions that are often used interchangeably in conversations: "Information Technology" (IT) and "Information System" (IS). Information technology is the technical IT culture. Information System is the corporate culture, including its processes, methods, and human resources.

It is now accepted that during mergers and acquisitions, IT auditors are involved in due diligence. They can identify the integration costs and their risks. These integration costs correspond globally to the upgrading of one technical environment to the other. Very often, the buyer wishes to keep his IT environment and integrate that of the purchased company. But this is not always the case, even if it is rare.

The integration risks concern the operational risks of integrating IT environments and the informal risks due to differences in culture and work methods. Despite this, one company may want to buy another, and the IT system of the acquired company remains within the new group. This is quite common in the banking and insurance sector because the information system produces the services of the bank or insurance company. You have the IT department of the acquired company which is maintained with its teams and therefore its culture, its "methods" of work.

The outline of the computerization of a company's information system is an important subject because it indirectly defines the analysis of the budget

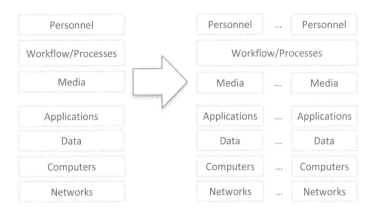

Figure 2.6 Information systems growing complexity.

and costs of the IT department. It is an exciting topic for controllers and auditors. Indeed, our perception of IT has evolved and continues to evolve. Just a few years ago (electronic) tablets were not considered a credible business tool in the enterprise. Does the rapid growth and evolution of connected objects extend the information system? Yes, because they already control information and connect to the corporate network to transmit it.

In Figure 2.6, our vision of the information system must reflect its growing complexity.

Only the process/workflow is more or less homogeneously understood by all stakeholders. They find that (following the figure from top to bottom):

- They are several people from different directions to participate in the same work *process* (workflow),
- They use different *media*, a machine tool touch screen, phone, or tablet, for example,
- They interact with different *applications*,
- They enter or modify part of the *data*,
- They use *computer* resources available on or off their site, and
- They are increasingly *connected* to a computer network component that communicates with other computer network components.

BIBLIOGRAPHY

AGR: Andy Greenberg, *"This Machine Kills Secret,"* 2012, Dutton, 978-0-75354-801-1
ATA: Énée Le Tacticien, *"Poliorcétique,"* Les Belles Lettres, 2002, 2-251-00106-9
AWU: Andrea Wulf, *"The Invention of Nature,"* 2015, Penguin Random House LLC, 978-0-385-35066-2
CAS: Charles A. Sweetland, *"Loose Leaf Book-keeping and Accounting,"* 1905
CGA: Charles Gasparino, *"Blood on the Street,"* 2005, Free Press, 0-7432-5023-0

CRO: Craig Robertson, *"The Filling Cabinet: A Vertical History of Information,"* 2021, The Regents of University of Minnesota, 978-1-4529-6372-3

DRA: Donald E. Ray, *"The Modern Invention of Information,"* 2001, Board of Trustees, 0-8093-2390-7

GNG: Jean-Baptiste Michel, Yuan Kui Shen, Aviva Presser Aiden, Adrian Veres, Matthew K. Gray, The Google Books Team, Joseph P. Pickett, Dale Hoiberg, Dan Clancy, Peter Norvig, Jon Orwant, Steven Pinker, Martin A. Nowak, and Erez Lieberman Aiden, "Quantitative Analysis of Culture Using Millions of Digitized Books." *Science,* 2010. Published Online Ahead of Print: 12/16/2010. DOI: 10.1126/science.1199644. www.sciencemag.org/content/early/2010/12/15/science.1199644

LVA: Louis von Ahn, *"The Taxonomy of Collective Knowledge,"* 2017, a16z podcast, 08/15/2017, https://a16z.com/2017/08/15/data-ontologies-diagnosis-collective-intelligence/

NSA: Nikil Saval, *"Cubed – A Secret History of the Workplace,"* 2014, DoubleDay, 978-0-385-53658-5

PAS: Paul A. Strassmann, *"The Politics of Information Management – Policy Guidelines,"* 1995, The Information Economics Press, 0-920413-4-3

PLU: Plutarque, "Vie de l'orateur Lycurgue," 1844, Chex Lefevre Editeur

PRA: Louis-Charles-François Petit-Radel, *"Recherches sur les bibliothèques anciennes et modernes,"* 1819

SEN: Sénèque, *"De la tranquillité de l'âme,"* 1860, http://bcs.fltr.ucl.ac.be/sen/ta.html

SZU: Shoshana Zuboff, *"The Age of Surveillance Capitalism,"* Hachette Book Group, 2019, ISBN 978-1-61039-569-4

Chapter 3

Information system audit

What is simple is always wrong. What is not simple is unusable.

Paul Valery, *Mauvaises pensées et autres*

3.1 CHALLENGES

Regulation, control, and auditing are a necessity for the proper functioning of companies and stock exchanges. Originally, they were applied to financial information. The digitalization of almost all the information necessary for the proper functioning of the company forces us to review the scope of regulation, control, and audit. This new perimeter, which covers all the information necessary for the company's operation, is called the company's information system.

Historically, companies confine the concern of digital information management to a dedicated department. The information technology (IT) management of information processing is the responsibility of the IT department. From an organizational point of view, it's very simple: The IT department takes care of the technical aspects and the user departments take care of their needs, passing them on to the IT department, which is responsible for implementation.

But IT is evolving, budgetary constraints are still there, and user management believes that the professional work methods implemented by IT specialists are too restrictive: At the end of the 20th century, they were not rapid enough and at the beginning of the 21st century, they were not agile enough. It is clear that the decrease in the cost of hardware and the evolution of software packages make it possible to meet the very specific expectations of user departments. Different solutions appeared over the last few decades as hardware and software possibilities have increased, such as information centers to search for data directly in files, minicomputers for management, interactive terminals, decision support systems or Executive Information Systems, data warehouses, personal computers, and recently tablets, telephones, robots or hand-held devices.

This description is a vision of an IT manager or director of the information system. But if we go to the workshops, the machines have more and more

DOI: 10.1201/9781003230137-3

important information processing and transmission capacities, equivalent to those of old computers. The IT department often learns by chance that equipment has been purchased by a user department, because it must be connected to the company network.

This equipment does not appear in the IT budget and not necessarily in the auditors' scope of analysis. Moreover, auditors often have a vision similar to the one of the IT managers, i.e., a vision of the company via computers, hence the historical name of IT audit.

What are the impacts of this global digitalization on the information system? There are many, but above all there are organizational changes, changes in responsibilities, changes in skills, changes in the understanding of what the IT budget covers, and changes in risk mapping. None of these changes appear alone, they all happen at the same time to varying degrees:

- It is impossible to modify the organization without modifying the responsibilities: The controls to be audited and the risk mapping must be updated, and
- It is impossible to change the budget without changing responsibilities and competencies: The risk map also changes to reflect the new budget allocation.

But let's first try to understand these impacts and then analyze their interactions. The organizational change essentially corresponds to the place occupied by the IT department in the company's organization chart. Historically, IT resources have been the responsibility of the financial or the accounting departments, which were the first departments to use their expertise. All the information processed is financial information such as accounting or cash flow. The IT support function is directly reporting to its one and only client.

Then the IT department became a support function for other functions, the general management, the purchasing department, the human resources department, and also the production and sales departments in addition to the financial department. In spite of this, it is still common to see the IT department reporting to the financial department, and the smaller the company, the more this organization is used. This way of looking at IT does not emphasize either the business process vision of the auditors, or the vision that the implementation of integrated management software packages (ERP) requires.

The digitalization of information is transforming the organization and processes of companies but should radically change the approach of auditors. It turns out that it does not. The service lines of leading audit firms cluster around three themes:

- Financial statement assurance,
- Non-financial statement assurance, and
- Data analysis.

This understanding of the company's operations is shared not only by the finance departments, but also by other departments.

Assurance over financial statements is the legacy activity of auditors. It mainly involves providing reasonable assurance on the financial statements, on reporting, and on compliance with financial regulations. The auditors' interlocutors are the financial departments. This data is historically considered to be the most important, as it measures the efficiency of the use of capital and the ability to pay dividends.

Both auditors and their clients know that financial information in the balance sheet, income statement and notes do not exist ex nihilo. It always comes from other departments. Until the end of the 20th century, accountants received paper documents and generally compiled the information by aggregating it. Now, detailed information is transmitted directly with a structure and format expected by the finance department's applications. The latter can consolidate the information and finalize the financial documents.

Assurance over non-financial statements is an operational view of the company. Auditors are concerned with the flow of information within and between departments. They must have a transverse vision. Their concerns are different from those of IT specialists, who are required to deliver a fully parameterized ERP module, such as the financial module or the inventory management module, within the timeframe of a project.

As the business becomes more digital, analysis of non-financial elements is essential to gain reasonable assurance of the proper understanding of financial results, financial forecasts, and associated risks.

Let's take the calculation of productivity as an example. More than two centuries ago, industrialists had to find methods to evaluate operational results without having to wait for financial results. Productivity was then calculated by the quantity of products per worker. The work of the scientific organization focused on the factory floor. Lean management is also concerned with workshops.

An auditor can easily cross-check the information in the financial reports with the reality of production. Depending on the degree of assurance required, he or she checks on site, for example, the production tool counters, intermediate stocks, finished goods stocks, and raw materials. This simple technique becomes less and less suitable as the size of the company increases. It is costly in terms of human resources and takes a long time to implement.

The most well-known example is the audit of inventories. To solve this problem, there are two options, one to limit the costs, the other to reduce the duration of the audit.

To reduce audit costs, and thus reduce the number of auditors assigned to the mission, statistical techniques are used in the same way as those used by survey institutes. A representative sample of the elements to be studied is defined. The definition of this representative sample is subject to the same rules and the same hazards as the representative samples of the polling institutes. There are two drawbacks to this method. The first is that the auditor obtains reasonable "statistical" assurance, i.e., with a statistical margin of error. The second disadvantage is that not all items are tested, so errors potentially reside in the untested items.

To limit the duration of the audit, the work of the auditors, instead of being carried out at the end of the fiscal year in a single intervention on site, is planned in several steps, quite often three. The first one is to prepare the work and the planning of the following ones, the second step is to audit all the possible elements available at the date of this first intervention on site and the third one consists, on the one hand, in auditing the elements not yet audited, i.e., produced after the second step, and, on the other hand, in finalizing the conclusions. In the case of inventory, a continuous inventory verification program, called perpetual inventory, is set up. It completes or replaces the annual physical inventory of stocks.

A win-win situation between the company and the auditors, the workload of the auditors is smoothed, and the interlocutors are not blocked by the auditors at busy periods (e.g. closing of accounts) or periods with few available resources (e.g. summer vacations).

Of course, these two options can be combined, as it is more cost-effective for the audit management or the statutory auditors. In the case of the auditors, this saving can be passed on to their clients, in whole or in part.

The digitalization of the company's information system makes it possible to combine the advantages of the auditors' historical method with the advantages of the options implemented in the 20th century: Data analytics is touted as the best of both worlds.

First, data analysis analyzes data, not information. This may sound trivial, but it is not. Data are numerical elements (0's and 1's) stored in the information system. This data is displayed or printed on demand and depending on the context provides information to the user.

This difference between data and information is also found in painting.

> No two persons looking at the same painting, sculpture, or drawing are having the same experience. Their eyes may receive the same information, but their brains process it in very different ways.

> [MFI]

Alain Baraton is a writer and head gardener of the Domaine national de Trianon and the Grand Parc du Château de Versailles, among other activities. With his gardener's eye, he has a specific way of understanding the paintings of Giuseppe Arcimboldo:

> Arcimboldo painted many pictures including The Four Seasons, a series of portraits composed only of plants: Winter, Spring, Summer and Autumn. "On his chest, Summer wears an artichoke. Its foliage is mottled, affected by one of the many cryptogamic diseases that occur when the weather becomes wet in the fall."

> [ABA]

The painting is the same for all visitors of the Louvre Museum, but depending on your knowledge, your experience you cannot help but look at the painting differently, even if you know that they were painted to show the timelessness of the power of the emperor Maximilian II. Computer projects do exactly the opposite, they start from people, their knowledge, their experiences and convert them into data. This difference between data and information or stories is a concern of anthropologists and sociologists.

In a long and thoughtful essay, Macquarie University anthropologist Greg Downey argues that

> in order to change popular understandings of evolution, we need not simply better data, but also better stories.

> [GRD]

The first phase of any IT project is to analyze the existing processes and define the future processes. The users and the IT people account for the future business processes by translating the users' needs with design methods. These methods transform user needs, i.e., words, into data, 0's and 1's, and verbs into computer actions, such as programs, themselves 0's and 1's.

From the company's point of view, the information system evolves with the IT techniques and is upgraded when the processes are no longer adapted: All this again and again with IT projects. Data is converted, i.e., redefined, from the database of the old application to the database of the new application.

From the auditors' point of view, there are two risks: The relevance of data analysis, which follows the evolution of software analysis, and the reliability of data analysis, which depends on the technical evolution of the information system.

Analysis software helps auditors spend more time on analysis. For example, we all use spreadsheets that allow us to easily sort, search, and process data. But these spreadsheets can't handle large data sets. These size limits vary depending on the spreadsheet and its version. If you perform several consecutive processes to arrive at your result, the spreadsheet does not keep track of these processes: There is no audit trail. In the same way a spreadsheet is not a project management software, a spreadsheet is not a data analysis software either.

It is very complex or impractical to prove the achievement of these results without an audit trail. It allows anyone to understand and follow the approach and processing of the data and achieve the same results. The audit trail is a mandatory and essential element in the work of any auditor, whether financial or non-financial, such as auditors of biomedical research involving human drugs.

It is a real challenge for auditors to get reliable data. The information system changes as projects are delivering and all data is affected. Let's take an example to understand this difficulty in obtaining reliable data. Let's consider that we have to establish the annual audit plan of an international company with sites spread all over the world. The company has tens of thousands of employees and buys and sells companies that join or leave the group as opportunities arise.

Of course, the audit department and the statutory auditors focus on the companies in the group that generate the most revenue. Those that have a strong impact on the consolidated accounts presented in the annual reports. But given the legal risks, you want to have better visibility on all auditable entities. Indeed, potentially, any company in the group that has legal problems can jeopardize the group. The risks taken by a group company can put the group's managers at risk in civil and criminal matters, such as the risks of corruption (third parties) or money laundering.

To define the exhaustive list of auditable entities (component in the audit lingo [IHV]), you tell yourself that it will be very simple. All you have to do is cross-reference the information in your accounting software with that of the lawyers and the companies you have already audited in previous years. But no luck, you don't have a single accounting software for all the companies of the group. Moreover, this set of accounting software is not particularly homogeneous. The list of companies in your accounting system(s) may not be exhaustive, either.

The IT department does not have the time to keep up with acquisitions and sales. Some companies send their accounting statements for group consolidation by e-mail, which are then entered back by headquarters into their software. Companies are identified and updated empirically in the consolidation and financial reporting software. The lawyers have no specific reason to consolidate legal entities electronically. They deal with files on a case-by-case basis and do their best to draft contracts. Lawyers may have lists of legal entities either by country or by region. But these lists will certainly not be up to date either.

So here you are with your list of companies you audited in the past years, the accounting list of consolidated companies and lists of legal entities. For each of these lists, there is a high risk that it is neither exhaustive nor reliable. You must therefore check the validity of the information in each of the lists, and then begin to match the elements between these lists.

All this to realize that you cannot match all the legal entities with the companies in your consolidation software or that you did not consider companies in the risk analyses of previous years. Of course, don't forget to consider in the audit plan that some of these companies might be sold in the current or next fiscal year. You have few auditors available and you have to make choices.

This simple example shows that:

- The same word used in different directions does not cover the same reality (here, a company),
- The segmentation of software and the absence of standardized business processes make auditors work complex (different departments, different needs, different formats, and information media), and
- Auditors spend a lot of time homogenizing or standardizing the data to be analyzed, for example, to define what is an auditable company or to analyze data that theoretically represent the same thing.

Data analysis can only be done once the data has been normalized and for that you need to understand it. So, you call on lawyers, accountants, and financiers to make the data consistent with each other, so that in the end they mean the same thing. To paraphrase Sherlock Holmes, you look for meaning in the data: "Data! data! data!" he shouted impatiently. "I can't make bricks without clay" [ACD].

The reliability of the data used by auditors therefore depends on both the extent of digitalization of the company's processes and the IT integration of these processes. IT integration can be represented by the number of different software packages used by a process. The greater the number of software packages used, the greater the risk the auditors will consider to be.

The transfer of data from one software to the next is a breaking point, which generates particular risks. This transfer of data can be done in different ways, handing over a document, sending an e-mail, computer interface between the two software. So, we have risks for each software and risks for each breakpoint.

The most representative or caricatural examples are those of companies with an international presence and a portfolio of applications that grows with acquisitions and new projects. The portfolio can include several hundred applications. It takes a long time to get a correct understanding at a given moment of how these applications support the business processes.

As a good auditor to identify risks, you make sure that the list of software specifies at least the version and the functionalities implemented for each software (we will assume that the version of a software from a distributor provides the same functionalities, whatever the country of sale). You can have the same ERP installed on several sites in different countries or not, but not have the same modules used. Of course, remember to have your updated portfolio validated not only by the IT departments concerned, but also by the management of each auditable entity.

You will always have at least one site for which it is not mentioned that the estimates are not made in the software package, but in an application developed internally by the sales department. You might as well know this before planning the audits. But to be able to compare the level of IT integration of processes, you need to have a common reference, i.e., what are the essential steps of each process for an auditor? It takes time, but this reference is necessary. For technical reasons, the simplest solution is for the auditors to define their expectations a priori. This decomposition will be the reference to be considered by the IT projects. For practical reasons, you will take the decomposition used to install the enterprise resource planning system that is supposed to be deployed to the whole group. Then you will create a summary diagram to communicate your risk analysis by integrating the IT interfaces. This diagram will show the different databases used by the various software.

You will thus communicate a simple and clear IT vision to make choices or justify them, and audits to plan.

Let's continue with the reliability of the data, the consistency of these data between them. The less reliable the data, the more at risk the processes are.

Let's imagine a process without defects, how can it function correctly with data that is not consistent or incomplete? Conversely, if the process is flawed, how can we imagine that the input data will provide reliable and complete output data in the accounts?

Fortunately, from time to time, for management purposes, a major project is implemented. A major project, quite often called a critical project, is a project that groups similar data by restructuring or simplifying processes. This major project will always be implemented to improve the processes, to make them simple ("lean"). Indirectly, it will by necessity homogenize the data used by these processes.

Let's take a company that is growing externally. It must have different software, if it does not have different settings, it will have different settings. Inventories are accounted for in different ways, and different management rules are applied. In short, the same data entered at the beginning of the process will undergo different transformations.

Auditors must reconcile data from different files when data is transferred from one software to another with what is called an interface. This interface transfers the data from one software to another, with all the risks of the media used for communication (e.g. networks, removable computer media). The more fragmented a process is, involving different software, the more interface control is a prerequisite for auditors to understand the risks to a process as a whole. As mentioned earlier, an additional difficulty for the auditors' reconciliation work is the case of the company using different software at different sites.

Once the reconciliations are done, the controls within the software can be analyzed. Auditors are again faced with the same difficulty of studying large amounts of data but multiplied by the number of interruptions in the information flow, i.e., the number of interfaces.

The implementation of integrated management software packages simplifies the work of auditors in theory. The data remains in the software package and is modified only by the management rules set up in the software package. The auditor must then verify the configuration of the controls and management rules in the software package, as well as the people who can modify them and the dates on which this was done. This is called an application audit.

3.2 DIFFERENT TYPES OF AUDITS

Figure 3.1 shows the different types of audit in relation to each other and to the elements of the information system that are directly concerned.

First of all, at the top, we have the investigations of possible actions by people in the company. This is not an audit as such, but audit techniques are used with discretion. The investigation may involve fact-finding on other elements of the information system that are related to the reason for the investigation.

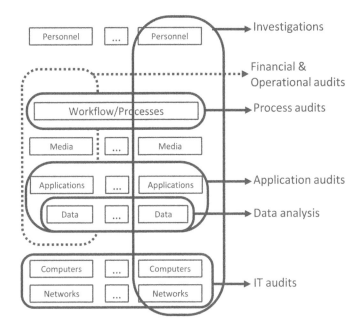

Figure 3.1 Different type of audits.

Then, the diagram is composed of two main groups of audits: The operational audits, and the technical/IT audits at the bottom.

The purpose of an operational audit is to analyze all or part of the processes of a department, the best known, of course, being the financial audit. The initial field of analysis is first the definition of the working methods, then their translation or parameterization in one or several computer applications and finally the data manipulated by these processes.

The audit can be limited to a process audit. In this case, the transverse vision of all departments is favored. This has the advantage of freeing us from a "silo" vision or one limited to one department. This transverse vision is symbolized in the diagram by a workflow, a process that crosses all the departments. Processes can be supported by one or more applications.

As the diagram indicates, if the processes are computerized, analysis of the application(s) and data are performed with the help of IT knowledge. Different IT knowledges are needed to perform the different technical audits: Application audit, data analysis, and IT audit.

To perform an application audit, it is necessary to have a technical knowledge of the software to be audited. Knowing the configuration of the SAP ERP software, for instance, is of no help if you have to audit the Oracle ERP software. In addition, knowing only the configuration of the SAP financial module is not sufficient to audit the SAP Sales and Distribution module.

Data audits all require the same skill set, that of knowing how to handle the data analysis software (e.g. Galvanize, IDEA). The data is extracted from the application and made available to you for integration. The main difficulty is that you must be sure to have requested the extraction of all the data that fall within the scope of your analysis.

It is wise for the auditor to either already know the structure of the software package's database, or to specify his needs precisely. Otherwise, the data extraction is incomplete. It is very unpleasant to waste time on incomplete data or to believe that a conclusion has been reached when data is missing.

If you perform an application audit with a process approach and follow the data from the start of the process to its conclusion in the financial data, you are performing a process audit. It's exactly the same audit techniques and IT skills required, but with a cross-functional view. In theory, if the company is using the same application end-to-end, application audit and process audit are one and the same.

Two questions arise: When do we process user access and data access?

First of all, user accesses must be audited keeping in mind the separation of functions. Does the right person have the right access, and only the access required for their responsibilities? The separation of functions is to the company what the separation of powers is to the State. The objective is to limit the abuse of power, which for the company means limiting the risks of circumventing controls at best, and fraud at worst. Recording tasks, operational tasks, and storage tasks must be performed by different people.

Apart from incorrect application set-up, risks of separation of duties may be due to lack of staffing that makes physical separation of responsibilities impossible. In addition, it may not be compensated for by adequate controls, which in practice would be weak or non-existent, such as the separation of authorization and approval functions.

It is not enough to check at a given moment who has the right to do what in the software. This observation is only valid at the time it is made. It is necessary to verify the management of access authorizations. To do this, the access authorization process is audited, and the access data is analyzed. Ideally, of course, the IT audit will have shown that an IT specialist does not have the ability to make changes to access authorizations and erase the traces of these changes. Only the person in charge of the application will have the right to modify the access authorizations in the application.

Users have access permissions that correspond to their responsibilities. They log in to the application, perform their tasks and modify data through the application's screens, controls, and business rules. But is it possible to directly access and modify the data? IT auditing techniques can be used to check this. You need to make sure that someone cannot access the data without going through the application or that the separation of responsibilities in the IT department is sufficient.

The IT audit is represented in the previous figure at the bottom. It directly concerns computers and networks. But IT is also a function of the company. For this reason, to better understand, we can highlight the IT department as shown in Figure 3.2 which thus becomes:

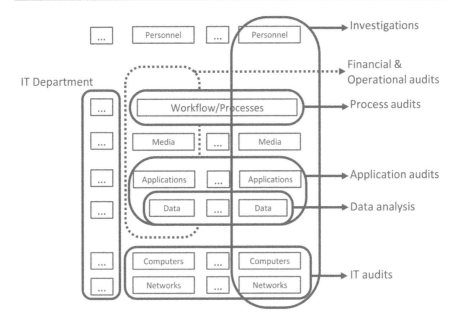

Figure 3.2 Adding the IT department in the information system.

IT risks and controls cover all items:

- Application audit,
- Data analysis,
- IT audit, and
- Operational audit of the IT function.

The Global Technology Audit Guide (GTAG®) issued by the Institute of Internal Auditors exclusively describes IT risks and controls and addresses data analysis, GTAG 16, application audit, GTAG 8 and 14, access management, GTAG 9, as well as specific controls for the proper functioning of the operational department, the IT department operational audit.

The international standards organization, ISO, has published the family of standards that address information security management systems. The Information Systems Audit and Control Association, ISACA, also defines IT general controls. In all cases, the use of the term "general computer controls" (GCC) covers the controls associated with the elements described in the diagram.

This diagram clearly shows the preponderance of zones over the traditional visions following the digitalization of the information system. Let's not forget that the information system is digitalized according to specifications described by the user departments. To function as they wish and to promote a common culture, all the departments will define a policy, procedures, methods, and rules.

All this documentation is available not only to all the staff of the department concerned, but also to the other departments. For the implementation of applications within a department, the latter will specify and detail its needs in terms of the configuration or development of the application. This information completes the existing documentation.

Auditors must first ensure that such documentation exists and is compliant and then verify its implementation. If the documentation is incomplete, the auditor relies on the state of the art to form an opinion. Professional bodies help to clarify the state of the art to a greater or lesser extent. More or less, because, for example, it is difficult for a professional organization to update its recommendations if the technology evolves too quickly: This is the case for computer technology. The state of the art must always be assessed according to the context of the company to evaluate the risks.

It is therefore possible to audit a non-digitalized information system, which is what was done until the middle of the last century. Computerization adds elements that must be audited. The technical risks increase because of this, but other risks decrease, thanks for example to the possibility for the auditors to analyze in real time a process or the completeness of a data set.

But we must take an additional factor into account when auditing the information system. The information system is always accessed by people who are not employees of the company, so with different contractual, legal relationships. These are the general rules that we rarely read to connect to Twitter, Sina Weibo, or Facebook, for example, but by doing so we accept the conditions of use of the application and access to the information system of these commercial social networks.

A person who is not an employee of the company may also be a supplier of products or services, a customer, a government agency, or a person who works for the company but is not an employee of the company.

The diagram used is centered on the understanding of the information system and highlights the company's personnel. Let's modify the diagram to include people who are not employees of the company, the third parties in Figure 3.3.

These third parties or external people interact with the company's information system, by talking, exchanging media or connecting to the computerized information system. These exchanges are multiple; all the company's departments are concerned, so we should not rely on the diagram that simplifies this aspect.

Talking is the easiest and fastest interaction. The customer walks into the store and talks to the salesperson or a supplier is invited into the company's premises to support a business proposal with one of the departments.

The exchange of media allows to keep a trace, usually the media used is paper, as for a report, a commercial proposal, mail. The medium can nowadays be for example a USB key/memory stick, a link to a file on a server (e.g. in the cloud), and in the past century a floppy disk or a CD-ROM.

The interaction with the strongest progression is the digital interaction. This is the possibility for a third party to connect to the company's information

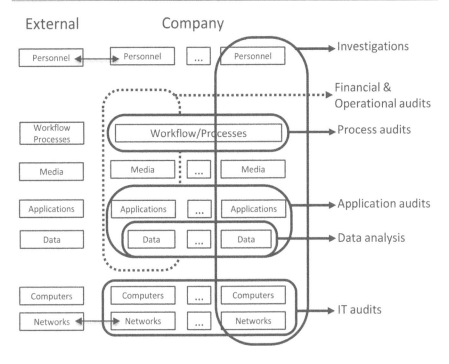

External   Company

Figure 3.3 Adding external parties in the information system.

system and enter the information requested by the application used. An interaction that we know well with the use of commercial websites that we access more and more via apps (short for applications) on our cell phones.

For each of these interactions, the risks are different and depend on the physical context of the exchange. In a store, controls against theft are put in place, in a shopping mall or in the city center, geolocation information is retrieved by merchants, allowing them to propose specific offers with the objective of avoiding lost sales.

Let us also note that these interactions are not exclusive. Let's take the example of in-store shopping, which has evolved to meet two constraints: The first is not being able to provide a sufficient number of sales counter to limit the waiting time at the checkout, and the second is only being able to provide a limited selection of products. The waiting time at the checkout is simply the payment that is involved. For the payment to be correct, it is necessary to check that the products purchased correspond to the amount. The traditional method of placing products on the checkout mat is a simple method where the check is done at the last moment before the customer leaves the store.

Current work is focused on how to bring up the controls in the purchasing process, a bit like the example of the inventory audit. The customer will therefore participate in these controls upstream, using a handheld scanner and scanning his products himself, or he will be offered automatic checkouts where he scans his purchases and pays. Of course, consistency checks are performed, such as between the weight of each product placed on the scale and the weight listed in the database for each product.

The constraint of being able to present only a limited selection of products to its customers is solved by virtually expanding the store. The customer starts the purchase act on the Internet, which can be limited to a selection. He can finalize it on the Internet, with a delivery or a withdrawal in store. He can finalize it in the store, to try the models in the store and listen to the advices of the salesman.

This physical constraint is also circumvented by the computerization of national libraries such as those in London or Paris. In both cases, they make available digitalized works that can be consulted remotely. But the architectural choices are different to consider the physical constraints to store in good conditions, on the one hand, and to make millions of works available quickly to tens of thousands of users, on the other hand.

The National Library in London decided to prioritize user access and greatly minimize the storage footprint on the new site. To do this, the information system has made it possible to bypass this physical constraint. The user selects in advance the documents he wants to consult and finds them available in the library: This is the interaction mode put forward in this new organization. The Paris National Library decided to store on the new site while increasing the capacity for users. However, the physical constraints are now becoming sufficiently strong that a similar organization to that of the London National Library must be envisaged, with a site outside of Paris while making the works available quickly. The computerized information system will have to evolve to take into account this new physical organization.

3.3 DIGITALIZATION

The digitalization of information helps bypass the physical constraints that have forged the operating modes and organizations of companies. In the same way, the challenge for the audit of information systems is to evolve its techniques to consider the impact of the digitalization of information. Indeed, facts are no longer only in the physical world, but especially in the computer world, the digitalized information system. Would it occur to the police during a search to take only the paper documents and leave the computers on site? No, of course not.

The ongoing digitalization of the companies presents of course challenges which should better be seen as opportunities. First reaction when changes happen, is to see them as challenges as they may modify our comfort zone. In addition, if we're not literate with IT, it's tougher as it is outside of our expertise. It requires involvement to figure out all the implications of what the IT tools usage implies. Time must be spent to be familiar with them, then envisioning them in our context. Figuring out the integration of these tools in our daily routines requires forward thinking exercise. This is for everyone and for auditors too. Auditors must evaluate the new tools in regards of their own work and the processes of the companies they audit. Reason is that automation could make audits faster, smarter and reducing the risk of error.

The new tools help automate basic tasks not requiring business knowledge, i.e., understanding the context. Driving 130 km/h or 80 mph is a fact, adding the context you're driving on the highway or downtown makes a huge difference in the risk analysis. Retrieving facts, or data, is an investment in itself and it takes more time than less to consolidate them. Once this is done, data analysis can start. Basic data analysis stays at the data level identifying discrepancies between data, odd data and so on. Then some basic correlation follows, where distinction must be made between correlation and causation between sets of data. Correlation is easy to visualize; causation is harder to define. Up to correlation, we may say that this is basic data analysis as it doesn't require business, processes or balance sheets understanding. Interpreting the data, being able to evaluate the pertinence of a value, the adequacy of the values between specific data, or the consequences of these values is not something you can see while reading the numbers. Well, even being able to predict anything by reading the coffee grounds of your Turkish coffee must be learned!

All this being said, if we agree on what that can and cannot be achieved, for sure data analytics is highly helpful once the caveats of the tool's implementation are resolved. It can analyze exhaustively data values extracted from one or different databases. It provides higher assurance and within an extremely reduce time frame. The set-up might be expensive and the return on investment must be calculated on multiple years. Each year, some fine-tuning must be performed to be aligned with the changes which happened at the client's information system. By-side benefit if the fine-tuning cost is less than you have estimated, you've got some budget left to build on top of what you have implemented already adding new controls, being more specific for current automated controls you perform, in short doing more for less (reducing costs) or providing a higher level of assurance, i.e., more extensive controls for the same price (reducing the risks of "missing" something).

How this looks like? Well, you will retrieve data at specific points you have defined in the business process and store it in your audit database, the thick arrows in Figure 3.4.

This is the ideal world, but reality is more complex, with the underlying IT layers having more than one software and multiple interfaces; the more data retrievals are required. Being positive, doing so if you analyze all the data each time, you lower the risks having issues or errors in the IT processes maintaining this business processes. IT processes, we will dive in a following chapter, are the processes used to monitor and maintain the automated information system.

Year 1, you developed the programs to gather the data and used them and tested them too by the way. Year 2, if the structure of the process hasn't

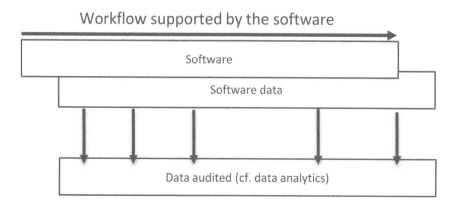

Figure 3.4 Ideal context for data analytics.

change, even if enhancement took place, it won't impact what you config-ured. Therefore, you have two options as said, either you're happy with it and based on your risk analysis, what you control is still valid or you think that additional controls should be implemented adding new data feeds or devel-oping new controls based on the data you're already retrieving. Economy of scale will apply if the process is implemented in the exact same way, i.e., same tools, for other countries or business units of your client's information sys-tem. The more an information system structure is simple, the more efficient, cost-effective the audit will be. The more that information system structure is used within the different departments, regions, companies by your client or within your group, the more efficient, cost-effective the audit will be.

That's when enters a new character in the IT show: Artificial intelligence. Be careful take it with a pinch of salt, you have to decipher the IT lingo. IT people are quite fast using words to describe their target but not the current state of what they're able to deliver. We have more powerful phones with a lot of features but are they "smart" phones? This is a challenge for auditors, see what's actually delivered by the new tools or what they can actually do, to adapt their workplans. As the technologies will improve, more should be delivered, your current workplan will have to be modified.

"Artificial Intelligence (AI) is intelligence demonstrated by machines, as opposed to the natural intelligence displayed by humans or animals" as stated by Wikipedia. Apart the use of the words demonstrated and displayed, the grouping of human and animals vs. machines, all these by themselves being subjects of discussion, questions could be what intelligence is and what intel-ligence is in the machine context? Yes, this question could be asked but really why linking these two words intelligence and artificial? It's the magic of IT lingo created by IT experts. In the 80s and the 90s, we had expert systems with different levels of engine (algorithm), being more and more complex. Again, it is because of the habit of using new concept expressing the future and not the reality. That's the reason why, a lot of exchanges takes place

around each new IT concepts arguing between what they can do and con-
jecturing on what they will do at some point in time. Again, we have to be
careful while auditing our clients or using these tools, do not oversell it internally, be pragmatic. Artificial Intelligence includes a subset of techniques aiming to enable machines to improve at tasks with experience, called Machine
Learning. Machine Learning includes a subset too based on neural networks
aiming to permit a machine to train itself to perform a task. The target is nar-
rowing the work to be done per subgroups of tasks for more automation, i.e.,
action without human intervention.

So each time we move to a narrower perimeter the expectation is to have
more automation, as a result, the auditor should be worried as risks are
induced by the perimeter and, appear if the implementation of the automation
was successfully design and tested, basic questions we have in our audit plan
that apply to any program. More automation implies wider and potentially
bigger impacts if something goes wrong. Testing is critical as usual, but we
may say more critical than usual. An additional risk here is that the set-up of
the system is performed once the programs are technically working without
bugs: It has been trained, i.e., configured using a set of data. The set of data
should be making sense against the objective of the training. Data being either
words, pictures, sounds, i.e., anything digitalized.

Let's replace data by language and you'll got the idea: If you learned
German at school, and you go to Spain it will be less useful than having
learned Spanish. You're a native Spanish speaker leaving in Spain, and you
move to South America, all the words you learned and used to communicate
were understood in the Spanish context. All this without considering other
often used languages within Spain. Do not assume that what the words actually meant in Spain is the same thing in South America. You can play around
with French, English, etc. and have more fun adding additional notion from
linguistics science to see how automation can be difficult applied to nature.

We are not diving in the "neural network" thing used in the machine learning definition because as an auditor, the risk is not due to the word in itself
but on what actually how it has been implemented and how it is maintained—
topics for Chapter 6.

These two tools, data analytics and artificial intelligence, are part of three
most often mentioned ones to impact how we audit. They both are about data
analysis and both manipulate data. The data analysis manipulates data before
facilitating the analysis, data analysis is not performed on raw data but on
retrieved consolidated data. This effort is often overlooked when the estimation of the workload is estimated.

The third often mentioned tool is blockchain. Blockchain is about data
modification. It is the result of many attempts in the 1980s to create an
encrypted electronic money allowing to bypass the public authorities. In 2008
in an article by Satoshi Nakamoto, a pseudonym probably for the collective
of the founders of bitcoin and the first blockchain, describes the functioning
of a protocol allowing the production of an unforgeable using a peer-to-peer

computer network "the blockchain" as the technological layer of a new technological layer of a new cryptocurrency, the "bitcoin." For some experts, this is at least as significant an advance as the invention of double-entry bookkeeping.

In 2017, Cyril Grunspan, the financial engineering specialist has the following general definition of a blockchain:

> a network of some kind where nobody trusts anyone a priori, but where everyone has the possibility to prove their good faith.

The bitcoin blockchain, like most of the blockchains that will be inspired by it, can be likened to a sort of unfalsifiable accounting ledger that makes the existence of a "trusted third party," which is traditionally required in digital transactions involving the transfer of securities or assets, unnecessary.

Blockchain technology existence is based on the Internet and its protocols. We're using the internet to send emails; the bitcoin leverages the blockchain technology to send "emoney."

Technically, blockchains are technologies for storing and transmitting data, allowing the constitution of replicated and distributed ledgers, without a central control body, secure thanks to cryptography, and structured by blocks linked to each other at regular time intervals. According to the professor and researcher in computer science Jean-Paul Delahaye, one must, in fact, imagine

> a very large notebook, which everyone can read freely and for free, on which everyone can write, but which is impossible to erase and indestructible.

The freedom to read the data being seen as a risk, some implementations restrict the access, allowing confidential data to remain as such when needed. The free of charge idea has become relative, because of the transaction fees charged today. So, a block (a record) is composed of a cryptographic hash of the previous block (previous meaning created before), a timestamp, the data. All this is useless for data in a database being modified through processes with the logic being in the programs. You may look at data here as a snapshot of a transaction performed. It has multiple practical and legal implications. Alain Bensoussan, lawyer, pioneer of advanced technology law, from Lexing, considers that

> this database [of records], which many compare to an accounting ledger—public and shared—contains an a priori unfalsifiable history of transactions, which is updated in real time by the users. Users validate each transaction and verify its consistency through the register.

This technology claimed as secure by design has found its most famous implementation with the bitcoin. Then different person thought about leveraging this technology and particularly Nick Szabo who proposed the concept of smart contract in 1994:

> A smart contract is a computerized transaction protocol that executes the terms of a contract.

Again, here the word "smart" for automated. Don't be impressed by the other word "contract," as these are not contracts in the legal sense, but computer codes that facilitate, verify, or execute a contract at the stage of its negotiation or implementation. Yes, this idea might be implemented in different ways, the auditor will have to be comfortable on how it has been implemented and maintained.

Because of their characteristics of immutability, global distribution and free participation, public participation, public blockchains pose new questions for national legislators. These questions concern in particular the tax regime, the legal framework, and the protection of personal data. Although alternatives are being developed or announced, no popular public blockchain today seems capable of removing all the legal obstacles revealed by bitcoin.

For sure, lawyers and legal professionals, are very enthusiastic about the potential of blockchain technologies. In particular, they mention the simplicity of audit and automation of contracts, echoing Lawrence Lessig's theories on "code is law." In terms of litigation, they note the importance of evidence recorded in the blockchain and a probable evolution of the legal profession, which will have to adapt to the issues arising from blockchain. In order to meet the demands of clients who want to know whether their use of blockchain complies with the law, they will have to be technically trained. For example, they will have to analyze a smart contract to certify that it will indeed carry out the envisaged operation, or even to draft one. The blockchain is also the technical underlay used for Non-Fungible Token (NFT). An NFT is similar to a certificate of authenticity, data stored in a blockchain, as it shows proof of ownership. Therefore, it is leveraged in the digital space to prove ownership of digital files (photos, videos and so on) so it enables art merchants to sell these easily reproductible documents. The documents become assets and the owner benefits of legal proprietary rights. Even if these documents can be duplicated and their copies shared. But as always when information technologies are involved, do not expect that this will stay forever. Some people are exploring the NFT potential to find new ways to use it. One of them is to have parts of a file being only accessible to the owner of the token. It looks like more or less to implement DRM without calling it as such. What is interesting is how new technologies are understood by the legal environment. On November 16, 2021, Miramax sues Quentin Tarentino over his Pulp Fiction NFTs for breach of contract, copyright infringement, trademark infringement, and unfair competition. Independent of the legal pertinence of the claims in the complaint, it shows that if a company buys such NFTs, for an auditor, it is worth being explicit of which technology is used in which current legal context.

For auditors, as for other information technologies, the key is to be confident on how these new tools have actually been implemented as we've seen that there is a huge difference between an IT idea and its implementation, what actually it does, and its maintenance, if it's still working as intended. This continuous changes on the IT layers supporting the business processes is an incentive to have annual audits evolving toward a continuous audit approach. Whatever the new IT tools or techniques being made available in the future, they will require new knowledge from auditors, analysis on how these tools are implemented and how they modified the current processes. These three examples of IT ideas/tools show that the digitalization of the information system has two main direct impacts. The first one is the mix between digitalized and non-digitalized information. The second one is the workflow, how information are being exchanged. In addition, there is a main indirect impact being the match between auditors' skillset and the evolving information system supporting technologies. Not having the comprehensive knowledge required by the information system creates gaps and so risks. Physical information and digitalized information are part of the same information system. The ratio between physical and digitalized information will modify the risks. What is to be considered then is the consistency between physical and non-physical data and the pertinence of the definition of the data. The latter is where there is a lot of challenges when wanting to perform data analytics.

Implementing a new tool changes a workflow, defining what has been modified from the computer/network up to workflow/processes in the previous figures, must be identified and risks analyzed accordingly. We spoke about the impact of digitalization on our audit approach and the opportunities created by the new tools. Well, let's just step back and look at all this. In fact, what digitalization does is that it makes everyone aware of the importance of information technologies. But everyone focuses on the trendy buzzwords from IT experts and forget that the impact is on the information system in itself. We moved far away from paper, drawers, physical stamps and signature, letters, etc. and it is not yet recognized and embraced by professionals: With digitalization all items in the information system are more connected.

The audit of the information system is the only approach that allows to apprehend the risks of the company and their complexity. It is no longer possible to consider only one part of the system, as with a financial or security audit. The more digitalization of the company develops, the more the interconnections of the elements of the information system make the controls interdependent.

Forming an opinion, obtaining reasonable assurance has become more complex to do and to achieve. It is no longer possible to reason per type of audit, such as an operational audit or a data analysis as all components from the IT Information System are imbricated. From now on, we must reason in terms of confidence level according to the risks faced by a company. A risk is "the possibility of a bad result" or "something that could cause problems" (Cambridge dictionary). The risk here is not related to audit risk, but to the risk that the company will get into trouble and be liquidated. Financial auditors distinguish between the risk of material misstatement of the financial statements and the risk of not detecting errors. The risk of non-detection of error is not within our scope and is the subject of comprehensive studies by professional bodies such as the Public Company Accounting Oversight Board (PCAOB) or the IFRS.

Auditors break down the risk of material misstatement of the financial statements into inherent risks and control risks. Inherent risks are the possibility that data or a set of data may intentionally (fraud) or unintentionally (error) result in a material misstatement of the financial statements, regardless of any consideration of controls. Control risk is the risk that data or a set of data will intentionally or unintentionally contribute to a material error in the financial statements without being prevented or identified by the company's controls on a timely basis. The company's controls are usually referred to as internal controls. Control risk is inversely proportional to the effectiveness of internal controls: The more effective the internal controls, the lower the control risk.

We will not discuss audit risk here either, which is specific to the way the audit is carried out and not to the information system of the company. Technical literature is available on this subject [AST]. It considers audit risk or audit engagement risk to be the risk that the auditor expresses an incorrect opinion when the financial statements are materially misstated. This risk includes both the risk that the information is materially misstated and the risk that an error is not detected.

It may sound technical, but it is real. Again, and again, an audit firm will be found by regulators to be negligent. A settlement is usually reached. The audit firm communicates its full cooperation with the judiciary, the confidence it has in the quality of the work done, most recently with KPMG/Rolls-Royce in 2017 or PwC/Tesco in 2014.

The risk that information is misstated is due to:

- Inherent risk: The possibility that an item of information may contain a misstatement independently of the controls, or
- A control risk: The control does not prevent, detect or correct a misstatement.

This vision of controls is certainly logical, but too technical and not very operational for the management of the audited companies.

Companies face other types of risks, a whole other taxonomy. The first level of this taxonomy is very simple. Even if all problems are conceivable and are the result of a specific risk analysis for each company, we can nevertheless group them such as in Figure 3.5 into:

- Legal risks,
- Operational risks, and
- Technical risks.

Figure 3.5 Legal, operational, and technical risks.

BIBLIOGRAPHY

ABA: Alain Baraton, *"Dictionnaire Amoureux des Jardins,"* 2012, Plon, 978-2-259-21948-8

ACD: Arthur Conan Doyle, *"The Adventure of the Copper Beaches,"* 1892, Strand Magazine

AST: Anthony Steele, *"Audit Risk and Audit Evidence: The Bayesian Approach to Statistical Auditing,"* 1992, Academic Press, 978-0-12664-140-0

GRD: Green Downey, 2012, http://blog.plos.org/neuroanthropology/2012/01/10/the-long-slow-sexual-revolution-part-1-with-nsfw-video

IHV: IAASB, *"2016–2017 Handbook of International Quality Control, Auditing, Review, Other Assurance, and Related Services Pronouncements,"* 2016, IFAC, 978-1-60815-318-3

MFI: Michael Findlay, *"The Value of Art: Money, Power, Beauty,"* 2014, Prestel Verlag, 978-3-641-08342-7

Chapter 4

Legal risks

All events are linked in the best of all possible worlds. says Pangloss to Candide

Voltaire, *"Candide"*

Legal risks concern compliance with the regulations applicable to the company, such as the Data Protection Act, data protection laws, labor laws, environmental laws, tax, and accounting regulations. Legal risks must assess the local regulations of the countries in which the company operates. The reduction of these risks is achieved by applying the most restrictive regulations to all sites. This simplification allows for better management of changes in regulations and simplifies the planning of compliance.

Operational risks include risks that may affect the proper functioning of the company, such as financial risks, subcontracting risks. These operational risks are broken down and analyzed according to the organization of the company, by department. They represent most of the company's risks. These risks are all linked to the performance of the company's activities and therefore indirectly associated with the personnel and their use of the information system.

Technical risks indirectly affect the proper functioning of the company and can increase the impact of operational risks. They are limited to the proper functioning of the software, hardware, and materials used by the company during its activities to deliver services or products. These materials can be, for example, the use of computers or machine tools that are no longer maintained because they are outdated, or the supplier no longer exists. Just as well, it could be the use of equipment by junior staff. In an information technology (IT) environment, these are the risks associated with "policies and procedures that the entity implements and the IT infrastructure (hardware, operating systems, etc.) and application software that it uses to support business operations and achieve business strategies" (IFAC definition). These risks therefore concern different components of the information system.

Legal risks impact all components of the information system. Operational risks and technical risks, on the other hand, have a direct impact on the workflow related components of the information system and indirectly on the other components. It is important to note that the more computerized the information

DOI: 10.1201/9781003230137-4

system is, the more important the technical risks become. Important for two main reasons, the first being that controls to reduce operational and legal risks are becoming more and more computerized, and the second reason being that the quality of controls to minimize technical risks has an impact on the duration of confidence in the proper functioning of these controls. All legal, operational, and technical risks will be defined for each company. They are then evaluated to define or modify the audit strategy. The elements presented in this chapter are used in the last chapter "Audit Strategy."

4.1 *SUI GENERIS* RISKS

Legal risks include all laws and regulations that concern the company as a legal entity and the company's operations. The company as a legal entity has a legal status and evolves in a legal environment just like natural persons. Through its organization, strategy, and operations, the legal environment in which it operates may change and no longer be identical to the one in which it was created. For Adam Smith already, the individual

> can know better the character and situation of the persons whom he trusts, and if he should happen to be deceived, he knows better the laws of the country from which he must seek redress.

> [ASM]

We can understand here the term "individual" as that of a company. Let us take the case of a company created in France, this one has a different legal personality according to its status. It can be a limited company or a one-man business with limited liability, for example. The first legal risks are inherent to the legal structure chosen when the company is created. Each legal structure has its advantages and disadvantages and always has legal constraints such as the constitution of the capital, the protection and the rights of the shareholders, the geographical location, the ownership.

The company as a legal person is a recent creation to preserve the continuity of the company's activity and not to protect the partners, even if they indirectly benefit from it. There are two reasons for the notion of a legal entity. The first is that the company could be threatened by legal proceedings against its partners. The second is that when the financial needs become important, with long-term needs, it is important to secure the continuity of the activity. The company's own assets must be isolated. It has a life of its own, that of the company. This need and this development of the companies are quickly well thought-out in all the legal environments of the industrialized countries.

The accounting system is evolving to take these changes into account. The appeal to investors is facilitated by this important change brought about by the double entry. Historically, the accounts of the first companies, which were then called companies, are not closed each year. They are open when the company is created and are closed when one or more partners change. A new company is created with new accounts with the new group of partners. The double entry allows the creation of equity accounts that formalize the company as a legal entity. It becomes important to regulate and standardize the life of companies. In the history of accounting, standardization is an upheaval. Accounting standardization, as we discussed in the first chapter, began in Western countries in the mid-20th century, with different technical approaches in different countries, but with similar political aims. The first claim of accounting standardization is to make a shift from the reference of "having to be" to the notion of "being"; the shift is from the notion of measurement to the notion of information. A good example is the notion of "fair value." Accounting used to record the past and make restrictive assumptions to avoid overvaluing the company's assets. Today, it recognizes the present and values assets according to an estimate of the resale value of these assets at the time of the estimate.

This evolution took place in France in the 1960s. The National Accounting Commission (Commission Nationale de la Comptabilité) revisited the history of accounting to become an ally of computers. Its 1968 report on the relationship between accounting and IT states:

> For centuries, accounting had been the only global system of economic information for the company, allowing facts to be classified and presented. The accountant was then the only provider of financial information.

Samuel Jube notes that

> this text makes this shift, where all of a sudden accounting will be presented as if it had always been an information system.
>
> [SJU]

This justification, this vision of things, can be found some 40 years later, in the discourse of global auditing companies. They are now trying to justify their "audit plus consulting" strategies once again to the SEC.

> One of the problems from which the accounting profession suffered in the late 1990s—which was evident at the hearings—was that it had bought into New Economy jargon. The leaders of the global accounting firms testified time and time again throughout the hearings that the "information age" required a "real-time reporting" so that "intangible value could be captured."
>
> [MBR]

This is one way to explain the historical hierarchical dependence of IT departments on finance departments in companies. While they want to take the turn of the digital transformation, what about the relevance of this turn if the company's organization does not evolve? Operational risks will appear. Accounting also helps or allows companies to structure themselves as they wish. They are equipped with the means to follow their evolution. They can be seen either in a legal way, as legal entities, or in an accounting way. Profits and risks are decoupled. How does this happen and why?

The objectives of managers are to make profits and not to jeopardize the company by doing so. The rise of pension funds in the ownership of companies is changing their management objectives. Managers must focus on making profits. The short-term return objectives demanded by pension funds even force them to build more complex legal structures. Let's take the case of an unlisted company with a single location, whose activity, shareholders, employees, customers, and suppliers all depend on the same legal environment. The legal risks are induced by the type of legal structure chosen by the company and by the contracts signed to pursue its activity. The accounting only reflects the operation and the financial flows of the company.

Let's take a company that is no longer a single-site company, but a publicly traded group with several sites. This group has its headquarters in a tax haven with its central management in another country. To reduce costs, so-called central (corporate) services are shared between subsidiaries such as human resources management, accounting, treasury, and research and development. Other activities are separated between production and commercial companies. The choice of location of sites increases the potential savings. The management of the group defines the strategic choices for the group and for all the companies of the group. The strategy is a political speech to increase the share price on the stock exchange. To implement it, the group's management defines the legal grouping of companies and the rules for the exchange of products and services between them. It thinks exclusively in terms of flows and increases in consolidated profits. It is the responsibility of the legal and financial departments to work together to optimize taxation while reducing legal risks. The legal risks therefore exist from the creation of the company and evolve throughout its life according to the company's policy.

But how does legal risk generate accounting risk? In the previous example, the legal risk changes when the company is split into a group. Whether the group remains in the same country or the activities are in different countries only adds additional legal environments. The perimeter of the company disappears as a place of mutualization, to make room for a group of companies placed in competition with each other. A company's accounts reflect its entire operation and activities. In this sense, the balance sheet and the income statement record the results of the decisions taken by the management. Ideally, it is seen as a whole. This whole includes all management, commercial and production choices. The responsibility for the results lies with the company's management, its management, and its choices. But this autonomy is no longer the same in a group. A company's own legal personality makes it possible to compartmentalize risks. The group can isolate this or that activity and the related liabilities within a watertight asset. A group can nowadays create companies with great ease. Each of them is supposed to benefit from the rule of autonomy of the assets of legal entities. For the group, this freedom continues in the possibility of transferring liabilities in the context of restructuring operations.

Put differently, a group decides on the specialization of its companies, on their commercial relations. They are no longer autonomous. Their balance sheets and income statements reflect the management of the group and not their own. The analysis of legal, operational, and technical risks is only fully relevant at group level. The risks identified for a company in the group must be weighed against its freedom of management. The group also makes it possible to limit the risks for its companies. It has many more means of action at its disposal than a single company. For example, after the financial crisis of 2008, banks are reluctant to grant credit lines to companies. High interest rates are charged on the debt, but little interest is paid on the credit amounts. More than ever, companies must limit both debit and credit amounts. Pooling cash between companies within a group allows for optimal use of available funds at the lowest possible cost, while strengthening the financial position of the companies involved. Cash pooling is therefore a means of reducing the risk of insolvency, particularly in difficult economic times.

In the same vein, taxes are a concern for the group and for each of its companies, regardless of their location in the world, from Asia-Pacific to America, Europe, and Africa-Middle East. Groups are organizing and structuring themselves to limit taxes and taxes on profits. The structure of the group is designed in such a way that the impact of taxation on profits is as minimal as possible. Robert A. Schultz sums up the situation by saying:

> In this case, everyone recognizes what corporations are doing and that it is unethical. It does, however, improve the bottom line.
>
> [RAS]

In the case of taxes, the idea is that group companies bill each other for services or products, so that the highest profits end up in subsidiaries located in countries with the lowest corporate tax rates. This intra-group invoicing is the result of considering the legal environments, the organization of the group, the activities adapted to these environments and the optimization of the business processes of the group companies.

An example of intra-group billing is the use of non-tax regulations such as property rights. A group company owns all the rights to the group's products and services. It is located in a country with a low-income tax rate. The other companies use these products and services and pay royalties, thereby reducing their profits. Nevertheless, reorganizations can also reflect the strategic will of a group as when Google renamed itself Alphabet in 2015, in part to allow the company to report the health of its core search business to Wall Street separately from its other divisions. In 2013 PPR (Pinault-Printemps-Redoute) renamed itself, Kering to demonstrate its new focus on the luxury and sports sectors, a move away from distribution, and a "caring" approach to cultivating brands, as well as acknowledging the roots of the company in France's Brittany region ("Ker" means home in Breton). From the mid-1980s onward, the major auditing firms took up these concerns and turned them into a substantial source of revenue, as Mike Brewster points out:

> Another manifestation of the firms' swerve away from audit services was their aggressive revenue-building tax products. The goal of these products was to help a company get its effective tax rate down and then take a percentage of the savings. There is no law against advocating for a client's aggressive tax position. But as firms made more non-audit revenue from audit clients, including millions on a single tax project, they opened themselves up to further curbs on their activities. In a way, any business that seek to add new products runs the risk of losing sight of its core activities. So, in a sense, the accounting profession made an understandable mistake in abandoning the audit. But bad audits have a bigger downside than a lot of products do—business failures and lawsuits.

> [MBR]

The main disadvantage is that each company in the group still has a legal personality. It must therefore behave in a way that respects the legal environment on which it depends. All this must be analyzed beforehand. Even if the legal environment changes relatively slowly, the increasing complexity of the group's organization and its financial flows increases the risks of non-compliance. To be sure that the risks are controlled or eliminated, the company sets up a compliance program. It also allows to avoid risky practices, to secure practices and to limit sanctions. Indeed, companies that undertake to set up or improve their compliance program can benefit from a reduction of up to 10% of the penalty incurred in the context of the no objection procedure. This reduction is in addition to the 10% reduction for the waiver of the grievance itself and the 5% reduction that may be granted for other commitments.

These compliance programs are composed of two parts, a substantive part (the prohibition) and a procedural part. In practice, therefore, it is a reinforcement of the legislative system, in particular with the links with criminal legislation. The legislator therefore grants a certain recognition to these internal company rules. If the compliance programs are properly implemented, they constitute an element likely to lead to the exclusion or at least the mitigation of the liability of the legal entity within which the offense was committed. Internally, the purpose of compliance programs represents a mode of organization, a paradigm of self-regulation, but externally, compliance is a new variation of the control instruments used by the State. Compliance programs must avoid conflict or contradiction with local laws, as they correspond in practice to the expansion of Anglo-Saxon law and its underlying logic, such as the US Foreign Corrupt Practice Act of 1977. It allows for the criminalization of acts of corruption carried out abroad. It was revised in the late 1980s to apply to any non-US company that might have had ties to the United States.

A second example is that of tax evasion, with many recent examples such as the Swiss banks that have made unusual agreements with the US Department of Justice. Measures taken by the US Office of Foreign Asset Control (OFAC) against terrorism by blacklisting certain states or individuals (e.g. BNP Paribas). The European Economic Community is also legislating with, for example, the regulation of the Internet to deal with terrorist risks or with the General Data Protection Regulation (GDPR) to better protect its citizens. The GDPR has made the United States more aware of data protection and has initiated discussions on this subject.

However, compliance programs have several advantages. The two main ones are, on the one hand, to go beyond the simple individual responsibility (specifically for the managers), and on the other hand, for the states, to oblige the companies to respect their legislation. Employees are always concerned, regardless of the legal risk, and they benefit from training and awareness-raising sessions included in the deployment of the company's compliance plan. Indeed, directly, or indirectly, a malfunction within the company is always the responsibility of one or more people. Legal risk is generated by the disregard of a duty, an obligation. To know when there is a risk, one must know when there is an obligation. Various people must be trained according to their respective responsibilities. This training must be kept up to date because commitments are made annually (cf. the periodicity of the validation of accounts), and the environment and legal texts change regularly.

If we return to the financial regulation discussed in the previous chapter, it is an integral part of legal risk. It evolves in response to scandals created by financial market actors. It limits the recurrence of the same malfunctions but does not prevent the appearance of different malfunctions. The main disadvantage of financial regulation is the time it takes to create or change it. The actors involved will either push or resist the changes. Each one proposes more or less self-serving arguments and does everything possible in terms of communication to support its position. Financial regulations must be respected, but they only serve to eliminate, or limit already known risks. The company can rely on them as good practices (mandatory of course), but in no case to anticipate the appearance of new risks. Financial regulations are one of the many regulations with which the company must comply.

A good knowledge of the legislation and its evolutions brings enormous financial advantages. The risks come mainly from a bad legal set-up or from not respecting the constraints of the legislations.

4.2 IDENTIFICATION AND PREVENTION

The legal environment is complex for two main reasons: The first is that it is complex in itself and concerns all the components of the information system; the second is that its contours change depending on the sector of activity and the third parties with which its business is conducted. So how do we identify legal risks? It is an exercise in style to assess legal risks, because they may or may not be of direct legal origin. The understanding of operational staff often stops at contractual risks:

- The regulations and their interpretation are constantly evolving. This is pure legal technique and requires active monitoring and lobbying,
- The legal environments of different countries may have different interpretations.
- Operational or technical changes can modify them: Making an object "intelligent" certainly modifies it but creates new legal risks or setbacks.

The "pure" legal risks or those of legal origin begin with the choice of the legal structure of the company and the information entered in the commercial register, such as the company's purpose, its sector of activity, its capital. Legal risks as a legal entity. Other legal risks appear as soon as the company is in operation. They concern all business processes such as manufacturing, research and development, marketing, and human resources. These are legal risks that are linked to operational and technical risks.

The 10 K balance sheets include explicit paragraphs such as the 2019 balance sheet of an international SEC-listed company:

> Compliance with and changes in laws could be costly and could affect operating results. In addition, government disruptions could negatively impact our ability to conduct our business.
>
> We have operations in ... that can be impacted by expected and unexpected changes in the legal and business environments in which we operate. Compliance-related issues could also limit our ability to do business in certain countries and impact our earnings. Changes that could impact the legal environment include new legislation, new regulations, new policies, investigations and legal proceedings and new interpretations of existing legal regulations, in particular, changes in export control laws or exchange control laws, additional restrictions on doing business in countries subject to sanctions, and changes in laws in countries where we operate. In addition, changes, and uncertainty in the political environments in which our businesses operate can have a material effect on the laws, rules, and regulations that affect our operations. Government disruptions may also delay or halt the granting and renewal of permits, licenses and other items required by us and our customers to conduct our business. The continued success of our global business and operations depends, in part, on our ability to continue to anticipate and effectively manage these and other political, legal and regulatory risks.

The departments and their managers are aware of the contractual legal risks and the regulatory risks specific to their profession. The Research and Development Department is sensitive to property rights and copyrights, while plant management is aware of environmental regulations and working conditions. Some regulations must be communicated to all members of the company, as they affect several departments, such as most of the regulations managed by the human resources department, for example discrimination. All of these are included in a more or less comprehensive way in compliance programs. But these regulations are an opportunity for economic reasons. It can be interesting to centralize the management of some of them in one department for economic optimization. The IT department or the purchasing department can centralize the purchase of software licenses (cf. ISO19770). Centralizing the management of licenses avoids buying licenses for one department when some are no longer used in another. The transfer of use is managed by the IT or purchasing department. However, this optimization is only possible if the legal entities are the same or the licenses are transferable within the same group. This is similar to cash-pooling but for licenses. From a technical point of view, centralized license management makes it possible to limit the number of versions of the same software with the ideal of having only one version used in production. This makes it easier to deploy software security updates and to ensure that the versions of the different software used remain compatible with each other.

Centralization makes it easier to negotiate contracts with publishers, the more licenses you buy the more discounts you can negotiate. Centralization decreases the risk in the event of a editor's control. Centralization allows you to adapt to frequent changes in the terms and conditions of use of the same publisher. Changes that database management system or enterprise resource planning publishers are fond of. The first ones will play with the technical evolutions to lead to contractual terms which become more complex with these evolutions, like the notion of virtual server or virtual processor, of the number of competing accesses to the data. The latter will invoice for all the modules of the software package, arguing that the modules you wish to install cannot be used alone. It's like renting a house, but you can only use the first floor and not the upper floors. The international standards body's ISO19770 standard is designed

> to enable an organization to prove that it is performing Software Asset Management (SAM) to a standard sufficient to satisfy corporate governance requirements and ensure effective support for IT service management overall.

Risks related to resources such as software licenses encompass the company's other resources. Although all resources are theoretically in the accounting system, this is not sufficient. For the same objectives as centralized software management, it is interesting to manage other company resources, because other regulatory constraints apply to them.

Among the resources used by the company, some are subject to special regulations and must therefore be followed by the company. Serious accidents are due to dangerous chemical products, but necessary to produce for certain industries. To limit the associated risks, a directive in France called Seveso was adopted in 1976, updated in 1996 and recently in 2012. This latest version of the directive, called Seveso-III, considers, among other things, changes in legislation on the classification of chemicals. It is necessary to be able to prove and therefore trace the management of these products, their purchases, their uses, their storage, and their access in particular. All this critical information must be computerized, as there are links with the accounting and physical security of the site. If all this information and its processing are computerized, then controls can also be automated. An example of a typical 21st-century resource is the personal data of users, customers, passers-by:

- User when you use a paid or unpaid website, such as Facebook, Baidu, Google,
- Customer when you visit a merchant site and place an order, such as Amazon, Alibaba, and
- Passerby when you are walking through a mall or store and you have opted on your phone to receive commercial offers based on your location or proximity.

Services and products are also affected by your personal data. If you wear an electronic bracelet or a "smart" watch to monitor your health, you know that you are regularly monitored. What happens to your data if the company that stores your data goes bankrupt or is bought out? Do you remember the scroll from the first chapter? We showed that it is very difficult to completely erase the data on a computer storage medium. What happens to these media if the company goes bankrupt? If the company is bought out, is the contract for the use of your data maintained as is by the new owner? But more practically, how a company can be compliant in case of a Tax audit? Is the information system able to demonstrate how the financial figures have been achieved? Up to mid-19th century, all was paper based, it was easy to show the documents to a tax auditor even if it required an on-going effort to keep at hand the most needed documents and archive the less needed one in a safe location.

With the digitalization, to demonstrate at one point in time how figures have been achieved, the applications and the data used at that time must be available. It is not mandatory as far as you can prove with a documented application development process which rules were implemented and which were the data before and after the main gates in the workflows. So, an alternative solution is to print out the figures before and after every major gate and the rules explained. Doing this implies that the correct release of the application and the data sample are available to be re-run. Regulations and their interpretation are constantly changing. It is a given that departments and managers must ask the legal department for its opinion as soon as they modify a process, a service, or a product, even if they have no doubt. Conversely, it is the role of the legal department to ensure that its advice remains relevant. It must keep an active legal watch on the evolution of regulations, on the opinions it gives and which are followed by the managers of other departments, but also make sure that it is always consulted by the management and the managers in the right way. It is better to avoid problems than to manage them.

We are a long way from the not-so-distant days when you had to walk up and down the lobby of the British Houses of Parliament to do lobbying. This practice has become so common that it was necessary to legislate in the United States with the Lobbying Disclosure Act of 1995; the European Community has not legislated on this subject, but the European Parliament and the European Commission merged in 2011 their respective registers of lobbyists into a European transparency register. It is therefore possible to influence the evolution of the regulation, but here again one must be careful. Poorly done lobbying is damaging to the reputation of a company or a federation even if there is no conflict of interest. Lobbying allows to influence the evolution of the regulations, but there is an indirect advantage for the company to be informed as soon as possible about the evolutions. The company can prepare itself without being in a hurry and thus obtain a competitive advantage. We are in the 21st century and the means to influence have also evolved with the use of the Internet and more particularly social networks, such as the debates on the influence of social networks on the results of the 2016 American election.

Three current topics that know no borders are private data, copyright, and intellectual property. The definition of what private data is and how it is used varies from one region of the world to another, and within the same region from one state to another. Copyright and intellectual property vary in the same way, with tax implications for the latter two. You have a Research and Development department with two locations, one in the US and one in India. The distance is eliminated thanks to your IT resources and the use of a secure private network. Engineers communicate easily by phone, video or video conference. They exchange files through internal messaging. It is wise to verify that these file transfers are not potentially taxable because of the creation of intellectual property in one of the countries. Prevention is essential, all law firms specialized in legal risks and information systems offer legal analysis, training, monitoring and audits. This is work done within the company. This prevention can be done outside the company with lobbying as we will see later. Prevention and awareness can be simplistic and boil down to updating the management of risks already known or identified by the managers of a department. The increasing digitalization of processes and operating procedures reinforces the need to address risks more comprehensively, by analyzing each business process:

1. Know the business sector and the business processes, i.e., the value chain of the activity considered,
2. Define the legal perimeter by identifying the legal standards concerned by the business process and evaluate the degree of legal uncertainty for each of the standards, do not forget to note the countries concerned by this process,

3. Identify the facts for each legal standard and estimate its degree of uncertainty,
4. Cross-reference the standards with the facts to qualify the legal risk,
5. Assess the impact of the legal risk according to the criterion(s) selected, such as in terms of value impact or reputation. If the analysis covers several processes, complete step 6, otherwise go to step 7,
6. Place the risks and business processes in rows and columns to visualize the risks that affect more than one process and reassess the risks in this context, and
7. Is it possible to simplify the processes to limit the legal standards involved?

Step 6 is very interesting, because it avoids making mistakes. Indeed, by default, we tend to think in silos, i.e., by business process, because we need to cut up/group the company's activities. But this grouping is arbitrary, it is usually based on a financial vision of the company. With the digitalization of the information system, these delimitations are permeable to legal risks. Once this simplification has been made, stakeholders must be made aware of and trained in legal risks and they must be notified and advised in a timely manner of changes to laws and regulations.

To better understand its customers and even its prospects, the company collects as much data as possible on each of them. Some data allows us to redesign the interface of a website to simplify the visitor/customer path and eliminate all obstacles to the purchase. Other data will either concretely define the customer, such as his address, age, gender, or analyze his behavior, his reactions, including when he left your site. Some data provide indications on the behavior of the visitor/customer of the site. We are familiar with loyalty programs with a card in the customer's name with the company's logo. Not to be confused with bank payment cards which also look like and accumulate a lot of payment or withdrawal data such as locations, dates, and merchants. Loyalty programs are part of the data we agree to share to benefit from additional services.

Internet shopping sites go further. You think you're in a two-way relationship, you and the merchant, but in fact there are at least three of you (if not more), because the way you use that site and the sites you have visited before and those you will visit after will be tracked by one or more third-party companies. When Apple Inc. changed the way its Safari browser works, e-marketing companies reacted very quickly. What Apple added to its Safari browser in the fall of 2017 was a new feature that blocks tracking, "smart tracking prevention" in addition to private browsing, website isolation and protection from harmful sites. The commercial "ad tech" industry is a market in the US of about 83 billion in 2017, almost more than 16% in one year. Their response is not long in coming. The Digital Advertising Community shares an open letter with strong positions like with this sentence:

> Apple's unilateral and heavy-handed approach is bad for consumer choice and bad for the ad-supported online content and services consumers love.

Let's continue our previous example with private data. The most widely shared view right now on how to improve sales and build customer loyalty is to transform the customer experience. The goal is to personalize the use of the site for each customer. The company must know each customer better, not only his name and surname, to anticipate his needs and desires.

It does everything it can to accumulate as much data as possible through each of its business processes. It makes hypotheses, tests them, and often confuses correlations and causality. This is the whole problem of these voluminous sets of data (big data) and their analysis with more or less relevant algorithms. Two legal pitfalls common to all resources and processes are the obsolescence of resources and the legal inadequacy of their use. This voluminous set of data is not necessarily unique within the company. Sometimes several processes accumulate massive amounts of data that relate to the same resource. The two cases that easily come to mind are Facebook and Google. But historical companies like Equifax in the US can accumulate personal data to provide a credit rating and facilitate access to credit. The data is only valuable if it is used in compliance with the regulations, in particular about the protection of personal data (Regulation [EU] 2016/679 applicable from May 25, 2018). In addition, in September 2017, the European Commission adopted a proposal for a Regulation on the free movement of non-personal data within the European Union. Data presents an enormous amount of potential business opportunities. Data scientists are in high demand. Cathy O'Neill, data scientist and author of the blog mathbabe.org, is more direct on this topic:

> The crash [of 2008] made it all too clear that mathematics, once my refuge, was not only deeply entangled in the world's problems but also fueling many of them. The housing crisis, the collapse of major financial institutions, the rise of unemployment—all had been aided and abetted by mathematicians wielding magic formulas.
>
> [CNE]

Without going into human, technical, or mathematical details, most of the legal and operational risks lie in the ethical use of data, the choice and use of mathematical tools and, of course, the interpretation of the results obtained with these mathematical tools. Equifax is a symptomatic case that allows us to make a synthesis. Equifax is a company created in 1899, based in Atlanta (Texas, USA). It is one of the three main consumer credit reporting agencies. It collects and consolidates information on over 800 million individual consumers and over 88 million businesses worldwide. It is continuously computerized to optimize its processing and to be in direct contact with its consumers through its website.

According to the Consumer Financial Protection Bureau (CFPB), Equifax accumulates thousands of complaints annually, most of which involve incomplete, incorrect, or outdated data. On September 5, 2017, Equifax reports that thieves (hackers) have accessed the data it stores and that the data of more than 143 million Americans and Canadians has potentially been stolen such as social security numbers, license numbers. Potentially, because the company can't identify the data that was copied. This is the third theft in two years for Equifax. It has accumulated a tremendous amount of bad practices that put the company and its executives at odds with many legal standards. The September 23, 2017, New York Times article "As Equifax Amassed Ever More Data, Safety Was a Sales Pitch" summarizes and describes the links between all the points we have just discussed, the management of resources (here private data), massive amounts of data and unsecured processes:

> Equifax's chief executive had a simple strategy when he joined more than a decade ago: Gather as much personal data as possible and find new ways to sell it. The company was making good money compiling credit reports on Americans. But Wall Street wanted stronger growth.
>
> The chief executive, Richard F. Smith, delivered, releasing dozens of new products each year and doubling revenue. The company-built algorithms and started scrubbing social media to assess consumers. In a big data collection coup, Equifax persuaded more than 7,000 employers to hand over salary details for an income verification system that now encompasses nearly half of American workers.
>
> As part of its pitch to clients, the company promised to safeguard information. It even sold products to help companies hit by cyberattacks protect their customers.
>
> "Data breaches are on the rise. Be prepared," the company said in one pitch. "You'll feel safer with Equifax."
>
> But this strategy means that Equifax is entrenched in consumers' financial lives whether they like it or not—or even know it. Equifax's approach amplified the consequences of the breach, reported this month, that exposed the personal information for up to 143 million people.

It's true that Equifax is in the news and Facebook is also in the news for its sales figures or the number of users. But did you know that Facebook has patented a new type of credit rating, based on our social networks? It is a basic trend to look for data other than the regulated ones:

> After all, our credit history includes highly personal data, and it makes sense that we should have control over who sees it. But the consequence is that companies end up diving into largely unregulated pools of data, such as click streams and geotags, in order to create a parallel data marketplace. In the process, they can largely avoid government oversight. They then measure success by gains in efficiency, cash flow, and profits. With few exceptions, concepts like justice and transparency don't fit into their algorithms.

[CNE]

4.3 INTERNATIONAL CONTEXT AND INNOVATION

Depending on the country, the same theme may have overlapping or different interpretations, such as the interpretation by international accounting standards of money, land, and labor as commodities. These international norms, mainly of Western influence, can be in contradiction with ancestral values in other parts of the world, as in India or China with article 90 of the Imperial Code on the ownership of land and the responsibility of the managing emperor (cf. Karl Polanyi).

Mark Herrmann even makes a wish in October 2016, on these issues of international laws not being harmonized:

> But it would sure be nice if we could reach an agreement that, for example, a company that is doing what it is required to do under one country's laws cannot be criminally prosecuted if that law conflicts with a second country's laws.

Since this will remain wishful thinking, it is best to be proactive. The international legal environment must and can be considered as soon as a service or product is created. Are you going to launch a project and worry about legal constraints only before marketing? No, of course not, but that is not what we do for most of our projects. Very sensitive sectors of activity are those that are highly dependent on a brand, such as luxury goods, or that integrate in their products a lot of intellectual property of the company or of other companies, such as electronics with aviation, or IT, with connected objects.

We are far from the concerns of citizens about copyright or intellectual property legislation. A very national historical vision as shown by this story told by Pierre-Antoine Frédéric Malapert:

> In the last century, it was noticed with a certain indignation that the heirs of the famous Barbin, editor of Boileau and other fine minds of the time, had become marquises and rode in gilded carriages, while the little girls of La Fontaine were in misery. The king's council was moved by the fate of these poor women. In 1761, a privilege was granted to them for the reproduction of their ancestor's works. Barbin's representatives, who were members of one of the companies called "les libraires associés," formed by the main publishers of Paris, attacked the new privilege before the parliament. There, in 1764, armed with the contracts made by Barbin with the fabulist, they had it decided that the privilege of La Fontaine's granddaughters should be declared null and void.
>
> [PFM]

Legislation creates constraints for companies already present in a market, but also for new entrants. If lobbying has been done properly, companies influence at least the status quo in the legislation. Companies can also invest in research and development and apply for or buy patents and not use them. Companies, including very small and medium-sized businesses, must avoid an overly national vision. If a company has no desire to go international, what is the point of forcing itself to think internationally? Because international companies may want to invest in their national market and find themselves with legal conflicts to manage. It is wise to protect one's brand, one's intellectual property at least in one's own country.

It can even be judicious to think about preserving one's trade secrets. This concern is not recent, as shown for example by this decision of the French Parliament of March 29, 1715, confirming a consular judgment of March 9, 1714:

> Foreign manufacturers are accused of placing their children, even as store boys, with the aim of surprising the secrets of the Lyon industry [of silk], and of suborning the skilled workers.

In the early 1980s, companies started to realize the importance of being present on the Internet, even with a minimal institutional site. Many companies found themselves having to buy domain names at prohibitive prices, because they were identical to the company's name, to the name of one of the products sold by the company or because the company wanted new domain name extensions, as if in addition to owning the domain name mycompany.de, it was necessary to have the domain name mycompany.com

If the owners of certain domain names did not want to sell, the company had to take legal action, with the uncertainty of the outcome of the judgment and the certainty of losing money for a lack of understanding of the digital issues by the company's management. On October 24, 1999, the Internet Corporation for Assigned Names and Numbers (ICANN), the Internet's regulatory authority, approved a uniform domain name dispute resolution policy to limit legal uncertainties. From December 1999 to December 2000, 75% of the 2500 complaints filed with ICANN were decided in favor of the trademark owner.

At the beginning of the 21st century, all this seems very far away, the media talk about it less, but in November 2011 in France, the Syreli platform was launched to implement the dispute resolution procedure for extensions managed by Association Française pour le Nommage Internet en Coopération (AFNIC). The success rate for the claimant for domain names that are more than three years old was 49% in 2011. Legal actions nowadays are about the jurisdiction to arbitrate a dispute and generate many cases of interpretation of the same legal texts. Electronic commerce is steadily increasing.

> E-commerce is global. Thus, even if national-level laws are developed to address some of the areas in which government regulation is desirable, e-commerce will suffer if these laws vary from country to country. For some issues, the law works best when it is harmonized at the international level.

[SKR]

These two examples demonstrate the extent to which the legal field is increasingly critical, as its intrinsic complexity is increased by the digitalization of information systems, the evolution of digital techniques and the diversity of digital uses. Outside of digital, the international legal environment must always be closely monitored. It is common to adapt your product to different regulations and obtain the necessary certificates to market your products. The more you differentiate your products to adapt to a market, the more complex your production becomes. The less you differentiate your products, the more you increase your production costs, because you must integrate the constraints of different markets.

Chandler Burr gives us an amusing example in his latest book "The Perfect Scent" on how to follow the evolution of international legislation:

> The Big Boy's [the international scent-maker corporations such as Firmenich or Givaudan] only growth sector (completely unproductive) is their legal departments as LVMH must rely on Firmenich lawyers and Givaudan chemists to establish, and maintain with constant National Security Agency—level international surveillance, that some bureaucrat in Tokyo hasn't suddenly outlawed Hedione, this instantly making 90 percent of Dior's perfumes the legal equivalent of poison sarin gas in Japan. (And speaking of regulatory environment, it is only getting worse. I was traveling around Tunisia with a perfume materials marketer who was talking about the growing List of Banned Materials incredulously. "No more polycyclics! No more phthalate musks!").
>
> [CBU]

However, legal differences are also opportunities. International standards tend to converge over time. For example, the evolution of safety standards for child seats in cars is a plus, because it brings products upmarket and encourages their renewal. If the company sells its car seats on several international markets with different regulations, the less restrictive local standards evolve toward the more restrictive ones. If you have expertise in the most stringent standards, you can easily seize the opportunity and sell compliant products as soon as possible. Each department of the company operates in a specific field, itself governed by a regulatory environment. An accountant will follow accounting regulations, a chemist will comply with food regulations, or a researcher will follow the protocols defined by the agency to which he or she reports, such as the drug safety agency. Knowledge of regulations is usually considered a must for managers.

On the other hand, not complying with a regulation can be a choice of the company. This is the criticism leveled at companies like Google or Facebook, whose approach is not to ask permission to test new features. Jonathan Taplin proposes several examples in his book "Move Fast and Brake Things" [JTA], two of which are very typical, the first one concerns Google and the second one Facebook:

> Google took a similar "don't ask permission" tack when Brin decided to digitize all the world's books. As he told Auletta, if they had asked authors and publishers, Google "might not have done the project."
>
> Mark Zuckerberg's initial letter to investors when Facebook went public was titled "The Hacker Way." He wrote, "The word 'hacker' has an unfairly negative connotation from being portrayed in the media as people who break into computers. In reality, hacking just means building something quickly or testing the boundaries of what can be done."

This willingness to take risks or not is a concept developed in recent years by various organizations including the Committee of Sponsoring Organizations of the Treadway Commission (COSO) and called risk appetite. COSO defines risk appetite as follows:

> The amount of risk, on a broad level, an entity is willing to accept in pursuit of value. It reflects the entity's risk management philosophy, and in turn influences the entity's culture and operating style ... Risk appetite guides resource allocation ... Risk appetite [assists the organization] in aligning the organization, people, and processes in [designing the] infrastructure necessary to effectively respond to and monitor risks.

It completes the enterprise risk management approach (see "Enterprise Risk Management-Integrated Framework" published by COSO). COSO develops a structured approach around this notion with the will that the company defines this notion for itself and the means it gives itself to satisfy it.

But this appetite for risk is rather dependent at a given moment on the personality of the founder, the management committee, the financial health of the company, or its relationship to innovation. It is legitimate to want to channel this appetite, to structure it in stages with milestones, but the practice is more human than administrative.

This willingness to test the limits of the legal environment is risky in one country, such as the case of Heetch in France. Heetch has been around since 2013, but the company had to start from scratch in 2017. In March 2017, the Paris court ruled that Heetch had illegally operated a transportation company and ordered it to pay 400,000 euros. Main reason was instead of having "drivers" sharing their journey for passengers to join and agree for the proposed price, Heetch had decided to do reverse, "passengers" were sharing where they wanted to go and "drivers" were proposing their "help." It had to suspend its cell phone application after this decision and rethink its economic model (business model). It obtained 12 million dollars from Felix Capital, Via ID and Alven Capital to finance its new service.

Exporting this strategy of testing the limits is even more risky, as with Uber, a company founded in California, which has succeeded in turning its name into a verb, used to stigmatize or decry its processes around the world. Its business model is being questioned from all sides with complaints from its drivers, associations, governments, and its employees. Several complaints are pending in 2017 and follow more than 130 complaints in the US alone in 2016 (The Mercury News, July 4, 2016).

These legal risks concern companies of the new economy. Digitalization also affects the legal world. We have this Epinal image of lawyers and jurists sitting in their offices with many paper files surrounding them. Katharina Pistor in her latest book explains that legal processes and lawyers must give way to people who master the digital world and its tools like smart contracts, digital money (bitcoins), digital property rights:

> The lawyers, who have taken center stage as master coders in the minting of capital, may have to cede most of their terrain to the "digital coders" who are already busily digitizing contracts, firms, money, and knowledge.
>
> [KPI]

In this effervescent context around the smart contract, it is appropriate to remember that we are talking about IT. But why this reminder? well that these are programs that automate these smart contracts and that they are subject to errors too like all other programs. It is important for any company to be first on the market to exploit new ideas and offer new services that will generate revenue and in the case of start-ups to be the foundation of their business model.

MonoX website on November 23, 2021, mentions:

> MonoX is a platform where new projects and developers can launch their tokens without the burden of capital requirements ... MonoX will revolutionize the DeFi [Decentralized Finance] ecosystem by fixing the capital inefficiencies of current protocol models.

Classic sentences from a team of well-intentioned co-founders, hardly working to provide breakthrough technology.

On December 1, 2021, a new post explains:

> ... Security has always been very important to us. We conducted a three-month testnet +bug bounty and conducted three audits prior to launch ... Roughly $31M was drained from the pool as a result of the hack. The exploit was caused by a smart contract bug that allows the sold and bought token to be the same ... This also goes without saying, but we won't even consider redeployment until we've been thoroughly audited again.

It is $31M worth of tokens on the Ethereum and Polygon blockchains. This is the latest hack at the time of the writing, Indexed Finance mentioned on October 15, 2021, a loss of $16 billion. Elliptic is a company founded in 2013

pioneering the use of blockchain analytics for financial crime compliance.

It can't be more explicit to describe the current context in a post on November 18, 2021, as that:

The relative immaturity of the underlying technology has allowed hackers to steal users' funds, while the deep pools of liquidity have allowed criminals to launder proceeds of crime such as ransomware and fraud.

BIBLIOGRAPHY

ASM: Adam Smith, *"The Wealth of Nations,"* 1776, W. Strahan and T. Cadell
CBU: Chandler Burr, *"The Perfect Scent,"* 2007, Picador, 978-0-312-42577-7
CNE: Cathy O'Neil, *"Weapons of Math Destruction,"* 2016, Corwn, 978-0-553-41881-1
JTA: Jonathan Taplin, *"Move Fast and Break Things,"* 2017, Hachette Book Group Inc., 978-0-316-27574-3
KPI: Katharina Pistor, *"The Code of Capital: How the Law Creates Wealth and Inequalities,"* 2019, Princeton University Press, 978-0-671-20860-2
MBR: Mike Brewster, *"Unaccountable: How the Accounting Profession Forfeited a Public Trust,"* 2003, Wiley, 0-471-42363-9
PFM: Pierre-Antoine Frédéric Malapert, *"Histoire abrégée de la législation sur la propriété littéraire avant 1789,"* 1881, Librairie Guillaumin et Cie
RAS: Robert A. Schultz, *"Information Technology and the Ethics of Globalization,"* 2010, Hershey, 978-1-60566-923-6
SJU: Samuel Jube, *"L'éclatement comptable de l'entreprise: constat et remèdes,"* Collège de France, Séminaire 15 mars 2016,
SKR: Norman Soloway and Cynthia K. Reed, *"Internet and the Dispute Resolution: Untangling the Web,"* 2003, ALM Properties Inc., 1-58852-113-3

Chapter 5

Operational risks

Seiri, Seiton, Seisu, Seiketsu, Shitsuke.

Taichi Ohno, *Workplace Management*

5.1 PROCESSES

Most legal risks depend in quantity and importance on the company's strategic and organizational choices. Operational risks, on the other hand, are inseparable from the company's activities.

The relevance of the company's activities is assessed by its financial results. To achieve its objectives, the company's management optimizes or changes its business processes. Internal or external auditors analyze them to assess the risks. The main business processes for auditors are those of the following departments, whether or not they are support functions:

- Customer Service,
- Finance,
- Human Resources,
- IT,
- Marketing,
- Operations, and
- Sales.

The Customer Service department plans, directs, controls, and implement all Customer Service activities. Depending on the company these activities could be call centers, order entry, credit check, credit limit, delivery issues, and returning process.

Finance department plans, directs, controls, and implements all Finance activities in the company including finance management, business planning, budgeting, forecasting and finance analysis, actual finance reporting, accounting, sales analysis, and planning.

The Human Resources department plans, directs, controls, and implements all HR activities including compensations and benefits, recruitment and

DOI: 10.1201/9781003230137-5

selection, career development and succession planning, training, employee motivation/satisfaction, performance practices and appraisal, HR administration, health and safety, legal affairs, and administration.

The information technology (IT) plans, directs, controls, and implement all IT activities in the company including such as IT infrastructure, network security, IT projects, budgeting, office equipment purchase, software, and network systems maintenance.

The Marketing department plans, directs, controls, and implements all marketing activities in the company including local marketing strategies, advertising, representatives and consumers' motivation, public relations, and Internet web page coordination.

The Operations department plans, directs, controls, and implements all Supply Chain activities in the company such as assembly line, warehouse, home delivery system, inventory control, excess planning, product supply, and facility security.

The Sales department plans, directs, controls, and implements all Sales activities in the company including development of sales force, motivation systems, sales leadership framework, sales support, field trainings, business planning, analysis and reporting, and career development.

As much as activities are specific to a department, processes are generally transversal. They start in one department and end in another. Between these departments, one or more other departments may intervene. This notion of process is crucial in the implementation of integrated management software packages (ERP). The software packages are broken down into modules that have access to common data. The modules automate the activities of a department. The sharing of data, i.e., the possibility for one or more modules to access, read, create, or modify data, allows the processes to be made real.

Let's assume that the purchase orders are considered by the sales department, and that they are then validated by the accounting department following receipt of payment. The purchase orders are created by the sales department and confirmed by the accounting department, which can trigger the preparation of the order and its delivery. Alternatively, the creation of the purchase order could trigger the preparation of the order which would be delivered following confirmation of payment by the accounting department.

Different options are possible, and the software packages are the most capable of taking them into account. Their modules can be configured to adapt to the activities and processes of a company, i.e., they can be customized to its needs. The configuration options avoid the development of external programs to carry out treatments not foreseen by the software package.

Once the software package is installed and configured, the company benefits from a completely automated work environment. The data shared by the modules is then visible to any person in the company according to their access rights to the modules and data.

The business departments and general management can see the status of the data in real time, as there is no waiting for information to be entered. The order form is entered directly by the salesperson and is immediately visible in the software package. There is no need to wait for the salesperson to return to the company at the end of the day to enter his handwritten purchase orders.

This visibility is the major stumbling block in the deployment of a software package in a group. If all the data is visible in real time in the software package by the general management, then the local management has more difficulty in arranging the results and the management monitoring indicators (Key Process Indicators) so that they embellish their management. This loss of autonomy is very difficult for them. They argue that the software package is not flexible enough to take their specificities into account, or that the functionalities of another software package for a particular task are so powerful that it is jeopardizing the turnover to use the less powerful functionalities of the software package.

It is therefore extremely common for the ideal world of integrated processes and data in a single software package to remain wishful thinking. Faced with this outcry from one or more subsidiaries and given the investments already made in the project, the group often decides to define a poorly tailored solution. The homogenization of the group's processes is then undermined. The basic or core model is amputated of all or part of the processes. It is reduced to what the group was able to keep during negotiations with the subsidiaries.

The auditor is in a situation that is both more similar and more complex than auditing manual processes. Similar, because the processes are unique for each subsidiary as if the processes were manual. Complex, because automation adds a layer of complexity, with all the technical controls. His ideal world (shown in Figure 5.1) of optimizing his work falls apart.

The auditor, either internal or external, as well as the management of the group imagined that the processes and data would revolve around a

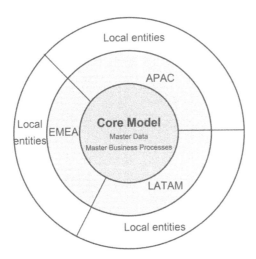

Figure 5.1 The core model concept.

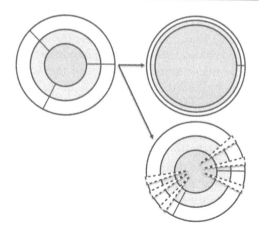

Figure 5.2 Core model from theory to reality.

core model, with specificities per region and if necessary, localizations. In Figure 5.2, the objective is for the central surface (the core model) to prevail over the grey surface, which itself prevails over the white surface. This implies moving from the basic idea (top left) to an ideal realization for the group (top right) and not to a reality that increases the risks (bottom right).

The dotted lines symbolize elements that differ from the choices made for the core model (disk at the center) and that are not applied at any level of the group's organization. This figure shows a vision centered around data and parameters common to the whole group. We can also visually compare the differences between the ideal world of a fully integrated process in a software package and the one that has been negotiated and implemented in Figure 5.3 infra.

On the left side of the drawing, we have the main selling point of software publishers, the internal justification of investments and return on investment calculations, equivalent to the three concentric disks. The desire to install a software package is to simplify processes and reduce costs for both the business departments, which become more efficient, and the IT department,

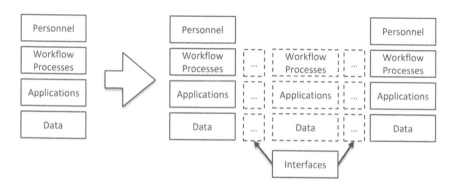

Figure 5.3 The reality is different from the initial understanding.

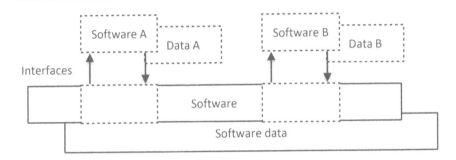

Figure 5.4 Automated processes the reality.

which has less software to manage and maintain. A staff that shares the same vision of how the company's processes work, a single software package with all the integrated management rules and that manages data access. A single database that reflects the state of flows at any given moment.

On the right side of the drawing, we have the reality, which can be much more complex than on this diagram. In the dotted line we have the added elements, additional software, data managed by this software and, of course, interfaces and personnel that are not those of the company (subcontractors or outsourced). All these elements add risks by their presence in the middle of the processes and by the need to maintain these different elements compatible as the software versions change.

A process with these interruptions can be diagramed as in Figure 5.4.

Each interface is a source of fragility. It must recover, in the right state, the data from one system to communicate it correctly to the next. As a result, when preparing for data analytics, they will have to be tested such as in Figure 5.5.

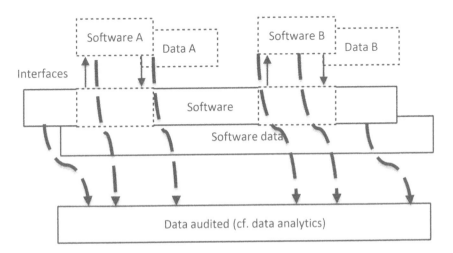

Figure 5.5 Example of data analytics implementation.

Let's assume that the software handles quotes over 100,000 euros, and that the other ones are processed in the software package (or vice versa). An additional risk arises, employees create several quotes below 100,000 euros instead of a single one. All this for good reasons, to limit more complex controls or to save time and satisfy the customer's request as soon as possible.

These processes are frequently weakened by interfaces. The additional difficulty is that these interfaces may be different between several subsidiaries. Software C and D will be used in another subsidiary instead of software A and B and perhaps for quotation numbers over 200,000 euros instead of 100,000. The content and the scheme itself may differ from one subsidiary to another. We feel helpless to audit the processes because of the different possibilities and the increasing functional and technical complexities.

Auditing a process of this type always requires as much preparation as a manual process. It is not cost-effective to audit the main model for all subsidiaries and then the local specificities, because the basic or main model is almost empty.

We are lost because of the technical complexity. The technical complexity is penalizing. The auditor must master his work programs. He must audit different software that he does not master or very little, and in any case, less well than the one targeted by the audit. To compensate for this, the IT auditor, who was once confined to technical IT risks with the Global Technology Audit Guide (https://na.theiia.org/standards-guidance/recommended-guidance/practice-guides/Pages/GTAG1.aspx), now intervenes in collaboration with or in support of the auditors to analyze the processes.

5.2 DATA

To solve this problem of technical unfamiliarity, and the processing of these volumes of data, the auditor uses data analysis software. There is software for auditors that facilitates this analysis, but a spreadsheet is not one of them. The data exists regardless of the complexity of the processes or the number of software programs used. This is the other way of looking at the ideal world of enterprise resource planning.

For auditors, data analysis has other advantages such as independence from users, or the possibility of continuous monitoring, because you do not need their availability to work on data, no planning is required. Once the tools for data retrieval are in place, the analysis can be done on demand or according to a predefined frequency.

But where is the difficulty because it seems too simple? Indeed, it is not as simple as it seems. To set up the data analysis, it is enough for an IT auditor to speak with IT specialists to identify the data sought in the database, the rights and access modalities to these data and finally to code the interfaces that go well to copy the data.

But the choice of data is only relevant if it is made by an auditor who knows very well the business process to be analyzed. He therefore lists the information he needs with his own vocabulary and ideally with the vocabulary used in the software package. The IT auditor translates this information to the IT people who maintain the software package.

As an aside for non-computer scientists, an IT project documents the implementation of a software package with three main documentations:

- Documentation of the definition of needs,
- The design documentation that translates these needs into processes and data that can be computerized, and
- The technical documentation that describes the choices made for configuration, programming, etc.

In other words, the auditor writes his needs (1), the IT auditor specifies the technical expectations (2) and the IT specialist details the necessary data and how they will be retrieved from the database. This is a job that must be precise and rigorous, with many round trips between these three people. The results of this work will justify, base an audit opinion and recommendations.

It is a job that requires an investment in time and money. In terms of time, it is therefore preferable to plan it and to carry it out before the on-site audit. In terms of money, the initial investment is not sustainable over time, you cannot come back 6 months or a year later and reuse the same programs, because, in the meantime, the software package's configuration may have been modified or it may have changed version. It is necessary to plan the time necessary to verify the relevance and the correct operation of the data recovery programs.

The company can make the investments profitable and manage the risks. It then asks the audit department or the operational department on which the analyzed processes depend to carry out this work regularly. This is called continuous or permanent monitoring. Continuous monitoring makes staff aware of the risks. It improves their practices about the points checked. This approach began in the 1980s and, according to the companies, is still in place in the 2020s.

The computing power of computers and their capacity to manage more and more data as well as data in a wide variety of formats such as images, sounds, videos, and text, have increased enormously (big data). The decreasing cost of computer resources facilitates their use for data other than those managed by integrated management software packages.

Many activities are not considered by ERP software that are specialized on the main processes. The big data takes into account the data extracted from ERP and other software:

> For a long time, mainly because of their "siloed" organization, this data could not be systematically exploited, and it was impossible to move from traceability to trace intelligence, or "mappability." This is precisely the transition that the major players in the big data technology market are promising, based on the development of storage databases that make it

possible to link large sets of data collected on various occasions and/or for various purposes, and to build from there a form of expertise that we could call "trace engineering."

[PMP]

Operational risks then spread to other elements of the information system that were not historically within the scope of finance people or software packages. Moreover, the business models of early digital start-ups are like the choice made by Google after its creation, as Andrew Keen recalls:

> Most of these Web 2.0 businesses have pursued a Google-style business strategy of giving away their tools and services for free and relying on advertising sales as their main source of revenue. "The best minds of my generation are thinking about how to make people click ads," one of Facebook's engineers dryly notes. Like Google, networks such as Facebook and YouTube have become big data companies able to target their users behavior and taste through the collection of their data exhaust.

[AKE]

These choices correspond to operational processes that are unknown to the auditors, and therefore to data that is also unknown. This lack of knowledge is in itself a risk, but an audit risk. Furthermore, the metrics used to qualify the activity of these start-ups are far from perfect and are revised and completed over time. New business models are also at risk because the underlying business processes and controls are also new. Business processes are either completely new or more complex, such as multi-channel sales processes. When you log into your Amazon account or simply through cookies left by Amazon on your device (phone, tablet, computer), the content of the page you are viewing is modified in real time based on your interactions with that same page.

Traditional process data analysis is still developing with new techniques being used in the early 21st century, as Geoffrey West reminds us:

> But there is a new kid on the block that many feel promises more [than big data] and, like Anderson, potentially subverts the need for the traditional scientific method. This invokes techniques and strategies with names like machine learning, artificial intelligence, and data analytics. There are many versions of these, but all of them are based on the idea that we can design and program computers and algorithms to evolve and adapt based on data input to solve problems, reveal insights, and make predictions. They all rely on iterative procedures for finding and building upon correlations in data without concern for why such relationships exist and implicitly presume that "correlation supersedes causation".

[GWE]

These new methods supported by increased computing power have the same goal as those used for data analysis: To identify new ways to increase revenue through a better understanding of customers or visitors. But data is scattered. It is even more scattered, as companies offer to enrich corporate databases with external data that is conditionally free, retrievable from the Internet or simply associated with you via your cell phone.

These companies offer a set of services to increase sales with data enrichment and predictive algorithms. The company therefore has at its disposal data with different legal constraints, data from its own activity, public data (open data) and other data from social networks, data available on the Internet and data from partners.

To better understand the risks, their complexity and the actors involved when viewing a website, I suggest you look at the graph of links between the NFL homepage and third-party sites. The graph shown in Figure 5.6 is created with the Evidon site in November 2017. Even if it is unreadable, it reads from left to right with the audited site nfl.com on the left and as you go to the right the links to the 107 other connected sites, sorted by purpose with different colors on the website. While the graphic is here in black and white, do not expect to have it more readable and understandable with some colors, it shows the complexity and imbrication of the links we don't see while using the NFL website:

- The publisher and its sites (Publisher),
- The advertising (Ad),
- The analytics (Analytics),
- The privacy (Privacy),
- The trackers (Tracker),
- The gadgets in the windows (Widget), and
- The unclassified ones.

Side remark, the funny thing with these links called Hyper Text Markup Language (HTML) is that they were designed in the early 90s as the innovation enabling users to more easily surf the web, and today they are mainly used by companies to track us. For auditors, it is a good example of a technic no more used for what it was initially designed and therefore potentially modifying the risks landscape.

Data is an issue in the design and management of websites. This dependence on data, whatever the activity of the company, increases the legal risks. Some of the data used or produced within the framework of the company's activities are protected. These protected data are divided into

- Personal data,
- Sensitive data,
- Data relating to private life,
- Data protected by an intellectual property right,
- Data protected by secrecy, and
- Data protected by contract.

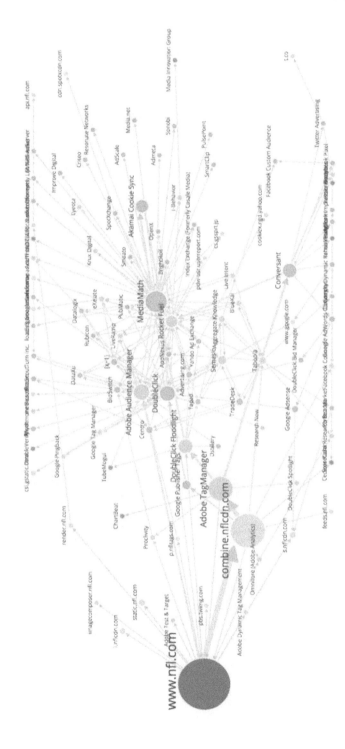

Figure 5.6 An unreadable graph reflecting the current tracking system complexity.

Each of these data groups is described below, in the 2018 European legislative environment. The conditions for obtaining, storing, and especially processing this data must be verified on a country-by-country basis, or according to international agreements if the company is storing data of citizens of one country in another country:

- Personal data are governed by regulations, in the European Community, the regulation has been recently updated the Regulation on the protection of individuals about the processing of personal data and the free movement of data (GDPR).
- Sensitive data are those that reveal, directly or indirectly, the racial or ethnic origins, political, philosophical, religious or trade union opinions, health, or sex life of a person. For example, genetic data, data on criminal offenses, biometric data are at risk. In France, the Cour de Cassation (~Supreme Court of the United States) limits data relating to private life to "family or friendly relations, marital or sentimental life, physical life or state of health" (Cass. crim. 14-2-2006 #0584384).
- Data protected by an intellectual property right such as copyright (economic and moral rights), trademark law or design law (property title conferring a monopoly of exploitation).
- Data protected by secrecy, by law or by a classification of secrets (e.g. confidential defense or secret defense) with risks of criminal liability.
- Data protected by contract such as in the context of data supply, licensing agreements, general terms of use and exploitation of data, or confidentiality clauses and agreements.

Open data can be legally separated into mandatory, voluntary, and openly licensed data.

> The diffusion of the term open data in the vocabulary of the debates around digital policies is only established after the Sebastopol meeting, held in 2007 in California, gathering digital activists such as Aaron Swartz, the founder of Reddit and activist of free access to scientific publications, Lawrence Lessig, the lawyer creator of the Creative Commons licenses, or Tim O'Reilly, at the origin of the notion of "web 2.0".
>
> [PMP]

Before consolidating them, the owners and the rights of use of the data must be defined, which can also be done, on the one hand, in order not to violate the law, but, on the other hand, in order not to risk having to make data available because of the misunderstanding of the legal constraints of using openly licensed data.

On the other hand, the company must protect its investments and keep evidence of its investments, financial, human, and material investments. The auditor must ensure that the IT controls are adequate and trace these elements and that the projects keep the proof of those.

The company completes this evidence and secures its rights up to the point of filing a database, through the proof of compliance with contracts, contractually frames its data, its use, or its exploitation. Let's take, for example, the Ryanair vs. PR Aviation case judged in January 2015. The court ruled in favor of PR Aviation:

> This request for a preliminary ruling relates to the interpretation of Directive 96/9/EC of the European Parliament and of the Council of 11 March 1996 on the legal protection of databases.
>
> (OJ 1996 L 77, p. 20)

> That request has been made in proceedings between Ryanair Ltd ("Ryanair") and PR Aviation BV ("PR Aviation") concerning the use by the latter, for commercial purposes, of data from Ryanair's website.

The court concludes:

> Directive 96/9/EC of the European Parliament and of the Council of 11 March 1996 on the legal protection of databases must be interpreted as meaning that it is not applicable to a database which is not protected either by copyright or by the sui generis right under that directive, so that Articles 6(1), 8 and 15 of those directives do not preclude the author of such a database from laying down contractual limitations on its use by third parties, without prejudice to the applicable national law.

As the plaintiff Ryanair had included restrictive clauses on the use of data on its website, it was able to force PR Aviation to stop using its data.

On the other side of the Atlantic Ocean, Southwest Airlines is the first American low-cost airline, founded on June 18, 1971. It, too, does not share its fares with flight information aggregators like Kayak and Expedia. But to date, no legal action has been taken that would provide details on the techniques used to avoid this sharing.

5.3 DIGITAL IMPACT

In addition to data, digitalization induces changes in work forms and modes. This makes the legal environment more complex. Lara Vivas Cuatrecasas summarizes this in the conclusion of her article on the International Bar Association:

> Technology has disrupted business, and disrupted work organization as a result. The new forms of work present new challenges for the law. While, in some cases, it is sufficient to adjust an interpretation to current laws, in other cases, new legislation simply needs to be passed (i.e. France requires

independent contractors who render services through online platforms to contribute to the social security system, but has also granted some protection similar to strikes). In any case, what is certain is that technology will continue to change at an exponential rate, and the changes derived from it will not only require new legislation but probably also a deeper change regarding how laws can be passed and adjusted to the exponential rate of technological change.

These changes in work forms and modes also increase the risk of fraud, as Mike Brewster notes:

> Joseph Wells is a former FBI agent, a CPA, and a certified fraud examiner (CFE) who founded a national association for CFEs. Wells has a saying: "Complexity is the killing fields of fraud." What he means is that as businesses get more complex, fraud is easier to hide. But even absent criminal intent on management's part, Wells said that the way the financial reporting is structured places the burden of proof on the wrong party—the auditor, not the corporate officer. "There is wiggle room in GAAP so that a client can forcefully argue a very questionable transaction, Wells said." Unless an auditor has a specific way of overturning the transaction, it usually stands. It really ought to be the other way around. You should have to demonstrate the proof of why you can book a certain transaction; the auditor shouldn't have to prove why you can't.

> [MBR]

The desire to simplify operational processes is not only due to the problems mentioned above. It is a corporate desire to simplify these processes, especially production processes, to reduce costs and improve their fluidity. Auditors also benefit from simple processes, as this reduces and limits risks.

Auditing a company's processes is therefore a challenge in itself for three reasons:

- For the same business processes, if the quantity of transactions increases, the risk of incorrect transactions increases,
- With the same business processes, if the products or services diversify and increase, the risk of error increases; and
- If business processes are changed, the risks also increase.

The audit approach must be different. Instead of waiting for the information system to be simpler so that the audit work can be simpler, it is better to simplify the audit approach. The company's processes are digitalized. The data needed for an auditor to form an opinion is also digitalized. Historically, auditors come with their work plan to verify the proper functioning of processes and to note any malfunctions or discrepancies. They also intervene on projects, considered by them to be critical or important for the company, to audit them before they go into production. The auditors must be independent and avoid being involved in the previous phases of the IT projects.

Rather than auditing computerized processes after the fact, it is more efficient to:

1. Define process checklists independently of their implementation, i.e., explicit work plans, and
2. Audit the controls defined in the deliverables of IT projects such as user requirements and their designs.

As discussed in the first chapter, the profession of auditor was originally a profession of numbers. Still and always at the beginning of the 21st century, this origin leaves its traces in the separation of financial auditors and IT auditors. Internal audit firms or departments train auditors respectively in IT or in the company's business or use new software such as artificial intelligence or neural networks.

To control operational risks, nothing is better than going back to basics, in our case the basic principles of the Committee of Sponsoring Organizations of the Treadway Commission (COSO) framework. Internal control is defined by COSO as "a process, effected by an entity's board of directors, management, and other personnel, designed to provide reasonable assurance regarding the achievement of objectives relating to operations, reporting, and compliance." In practice, there are three points to remember about internal control:

- It is a process,
- It provides reasonable (but not absolute) assurance of law-abiding leadership and management (cf. COSO: "tone at the top" vs. "tone in the middle"), and
- It is adapted to the achievement of the company's objectives.

The trend today is to make operational management responsible for ensuring that the internal control system is properly designed and operates correctly. The 2013 update of the COSO framework improves internal control by bringing in the expertise of support functions such as risk management. The internal auditors provide an independent view and carry out appropriate reviews to improve the organization's internal control.

Digitalization has a new impact. Globally equivalent processes can be different by replacing the work of employees with the involvement (work) of customers. This replacement is not a subcontract governed by a contract. These changes are visible in all service professions, with users taking over work that was previously done by employees, such as self-service and automatic checkouts.

Websites are way ahead of the curve in engaging the customer, with a huge amount of work going into analyzing the best possible interfaces to guide the customer. Social media is a caricatured example with customers posting 455,000 tweets on Twitter, adding 4 million "likes" and 510,000 comments on Facebook every minute, and uploading 400 hours of video to the YouTube server every minute in 2017.

This involvement generates risks that are difficult to control because of the difficulty of controlling the work of users. Compensatory controls are put in place such as moderators (possibly employees of the company) who will review the posts on a site and check that they comply with the site's instructions (guidelines) or by subcontracting (most often), human raters as they are called, Internet evaluators or Internet assessors who work indirectly for Google, Amazon or Microsoft, for example. If this work is poorly done or poorly controlled, the risks to the company's reputation increase. The only way to counteract this is to manage the company's institutional communication properly.

The auditor needs to understand what is behind these changes on a business model based on the number of clicks or the number of users, for example. It is very easy to distort this information. We tend to imagine people working in a low hourly rate country creating user accounts, continuously viewing, and clicking on company pages to increase these metrics that allow these companies to get funding from investors. More prosaically, it is enough to buy programs that will do this work (bots) and simulate instead of humans, the consultation of pages or the creation of user accounts.

These operational changes require auditors to change the way they work and upgrade their skills. Mike Brewster gives us a representative example:

> In 1984, Nicolls himself went to work for one of his S&L clients as a loan workout specialist. "There was a lot of pressure to put up more and more loans," Nicolls said. "And the auditors that we had out there were virtually clueless." As Nicolls observed, both as an auditor at Ernst & Whinney and later as someone who dealt with auditors in his job at the S&L, auditors had great difficulty trying to account for the risk that bank loans inherently contained.
>
> [MBR]

Non-strategic risks have been discussed, but how does the company's strategy affect operational risks and their importance? These concerns are considered in the due diligence.

Our analysis of risks and operational risks in particular is influenced by our resistance to change and the illusion of an ideal IT world. We think that the company we audit is eternal, that it will somehow outlive us. This perception is more or less strong depending on the country we live in. But as Geoffrey West notes:

> Half of all US publicly traded companies have disappeared within ten years of entering the market. Although a small minority lives for considerably longer, almost all seem destined to go the way of Montgomery Ward, TWA, Studebaker, and Lehman Brothers.
>
> [GWE]

The second bias is that the commercial discourse of hardware and software vendors penalizes our understanding. After having detailed the problems of companies at a given moment, they develop a product. Legitimately, they want to convince us that it is the solution to our problems.

They tell us about the ideal world that our company will be able to achieve by implementing their products. Progressively, these manufacturers and editors propose equivalent solutions. The marketing vocabulary and the disruptive ideas and concepts of the moment are flourishing in the press and in our collective unconscious.

From the 1980s onward, integrated management software packages were the solution for reducing IT costs and dealing with the shortage of IT specialists. The marketing discourse was in full swing. We have the ideal world of the core model that we mentioned earlier. This ideal world is linked to the usual organization of the company as a pyramid with strategic decisions at the top, tactical decisions in the middle, and operational decisions at the bottom. This gives this correspondence as described in Figure 5.7.

Moving away from this concept creates operational risks, but the notion of a pyramid does not exist in groups. The reality is more like a group of pyramids.

If the group has an important external growth strategy to which you add asset sessions like sites or subsidiaries, maintaining a stable core model is very difficult, if not impossible. Maintaining a stable core model in such a group is extremely costly in terms of time and money and it is also extremely risky. The ideal world of computer scientists is not the solution. On the other hand, some of these ideas can be used, but in different ways. For example, groups are more or less quick to reorganize, but they all end up enhancing their profit lines. These profit lines are known as Business Units (BUs), Business Lines, or Product Lines. If the group buys or sells a company, it does so consider the forecast for one of its profit lines.

It is preferable to limit the configuration of an ERP system to a BU. A BU is a grouping of legal entities decided by the management of the group. If

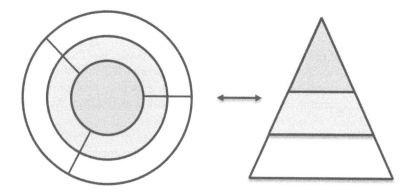

Figure 5.7 The theoretical core-model and organizational charts.

they are heterogeneous in terms of their geographical location, legal status or products, the creation of a core model for the entire BU is complex and risky, as will be its maintenance.

The geographic separation of a company's sites is an additional source of operational risk. People, products are transported from one site to another or to customers; data, electronic documents are transferred from one site to another. Every time people, products or documents leave one site to another or to a customer, the company is liable.

The risks of digitalizing a process come not so much from the digitalization as such as from the poor design of the changes to a process. One impact of digitalization on risks is simply that it has not been understood. In the current race to innovate using any technical possibility, some effects of digitalization are forgotten. The technical improvement of a process can turn against its original purpose. As a first example, let us take the legitimate concern of preserving endangered animal species. To manage the population of a species over very large territories, it is costly, random, and complex to carry out surveys and statistical calculations. However, this information helps to alert governments and to implement actions to improve the situation of the species studied. The geolocation of individuals of an endangered species is a simple and effective technical means to facilitate the management of individuals of the species at low cost and with excellent accuracy. The geolocation of wild animals (e.g. rhinoceros) is also designed to better protect them. But it also allows traffickers to track the animals.

Moreover, the availability of photographs of wild animals on the Internet also allows the location of these animals. Digital photographs contain additional data such as the type of camera used and the location of the place where the photograph was taken. The traffickers then circumscribe their search area around the location of the photograph. This saves them costs and search time. In fact, it was thanks to the metadata of a photograph posted on Twitter on December 3, 2012, by Vice editor Rocco Castoro that the police ended the run of John McAfee, founder and former boss of the computer security company that bears his name. He had been wanted for three weeks by authorities in Belize in an investigation into the murder of a man found dead on his property.

As a second example, let's take the risks related to information leaks. These have always existed, but they are complex to carry out and very risky. Andy Greenberg in his book "This Machine Kills Secret" [AGR], summarizes the changes:

> The barriers to modern megaleakers like Manning have scrimbled: They needn't spend a year photocopying [as Ellsberg]. They needn't be Eagle Scouts or war heroes who penetrate the government's most elite layer only to rogue just one of the millions of Americans with access to secret government documents or the many, many uncountable millions more with access to secret corporate information.

And perhaps most important, they needn't risk reprisal by exposing their identities to the journalists they hope will amplify their whistleblowing.

The forces that caught Manning are real and significant: The greatest vulnerability for any leaker remains his or her human connections.

Andy Greenberg also links this to the risk of too much process complexity (a point we discussed earlier):

Ironically, our government's tendency to overclassify information—and the sheer complexity of the rules for dealing with classified information—ends up increasing the number of cases involving the mishandling or unauthorized disclosure of classified information.

He quotes Julian Assange:

These megaleaks ... they're an important phenomenon, and they're only going to increase.

Digitalization also has unknown, unexpected or unintended effects. Daniel Ellsberg is a military man who for two years from 1969 to 1971 spent hours and hours at night in front of photocopiers duplicating top secret Pentagon documents about the US involvement in Vietnam. He would take the copies out every night in his briefcase and eventually deliver them to the New York Times and 17 other newspapers.

Today's photocopiers and printers are closer to a computer than to a 15th-century print shop. Both sign their work on each printed page. Each weapon has a particular signature when it fires. The marks on the casings are specific to it. Ballistics can confirm whether a weapon fired at a crime scene by comparing the signatures on the casings. Every copier and printer also have a specific signature when it prints. The marks and the way the pages are printed are unique due to the wear and tear of the machine.

But the most interesting point is that the machines indicate on each page they print information that is invisible to the naked eye. This information uniquely identifies the copier or printer, such as its make, model and even its serial number. This feature called "watermarking" is available in Microsoft Word, but here you know you are identifying your document.

Robert Graham summarizes the changes for leaks with these new machines in the case of the leaks about the 2016 US election hacking by Russian hackers:

The Intercept released documents on election tampering from an NSA leaker. Later, the arrest warrant request for an NSA contractor named "Reality Winner" was published, showing how they tracked her down because she had printed out the documents and sent them to The Intercept. The document posted by the Intercept isn't the original PDF file, but a PDF containing the pictures of the printed version that was then later scanned in.

His article "How the Intercept Outed Reality Winner," Monday, June 5, 2017 presents photos that allow you to visualize these signatures. As pointed out in Chapter 2, complexity increases risks, all of them, legal, operational, security, and IT. It increases the auditor's workload, the time required to understand the processes but also all the time spend to audit IT processes. It is no more possible to audit a company without performing at least basic duties on the IT department, i.e., more than SOX needs. Let's dive in the IT processes from an IT department in the next chapter from the administrative ones to service management and project management. Administrative processes are about managing an IT department, Service management processes are about keeping the lights on, i.e., ensuring that IT won't create any incident and if so its resolution. Project management is all about helping the companies achieving its business goals.

BIBLIOGRAPHY

AGR: Andy Greenberg, *"This Machine Kills Secret,"* 2012, Dutton, 978-0-75354-801-1

AKE: Andrew Keen, *"The Internet Is Not the Answer,"* 2015, Atlantic Books, 978-1-78239-342-9

GWE: Geoffrey West, *"Scale: The Universal Laws of Life and Death in Organisms, Cities and Companies,"* 2017, Weidenfeld & Nicolson, 978-0-297-86966-5

PMP: Pierre-Michel Menger and Simon Paye, *"Big Data et Traçabilité Numérique,"* 2017, Collège de France, 978-2-72260-467-4

MBR: Mike Brewster, *"Unaccountable: How the Accounting Profession Forfeited a Public Trust,"* 2003, Wiley, 0-471-42363-9

Chapter 6

IT processes

> Pray, Mr. Babbage, if you put into the machine the wrong figures, will the right answers come out?
>
> Charles Babbage, *Passages from the Life of a Philosopher*

This chapter is about traveling in the unknown for non–information technology (IT) specialist, and for a lot of IT specialists being for reasons highly specialized. The digitalization is the move for an information system to have more and more data and processes supported by Information Technologies. The more it is digitalized the more IT processes audits are mandatory. Auditors must understand how processes and data are maintained up and running and how they are improved. To have a successful maintenance and project deliveries, administrative processes must be in the audit's scope too.

While the importance of IT processes increased, the professional organizations (audit or project related) added more and more topics to their initial works. Efforts have been made by professional bodies since the 80s. There is Information Systems Audit and Control Association (ISACA) on the audit side with the Certified Information Systems Auditor (CISA) certification and the COBIT framework formerly known as the Control Objectives for Information and Related Technologies. First released in 1996, it was originally a set of control objectives to provide IT auditors with a book of knowledge initially addressing financial auditor's needs, i.e., filling a lack of expertise. The framework has then been expanded several times to, in a way, recognize that IT doesn't stop getting more and more essential to companies, with the latest release in 2019 as shown in Figure 6.1. ISACA presents COBIT as "a framework for the governance and management of enterprise information and technology, aimed at the whole enterprise."

The 2019 framework defines 40 processes grouped in 5 domains:

- "Governance objectives are grouped in the Evaluate, Direct and Monitor (EDM) domain. In this domain, the governing body evaluates strategic options, directs senior management on the chosen strategic options and monitors the achievement of the strategy (5 processes.)
- Align, Plan and Organize (APO) addresses the overall organization, strategy and supporting activities for I&T (14 processes.)

DOI: 10.1201/9781003230137-6

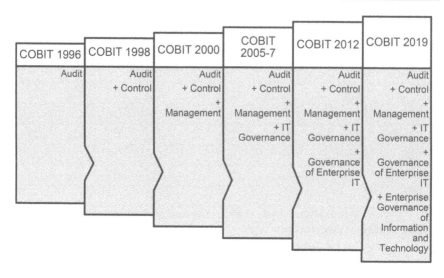

COBIT 1996	COBIT 1998	COBIT 2000	COBIT 2005-7	COBIT 2012	COBIT 2019
Audit	Audit + Control	Audit + Control + Management	Audit + Control + Management + IT Governance	Audit + Control + Management + IT Governance + Governance of Enterprise IT	Audit + Control + Management + IT Governance + Governance of Enterprise IT + Enterprise Governance of Information and Technology

Figure 6.1 **COBIT framework evolution.**

- Build, Acquire and Implement (BAI) treats the definition, acquisition and implementation of I&T solutions and their integration in business processes (11 processes.)
- Deliver, Service and Support (DSS) addresses the operational delivery and support of I&T services, including security (6 processes.)
- Monitor, Evaluate and Assess (MEA) addresses performance monitoring and conformance of I&T with internal performance targets, internal control objectives and external requirements (4 processes)."

As you can see, there is no dedicated detailed information for service or project management processes. For help on this, we can rely on the Information Technology Infrastructure Library (ITIL) and the Project Management Institute (PMI). ITIL is touted as

> "the framework for the management of IT-enabled services" and being "an adaptable framework for managing services. Through our best practice modules, ITIL helps to optimize digital technologies to co-create value with consumers, drive business strategy, and embrace digital transformation."

(Axelos)

Nowadays we have ITIL 4, but it already has a long history:

- In the 80s, the UK Government's Central Computer and Telecommunications Agency developed a set of recommendations designed to standardize IT management practices across government functions, built around a process model-based view of controlling and managing.

- In 2006, the ITIL Version 2 glossary was published.
- In 2007, ITIL Version 3 was issued consisting of 26 processes and functions, now grouped into only 5 volumes, arranged around the concept of Service lifecycle structure.
- In 2011, the 2011 edition of ITIL was published.
- In 2019, the ITIL 4 Edition starts with the ITIL Foundation book. Twenty-six processes of ITIL V3 are now replaced by 34 practices in ITIL V4.

The PMI released the first Project Management Body of Knowledge in 1996. The sixth edition, released in 2017, defines 49 processes consolidated in 12 project management standards from 39 processes in its third edition (2000):

- Initiating process group—processes performed to define the start of a new project with the required authorizations.
- Planning process group—processes required to establish the scope of the project, refine the objectives, and define the course of action to achieve the project's objectives.
- Executing process group—processes performed to complete the work defined in the project management plan.
- Monitoring and controlling process group—processes required to track, review, and regulate the project's performance; identify areas of change required and initiate necessary changes.
- Closing process group—processes required to officially close down the project.

The seventh edition released in August 2021, still keeps the processes but communicates on principle-based approach instead of a process-based approach.

In addition of these main three frameworks there are all the ISO standards and directives applying to IT, to name a few:

- ISO/IEC/IEEE 90003:2018 | Software engineering—Guidelines for the application of ISO 9001:2015 to computer software,
- ISO/IEC 20000-1 is the standard for service management, presenting a number of requirements for managing the design, implementation, operation and improvement of services,
- ISO 21500 series for project, program management, and
- ISO/IEC/IEEE 16326:2009 for Systems and software engineering—Life cycle processes—Project management.

With all these organizations taking care of the digitalization and maintenance of our information system, there are a lot of reasons to be afraid entering the IT environment. This is the reason why, a lot of analyses are provided by these private companies selling standards to present alignment between these standards. They are regularly updated as each standard is being regularly updated. And all this is without taking account additional more private endeavors, dealing for instance with agile. All this requires some training, some certifications with different levels for all the IT people. It's amazing that the 20th-century methodologies were highly criticized as too complex. When looking at the IT landscape nowadays, it looks complex and it is. The landscape is a moving one due to the recurrent new releases of these frameworks. As a result, these frameworks tend to overlap more and more. This shows why in real life there are IT auditors. Basic IT knowledge (ITGC for IT General Controls) is mandatory but useful for an overall understanding of the IT risks only. It helps for identifying areas of risk requiring deeper analysis, this is when more knowledgeable IT auditors come in.

Good thing is that it is possible to group the IT department duties: Administrative, service management, and project management duties. Administrative for all activities required to manage the IT team and the budget, service management to manage all the assets and keep them up and running, project management to enhance or create new assets. For ISO, an asset is anything that has value to the organization, its business operations, and their continuity, including Information resources that support the organization's mission [ISO/IEC PDTR 13335-1].

6.1 ADMINISTRATIVE PROCESSES

The administrative processes of an IT department are identical to those of other departments. It is about managing internal and external human resources, managing a budget, and monitoring the technical relevance of the information system and of the resources too. Administrative concerns are about keeping the current IT information system working flawlessly and scheduling changes, i.e., building the to-be IT information system, enabling the business to move forward with its strategy.

IT administrative processes must enable the CIO to:

- Monitor the budget (e.g. hardware, software, resources),
- Optimize the assets usage,
- Ensure full capacity usage of the resources, avoid cash-out, and
- Manage the projects.

An IT department is at the same time a service and a body shop. It produces new services and delivers services. As such people are key in its success. So, the organization chart must be aligned with these duties. Defining an organization structure has always a meaning as it supports the business strategy and compensates IT constraints. They are different options to ensure that administrative, service and project management activities are fulfilled and correctly staffed. There are different ways to break down an organization chart, some riskier than others.

Ideally an organization chart shouldn't be split per technology, reason would be that the resource profiles are completely different. It could be between some development technologies between waterfall, agile or DevOps, or between different operating system, e.g. Windows™, macOS™, and Unix™. People mindset is around the technique or the technology not focused on delivery to the business. Moreover, how can a team spirit be built not having everyone sharing the same objectives related to service or project management. How transitions will be managed while new IT tools are being developed? In short, the organization chart should be consistent with the IT objectives.

On a human resources point of view, whatever the work, it can be done internally or outsourced. If done internally, it can be done by a mix of internal and external resources. The main difference between the several options is the mix ratio internal vs. external. Risks can rise up to a complete lack of internal knowledge on the design or the techniques implemented if fully outsourced or with only external resources assigned. Auditors already know this ratio but with a financial point of view, with the expenditures and the cost difference between internal and external resources. As IT resources are critical for all the business processes, two things must be looked at, first what is the pertinence and coverage of the methods and best practices and second, are these methods and best practices being applied. Reasons are the work must be performed in a reliable way within all the company, and the assets must be created and delivered in a consistent manner. In an ideal world, processes are in place, so assets are identified and correctly documented, as a result IT resources are substitutable. In fact, the IT resources are not therefore auditing that the knowledge is not only in people's brain but documented is critical. The organizational chart and the distribution of interns and externs must be analyzed in this light.

It happens that an IT department is structured against technologies. The organization of the IT department favors the appearance of risks, such as an organization by techniques, while techniques change, for example, an organization by operating system was fashionable in the 1980s. The intention was good but the methods used for the mainframes were barely applied for departmental computers (minicomputers) and not at all for what IT specialists call "Open Systems." These open systems are issued from an OS from the mid-1960s but now owned by different vendors. There are no reason why best practices couldn't be applied to this environment. The organizational structure should be such that the work teams are all performing functionally cohesive tasks.

This principle lends itself to specialization and allows one to utilize specific skill levels when needed. Someone performing tasks linked to a specialty of that person, will be more productive and have higher quality results than a generalist, i.e., someone with limited knowledge in the given area of work. This implies that the assignment of a resource is based on the nature of the work to be performed. A by-side benefit is that this usually improves staff motivation and job satisfaction. A step further if the IT department is big enough, the teams could be functionally grouped within an organizational hierarchy in a manner such that related work is under one manager's area of responsibility, and not spread across different organizational lines. A constraint is that it implies a well-conceived grouping of the work teams and careful delineation of responsibilities.

The organizational structure should be compatible with the systems development methodology in use at the installation. This involves that the structure must support the manner in which the methodology will be used, and the methodology, in turn, must support the organizational structure. It should be amenable to a project orientation that allows co-sharing of responsibilities between IT and user departments. The use of some sort of a matrix structure allows the co-existence of both functional and project managers. It also provides the foundation to establish a project continuity as one rolls the project from one work team to the next. In the 21's wording, it will look like:

> "It aims to shorten the systems development life cycle and provide continuous delivery with high software quality." *This is for the sales pitch found at Wikipedia for DevOps, it* "is a set of practices that combines software development (Dev) and IT operations (Ops)."

This definition falls short on users and IT specialists co-sharing responsibilities.

Matrix organizations might have an appearance of complexity for some of us. This is mainly due to the fact that we are accustomed to organization chart as a breakdown hierarchical structure. Yes, matrix structures are best used in environments that are disciplined and observe formal planning and control procedures.

The administration body should maintain the information on the expertise of the IT specialists, knowing that a person is a network specialist is not enough to correctly assign the expert to the right projects, to nurture the expertise with new certification or to enlarge the expertise to related fields. In addition, the organization to perform efficiently needs to rely on a corpus of standards and best practices. This is where we find our ISO, ITIL, COBIT, PMBOK friends for example. A body within the IT department should be responsible for issuance and maintenance of all the governing policies, procedures and guidelines that are applicable to and used by the IT department.

The main risks are the difficulties managing resources, having the right people at the right time with the right technical background, enough professional experience or simply the knowledge of the IT department's operating procedures. It relates to how the budget needs are usually taken care of. Quite often, a FP&A person will prepare the budget breakdown based on the following meetings with the CIO and his/her direct reports. This budget includes business as usual activities (Service Management) and project activities (Project Management). A gross estimation is done for all the activities indicating the amount of workload, i.e., the number of man-days. This workload must be compared with the resource's capacity. If the IT department is composed of 10 persons, assuming 220 workdays per year, the team can produce 2,200 man-days. They can produce it during a year, meaning they can produce ~183 man-days per month. If all the activities consolidated are less or equal to 183, there is no risk of capacity shortage. However, if it is more, more than the contingency we used being 220 workdays per year, external resources or external services should be contracted. This a high-level point of view as some fine-tuning is required. Reason is that we know now that the IT resources are not easily interchangeable. Therefore, capacity could be there, but not the one needed. If an additional database specialist is required and only a network engineer is available, it won't work. The capacity calculation must be performed based on the workload required per expertise.

Speaking about resources and their workload, an expert should take less hours to perform a task than a non-expert. The point is how a person is considered as an expert? There are two ways, one based on trainings and the other based on professional experience on this topic. For all the frameworks we spoke, certifications are available in addition of trainings to get rid of on top trainings. In addition, for almost all the software bought by the IT department such as operation systems, software packages have also, on top of trainings, different levels of certifications. Recent studies and practical experience show that the more a person is expert the less errors are made. The relevance of resource profiles to the tools used to maintain and develop the information system is a point of interest for auditors.

That's why in the IT organization chart, a body should be in charge of capacity management. It is called Program or Project Management Office (PMO). Nevertheless, it is not because such a PMO exists that it performs all these duties. Actually, only a few of them do. They are usually responsible for administering and managing project-related activities. They at least take care of tracking time being spent on the different activities, eventually manage project with some forecast. In that case, the risk is that the focus is made on projects for the sake of projects without regard to the other activities assigned to the resources. If there are critical projects for the company, the auditors should wisely check how the IT department handle its capacity, are there formal processes in place being followed? A budget is only making sense if the capacity has been checked before approving it. All the numbers might make sense financially but not operationally which can lead to budget overruns.

The relevance of the workload estimates is critical to finalize a successful IT department budget. Estimating the service management activities is an easy task based on previous workload and estimated business growth. Additional on-going costs such as licenses renewals, hardware maintenance costs, network costs, pure application maintenance costs, must be added to have a full picture. Based on key metrics built on assets such as number of servers, number of PCs, number of sites, outsourcing costs, ratios are calculated and compared with the current incidents impacting the information systems as an average. The business strategy will modify some of these metrics while the forecasted projects will change others.

Estimating the workload activities for the planned projects at such an early stage is a challenge, but it must be done. In an ideal or pragmatic world, a person should be in charge of the estimations, perform and assist eventually in the work planning and estimating process for all the projects. The deliverables of the projects should be identified and provided to update the service management budget. Deliverables in a project are not only adding new assets but also decommissioning or retiring some active ones too, being counted in the current service management costs.

Another duty that could be centralized or transverse to the IT department is the ownership of the assets. An asset as multiple aspects, for accounting, it has an initial financial value, capex and opex associated, for IT support, it is a component or configuration item, it has a location, a release number, links with other assets, for IT administration, it has a life, with different releases associated costs, associated change requests, the contract's details.

Asset means here any item representing a cost for the company such as having been bought or developed by the IT department or linked to an IT asset. For instance the site where end-users are working is of interest as it provides information where IT assets might be used or stored. All these assets, including their multiple aspects, must be stored centrally in a Configuration Management Database (CMDB) (ITIL wording). They are critical for both service and project management activities and as such for auditors too. It is not possible for a CIO to efficiently monitor the IT department activities, define a strategy and proactively avoid incidents.

Having all this information available at hand facilitates analysis, such as financial analysis, incidents and problems analysis, strategy analysis. Knowing how many assets are actively managed by the IT department and used by the end-users is a point of interest for the auditors. It is interesting as these assets are assets, and they support the business processes. It is interesting to know that when someone is leaving the company, the leaver returns the laptop, the mobile phone, etc. provided to him. Cross-referencing who left the company and where are the assets the person was using help identify if information in a laptop are left with no company control, or if the accesses are canceled even before the hardware has been returned. Similarly, it helps knowing who has access to what within the information system.

Where the PMO has the overview on on-going and forecasted activities, the CMDB is required to proactively maintain assets. It is the sine qua non-condition to monitor costs.

6.2 SERVICE MANAGEMENT

Service management in an IT context, is composed of all the activities keeping all IT assets in operational condition. Maintaining a digitalized information system can't be done without knowing the IT assets used and their relationships. IT assets used means active assets needed by the end-users to do their job. We may think of keeping updated lists of the different assets and go from there. It might be OK for a small enterprise but no more. The number of assets

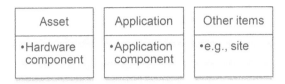

Figure 6.2 Common understanding of configuration items.

to track increase fast along with the size of the company and the digitalization. The more assets, the more relationships there are between these assets,
they have to be tracked too. The best solution is to store the information in
a database. The structure of such a database is more or less standard and is
CMDB we spoke about. It is mandatory to provide good services. The CMDB
will store basic details for the different assets plus additional ones the enterprise would also like to have visibility on.

Quite often, the word asset refers to hardware item. Distinction is being
made in the literature with application component being part of an application library. As a result, it looks like as in Figure 6.2.

On a pure service management point of view, this distinction is useless.
Nevertheless, it is useful to have an attribute to categorize the type of asset
such as in Figure 6.3.

This structure better reflects that all the elements required to deliver the
services: These elements are called configuration items. A configuration item
is either something directly with an IT financial cost assigned to it or a component required to be known to perform the service. You are at your desk
and need help to have your laptop serviced. You will have to tell, at least,
where you are seated such as which building and where in the building: Your
laptop is an IT asset and the site is another component. An IT asset is of
interest because it costs to buy, develop, or maintain. As such, any deliverable
produced by a project is an asset. An asset is always link to another asset, for
example, a program to another program, a laptop to a site, an object to an
internet link. It is also linked to a person or a site, meaning things that are not
IT managed. These information therefore should be created and maintained
through interfaces with the applications managing them. Doing so, it avoids

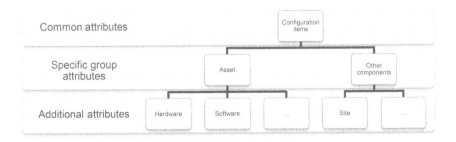

Figure 6.3 All items consolidated.

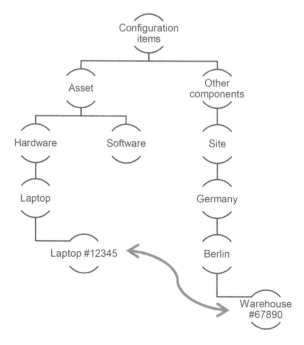

Figure 6.4 Relationships between elements.

the risks of having incorrect data or outdated data. The word item is a better word to describe all the information required in the CMDB to maintain the information system assets.

So, the representation in the previous figure misses the link between the two components, thick arrow shown in Figure 6.4.

At the end due to digitalization creating configuration item which were not existing previously as IT asset and extending the relations between configuration items, the figure looks more like a network than a hierarchical structure.

In real life, when auditing a CMDB they are all made different. They are different on:

- How many types of items are managed,
- How the configuration items are grouped, and
- Which relationships are monitored?

Creating from scratch a CMDB, is time consuming and expensive, so choices are usually made to target some critical items first and schedule other ones afterwards. Assets are targeted first, and the other components should be populated by the applications owning them. For instance, active sites might be populated by the Real Estate application. Such a solution might be applicable for assets too, for example, leveraging a software to discover network assets. Grouping the configuration items is up to the team designing the breakdown structure. Due to all relationships created along, it may not be easy to ungroup or group configuration items in a different way. As an example, laptops and desktops could have been split and due to COVID-19 forcing everyone to work remotely, desktops and laptops might be grouped.

To try to make things simple, it is wise during the design of the database to limit the types of relationships managed, i.e., trying to avoid the number of thick arrows in the previous figure. It makes sense to minimize the type of IT assets also.

The number of relationships will increase dramatically the more the assets are managed. In addition, the relationship between two items changes as time passes by, for instance, a person used to be assigned to a site but has been moved to another location and is using a new desktop or the same laptop at that location. As for any other stored information, files, or database etc. processes must be defined to create, update or un-activate them, and if required delete or archive them. Maintenance activities mainly update or un-activate assets. Project activities mainly create assets. It will update the database as they go along. To fill a CMDB as fast as possible, an initiative can take place to retrieve or upload data, but defined maintenance processes and project management methods are anyway mandatory to keep the database content aligned with the reality.

Based on all this, what is an IT asset for us in this book? An IT asset is any item from the information system with a cost assigned to it. To make is simple, what is mandatory as IT assets worth tracking are assets with a financial cost attached to them. Why do we consider an asset with a financial point of view? It is not a by-default option in ITIL, but it is pragmatic for project management and for auditors:

- With costs, the database can be easily seen with Pareto eyes, which are the 20% of assets representing 80% of the costs?
- Are these assets representing 80% of the costs being part of a similar group? For instance, if these assets constitute an application, question will be if the application should be redeveloped or rented as a service, etc.
- For each asset, knowing if its maintenance costs are more expensive than investing in a new one.
- Pro-actively, checking if replacing an asset before making any work on it as its replacement would be less than the maintenance costs or the maintenance costs would be greater than the remaining amortized value of the asset.
- Identifying which assets not having active links and therefore should be discarded or re-used, re-assigned.
- Detecting the assets associated with too many incidents.
- Scheduling pro-active operational maintenance duties on a regular basis to avoid incidents.
- Auditing the consistency between the information in the database and the existence of the assets.

For an auditor, if an enterprise is able to tackle these types of question, one may assume that the CMDB is pretty OK, the operating expenses are making sense and that almost all the assets should be real.

As IT assets are used by more and more business processes, service management is critical to avoid workflow disruptions. That's the reason why the improvement of services provided by IT departments is studied by various organizations around the world. The two main ones, mentioned previously, are the Information Technology Infrastructure Library (ITIL®) and ISO with ISO/IEC 20000. Where these products overlap with COBIT guidelines, they ensure that they are consistent with it. They describe different processes to deliver the services. Some of the processes take care of the points raised previously for the CMDB. The other ones are related to ensuring that if an end-user is facing an issue to perform his job, it is taken care of in a timely manner.

Let's assume that an accurate CMDB is available, and that an asset is not working. It impacts directly or indirectly an end-user. The end-user calls for assistance. The helpdesk asks for details, these details help analyze the issue, retrieve data in the CMDB and further narrow down the root cause. Depending on the asset and the type of root-cause, dedicated services take care of the resolution. If it is software related, the end-user support becomes prevalent to provide consulting, training, and technical assistance in the application of end-user tools. More specifically, the end-user support team provides consultation to determine if an application is suitable for end-user computing and if so, how best to do it, training to make the user comfortable with a tool or procedure, technical assistance encompassing a broad range of on-call services and at keeping the user functioning and productive.

All the processes target the shortest disruption time. The disruption affects business workflows. Its resolution takes obviously more or less time. One of the reasons it might take more time than less is the quality of the information in the CMDB. All what we said previously about the importance of accurate data in a CMDB is mandatory also for the operational performance of the enterprise. This is the reason why it should take less time. A disruption impacts a process in two folds, first one being the lack of production and the second the cost of catching up to be back to normal. Moving forward with more and more leaner processes the disruptions have greater financial impacts. If employees can't work, they may be assigned to some other tasks not impacted but it might not be for the all duration of the incident, so not all the expenses may not be put on the incident. The same team or the next one will have to do the work not done while keeping the pace with the work scheduled to be done.

If an operational excellence team exists within the company, it should be able to provide an estimate of the impact of a disruption. For instance, an application bug or a network breakdown may stop many sites, each of them with thousands of employees, all this sum up quite fast. These costs can be added to the pure financial analysis when we looked at the CMDB with costs in mind. It helps justify the return on investment on upgrading or renewing assets, both for capex and opex.

We are all familiar with the intricacies developing and maintaining software, we are less conscious that digitalization adds a "virtual" layer or aspect to every hardware item, such as the "Internet of Things," as it is called. This aspect must be tracked and the CMDB is an answer to make it more visible. Having it in the CMDB allows us to identify with which other items it is communicating with. Communications or links between items is the other way to identify assets mandatory to be known by the enterprise. Usually, identifying all items associated with a cost identifies almost all what is worth knowing.

The common support services provide development-type services to the user organizations to keep their system running bug-free and according to the specifications (maintenance), the system evolving with the changing working environment and needs (enhancements) and having the system back to normal as fast as possible. The main way to update the CMDB is through projects. Projects helps an enterprise move from a stable information system (the one active in the CMDB) to a new stable active information system. Active because it shows which items are being used by the enterprise and stable because it must be bug or incidents free.

This is a usual practice or usual way, in the legal context, to look at the evolution of the law. The law that applies is the one that was active at the date of the fact. For example, you have filed a trademark, the law that applies is the one at the date of filing the trademark. That's the way the active information system in the CMDB should be looked at, i.e., active at some point in time.

6.3 PROJECT MANAGEMENT

Project management is not a topic specific to IT departments. However, IT specialists do a lot to innovate and leverage the potential of new tools or technical advancements. On a regular basis, consultants are firing on all cylinders to propose new approaches, new methods, or methodologies. It is a crowded environment. Methodology changes are confusing for IT and non-IT people too, with some of them embracing them heartedly to others being reluctant.

Reasons is that as always and, in the future, too, projects will fail while others won't. The projects failings are used ad nauseam to guess the root causes of these failures and propose ways to avoid them. Auditors should be cautious about the following points:

- The level of maturity of the people using the old and the new methods,
- The change management and associated risk, and
- The method's coverage.

There is no standardized method for managing IT projects like there is for accounting or financial management. Of course, the fundamentals are always the same: You must deliver a reliable product on the agreed date for the approved budget. But the practicalities are different at different times. Their

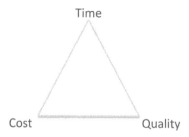

Figure 6.5 The project triangle.

changes over time are essentially justified by technical evolutions in hardware as well as in programming tools and methods. Still in 2020, project management methods must be agile. Various organizations market products around this concept of agility and sell training and certifications.

When auditing a project, an auditor can easily fall into the trap of auditing the conformity of the use of the method. This type of audit focused on the processes has little added value, it notes possible dysfunctions after the fact and not on what has been produced. It is advisable to prepare a specific project audit work plan structured in four parts. Each part focuses respectively on the risks for the deliverable, for the budget, for the reliability and for the deadlines. For IT specificities, additional questions can be annexed.

Given the increasing importance of IT in projects, it is preferable to have a single work plan that identifies risks in the same way. This makes it easier to analyze the results of consecutive audits on the same project, to compare audit results between different projects, and to communicate with third parties with results presented in the same way, regardless of the project audited. The risks are mainly related to the future turnover due to incorrect project management. Poor security management increases these risks as well as the reliability of developments with the bypassing of controls for example, and indirectly on the budget and deadlines.

How an auditor might handle the complexity of IT lingos and methods? A project is about delivering new services, new products, in short new assets to the company. If it doesn't, the spend can't be capitalized and the expected financial benefits won't be achieved. Let's focus first on the journey of a project and second on the methods' coverages. In the literature, a project is often described as a challenge between time, cost, and quality to deliver the services or the products. The challenge is represented by a triangle in Figure 6.5.

However, if we agree that a project must deliver a reliable product or service for a budget at a specific date, any method will have to maintain the balance between:

- Deliverables,
- Budget,
- Duration, and
- Reliability.

Figure 6.6 Beyond the project triangle: The project pyramid.

We may represent the challenge as in Figure 6.6.

Why adding deliverable? Let's say that you plan to go on vacations with your family and it's an opportunity to strengthen bounds, spend time with your kids and build memories. While planning your holidays, you split all what you would like to do between what is a must for your kids and your family and what you would enjoy doing. The deliverable here, is the overall journey with key items (also called features, stories for instance) and nice to have items. Let's say you won't have time or budget, or an item can't be performed or doesn't match what you have expected, then you will cancel noncritical items. They are not critical as they don't impact your overall objectives of enjoying family time.

As an auditor, we will easily face two words, one for an "old" method and one for a new method. Nowadays, waterfall and agile or an equivalent agile based trademark method, such as SCRUM™. The "waterfall" method does not exist as such as it is not documented but referred to as an old ghost to terrify new generations of IT specialists and promote new trendy way to do things. Therefore, if waterfall is being used it should be documented. Accountants however have defined a standard work breakdown to help themselves navigate through the different ways of managing projects used by the companies they audit. When a new method is created its focus is on application development, then, will step by step add new layers to cover from the idea or proposal or requests for a project up to the hyper care once live or even maintenance. The cross-references between the method used and the accounting project model should be done upfront before going into details about a project. It will help understand if anything is missing in the method and where risks lay.

There two reasons why it makes sense to be vigilant for a project, either it is important for the company or because it isn't as important but being red on deliveries, budget, or timelines. Auditing a project with a high capitalization percentage vs. the IT department budget is beneficial to have a better understanding on how methods are being applied, identified the root causes of these issues. Root causes are analyzed to identify areas of improvement and proactively check if any active project might be at risk.

Auditing a project is a standard work for auditors. It is performed in a lot of different ways, and at different project stages. The most often used stage is before the go-live to support a go or no-go decision. This might work for a small project but actually too late for an important or critical project if nothing has been done proactively at previous stages. If it is a no-go, it leads to additional expense reverting and correcting issues, to new business revenues delayed, plus the need to perform a follow-up audit.

Ideally, a list of basic audit requirements should be provided to the project team before the project starts. These requirements should include all basic business controls and segregation of duties requirements. We will go into more details in Chapter 10, "Risks management." They should be implemented in the new application plus additional ones requested by the auditors based on the applications high-level design and legal constraints.

A project health check or audit can be useful. It is dedicated for auditing the balance between the four pillars, deliverable, budget, time, and reliability. The current agile methods are focused on delivering something in a time-box. It is the latest update of the rapid application methods of the 90s. The focus is on time first, second on deliverables. On a timescale, it looks like what is being shown in Figure 6.7.

It is a consecutive chain of timeboxes. A timebox last N weeks. It looks like a train. Each timebox delivers features, the features delivered by a time box may change. For example, a feature is more complex to develop than the initial estimation and its delivery is postponed to a following timebox. That feature might be replaced by another one, so the timebox delivers the same number of features.

Obviously, there are dependencies between the features, some must be developed before others. The contents of the timeboxes must reflect that. What's beneficial is the workflow looks predictive, on a regular basis, each N weeks, a timebox delivers new features in production. The resources see each N weeks the usefulness of their results. The communication channel between end-users and the project team is therefore an active channel due to the regular deliveries. Not knowing what the project team is doing used to

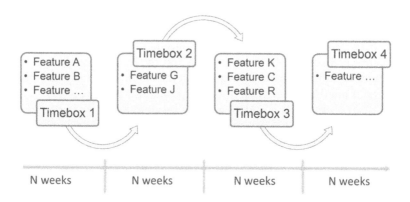

Figure 6.7 Timeboxes and timelines.

be a common end-user complaint. This issue was attributed not to the project manager management style but to the method, mainly the waterfall approach. As auditors we know that it is not because you have guidelines that they are correctly understood and implemented.

The regular deliveries provide a feeling of control. One may expect that the budget, duration, and quality is correctly monitored, and all the features will be produced. Let's focus on quality of the applications being developed, not on all the bugs, not the ones being so obvious that everyone can notice them, but the ones more insidious.

Let's see how bad it can be with a recent example from UK, and it went really bad. The Post Office Limited (POL) or Post Office as per the registered trademark, provides in UK a wide range of products including postage stamps and banking services. The banking services are provided by partners, called "sub-postmasters" (SPMs). They are self-employed sub-post officers running small firms. They provide services using software provided by the Post Office.

In 1999, the Post Office deployed a highly distributed computing system, called Horizon IT. The SPMs started complaining that the central accounts were not aligned with the local accounts. The Post Office was lax on its service management duties, it did not investigate the complaints, nor check the audit logs to understand what was going on.

From 2000 to 2014, the Post Office instead brought cases against 736 SPMs, as noted by the BBC, "an average of one a week." To make it short, the Post Office successfully had some of them gone to prison for theft, some lost home and pensions, some were ruined, bankrupted as they paid off the Post Office claims, because if some accounts were off by thousands of pounds others were by way more than that. This was possible because in the English legal system, specific private entities can serve as prosecutors.

In 2015, 555 SPMs brought a civil case against the POL not knowing the software deficiencies. They had no clue as why there were "missing funds" as claimed by the Post Office and couldn't have access to the software configuration and design provided by the Post Office. So, the Criminal Cases Review Commission, an independent board that considers cases of miscarriage of justice in England, Wales and Northern Ireland began investigating in 2015. The extensive investigations confirmed many dysfunctions, bugs, errors, and defects that causes discrepancies in accounts, for instance a simple one, transactions appeared while the branch was closed. In 2019, in an amazing 400-page ruling, Mr. Justice Fraser said that the contract terms were unreasonable and onerous, and so having the Post Office in a too powerful position vis-à-vis the sub-postmasters, being tied hand and foot. Up to 2018, the Post Office withhold information about the audit logs. The audit logs were a known practice to track all defects and find solutions (basic service management service), it was called the Known Error Log—side apart, it is hard to think about an Unknown Error Log.

Twenty years later, some have since died, campaigners won the legal battle to have their cases reconsidered. They did so by claiming that the computer system was flawed.

In 2020, while case was wending its way through the courts, Peter Ladkin, Bev Littlewood, Harold Thimbleby and Martyn Thomas, four experts in the reliability of software-based systems wrote in the volume 17 "Digital Evidence and Electronic Signature Law Review" (2020-11-02) a paper concerning dependability of computer evidence in the UK legal context:

> "The reliance on computer evidence should be subject to proof of its correctness," "First for any moderately complex software-based computer system, such as the IT transaction-processing system Horizon used by Post Office Limited, it is a practical impossibility to develop such a system so that the correctness of every software operation is provable to the relevant standard in legal proceedings. Any such proofs require the use of mathematical-logical analysis methods (called formal methods) in the development of software.... Second, no matter the quality of the software, the computer hardware on which the software runs is necessarily constrained in the resources available to it. Hardware may, in the course of operations, be modified or constrained. By way of example, it may be exchanged or upgraded for other hardware, which may have different constraints on resources (such as size of memory or available disk space), or otherwise. These actions may cause the operations of even logically impeccable software to act in such a way that they no longer fulfil their original intent; they may even behave unpredictably. This phenomenon is manifest in the increasing numbers of cybersecurity incidents, in which malware is inserted into running systems to subvert their operations." *They follow on writing:* "In electrotechnical terms, 'reliability' means 'ability to perform as required, without failure, for a given time interval, under given conditions.' That is a notion of absolute perfection. However, as we shall note below, most software contains defects, at the rate (see our discussion below) of generally between 1 and 100 defects per 1,000 lines of source code (LOC; 1,000 LOC is often referred to as 1 kLOC). The lower defect bound of around 1 per kLOC is generally attained only by carefully developed specialist safety-critical OT software, and not always. In general terms, none of us are aware of any non-trivial software-based system which can be shown to be reliable in the absolute sense given in the IEC definition."

> [ISO/IEC 27001 Information technology—Security techniques—
> Information security management systems—Requirements]

This paper reminds us and particularly auditors to be careful with evidences shown to them and never assume that all is perfect because they have been told that it was the case:

> We apply a new method to make the old demons disappear, and in fact they did.

A basic trend in software development is the use of code that has already been written elsewhere. This practice exists with pieces of programs or complete programs to integrate them into a new feature. This trend has grown with open-source software. This practice brings additional risks to those of the project management but related and known by all the companies of construction of buildings, manufactured products, what is the quality of the reused components? Is there a certification or do we have to test them whether they have this certification or not? The easiest answer is to test before reusing, with a focus on does the component do what it was designed to do and nothing else? This is an important risk that should be included in the information system auditor's work plan, even though it is an interesting subject to analyze but outside our topic.

Before pursuing the analysis of risks with the new IT trends in Chapter 8 "IT risks," it is worth looking at human uncertainties in the digitalized world.

Chapter 7

Human uncertainties

Looks are one thing, and facts are another.

Hermann Melville, *The Confidence-Man*

It's common to read that a car crashed, it provides the feeling that's the car is autonomous. It makes sense to be careful not speaking about a potential driver's error, as the accident might be due to a technical issue. However, the Global Status Report on Road Safety 2018 from the World Health Organization lists the key risk factors as being: Speeding, driving under the influence of alcohol and other psychoactive substances, and distracted driving. Changing the technology doesn't change this. Human uncertainties are common whatever the context and it exists to in the use of the information systems. In addition, due to assets managed by an enterprise, insiders or outsiders will intentionally try to take ownerships of these assets or the turn-over created by these assets.

The European Union Agency for Cybersecurity (ENISA) presents in its methodology for sectoral cybersecurity assessments 2021 the following high-level decomposition of threats into natural and human causes, as well as unintentionally and intentionally acting adversaries in Figure 7.1.

ENISA calls people acting intentionally as attackers. The National Institute of Standards and Technology (NIST) defines an attacker as a person seeking to exploit potential vulnerabilities of a system [NISTIR 8053]. It's a generic term covering multiple profiles from insider attackers to competitors including cyber-terrorists. This chapter is called human uncertainties as our focus is why an information system can be prone to usage unintended by its objectives. The previous chapters were about technical challenges due to the increase of digitalization of the information systems, now let's dive in how the design of an information system and the technologies implemented create opportunities for unplanned usages. To do so, we focus on the unintentional uncertainties, as it is directly related to the quality of the design of the workflows: By default, it should have been tested, validated for us as auditors to be able to rely on accuracy of the data provided. Then, it is worth checking how intentional uncertainties may leverage that design and how it might be prevented. We will end this chapter focusing on forensic investigations particularities, how it is different from auditing, and how important there are.

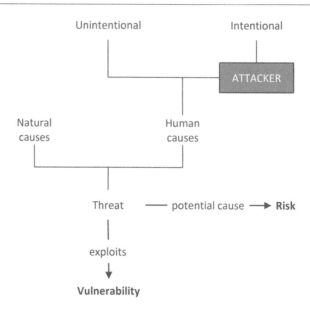

Figure 7.1 ENISA high-level decomposition of threats.

7.1 UNINTENTIONAL ACTS

Operational risks increase when processes and procedures diverge from the reality on the ground. This divergence increases progressively. Scott A. Snooke notices "the slow uncoupling of practice from procedure" and call it the practical drift [SSN]. For him, the typical response is to tighten controls and to increase sanctions for failure to comply. It can only inevitably lead to the same risks because in time, the new controls would also be circumvented or simply ignored. Scott Snooke proposal is to consider human nature while designing processes. The challenge is not how to fix the human error or unwanted behavior but to design the business processes, the internal controls with the practical drift without making in fine the business processes more complex than needed.

The specialists in charge of the methods within the company are less concerned with maintaining the efficiency of the methods by making them follow the evolution of the company. They start to worry about justifying their knowledge and go less into the field. A certain amount of bureaucracy is then put in place, to the point of slowing down or blocking the processes.

Like when safety specialists talk among safety specialists and forget to listen to and take into account the remarks of operational staff. As when manufacturing methods have accumulated to be known only by method experts and no longer by the operational people who are supposed to apply them. Lean management is a state of mind that aims to counteract this tendency to bureaucratize processes and procedures.

Two moments of risk are when procedures and directives have become too complex, and when the company decides to implement new procedures and directives. In the first case, the operational staff will bypass the constraints considered to be blocking them from achieving their work objectives. In the second case, the lack of knowledge of the procedures and directives will create involuntary dysfunctions.

Operational risks therefore increase when they are no longer everyone's business. In other words, knowledge is collective through the contribution of individual skills. The reality in the field is, for example, that two identical valves of the same color do not have to be opened in the same way to obtain the same flow rate; only the operator in the field will have this knowledge, not written into the procedures. The loss of this individual knowledge on the practice of operations is flagrant when, following restructuring or because of an age pyramid badly managed by the company, a high proportion of experienced workers leave the company. At this point, operational risks increase.

Complex processes increase operational risks, as they force people to pay attention to too many different elements at once. You know this disadvantage very well; it is described in your country's traffic accident statistics:

- If you use the phone while driving, the risk of an accident is multiplied by at least 3, and
- If you read a message while driving, the risk of an accident is multiplied by at least 23.

How has aviation managed to control and maintain aircraft accidents close to zero? By keeping the process simple and the operator (here the pilot) focused on one task at a time.

"The rate of air accidents in the United States over the past 10 years has been close to zero percent," writes Steve Casner [SCA], in large part because pilots, in addition to training themselves not to make mistakes, also use a variety of systems designed to combat them. Each flight has two pilots, two air traffic controllers and two flight computers. The pilots rely on checklists to ensure that no step is missed. They use loud announcements to make sure everyone is paying attention. Pilots do not multitask. If a pilot realizes he needs to look at a map, he says to his copilot, "This is your plane," and waits for an affirmative response—"I have the plane"—before turning his attention to the map.

Duplicating hardware and network lines is also a best practice to avoid costly workflows disruptions. In parallel, it is wise to ensure that information technology (IT) expertise is duplicated, and knowledge shared within the IT team. Similarly, end-users should be trained and informed when an application changes before it is implemented in production. Users should know the different type of accesses defined, the duties and responsibilities associated with them. Providing access is key and should be part of even the simplest audit. It's like having your blood pressure checked by default by your doctor when you're visiting him. That's the reason it is part of the basic controls performed for SOX reasons.

When speaking of access, we usually think of application access enabling an employee to be part of a workflow: This is part of the next chapters. However, there are highly powerful access called system or admin accounts. They are part of IT SOX controls too. IT audit should verify these powerful accounts accessing the different layers of the IT infrastructure from top to bottom and the specific safeguards in place.

Being practical, for all these accesses, a user layered approach should be used. If you remember, we split the information system in different layers from the most visible ones by the end-users to the less visible ones, even unknown by the end-users, Figure 7.2 describes these layers, adding more technical details such as database security and physical security before the user can access to the data.

There are multiple standard dealings with user access management directly or indirectly, in particular one standard the ISO 27001 Standard for Information Security Management Systems. There are of course other bodies taking care of this hot topic. ISO 27001 expresses that the main objectives of user-access management are to ensure that only authorized users have access and to prevent unauthorized access. We are tackling here the first objective as it relates to the basic best practices to have in place and the second objective is more related in the Subchapter 10.3 "Technical risks."

To provide access only to authorized users is often understood as providing access to human beings, physical persons, but I propose you to expand the term user either to a person, an object, a program. Interfaces between applications and of objects as in Internet of Things are expanding at a great speed and can't be ignored anymore. Including objects and programs ensure that all interactions are fully monitored. Not doing so would relegate the management of these accesses to IT people, it is a risk. In addition, the policies you would define wouldn't be comprehensive and homogeneous.

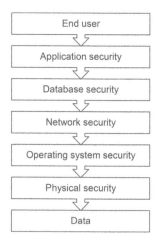

Figure 7.2 A user access layered approach.

A basic set of business-level objectives for user access management can be defined as follows:

- Allow only authorized users to have access to data and resources,
- Restrict access to the least privileges required by these authorized users to fulfil their business role,
- Ensure access controls in systems correspond to risk management objectives, and
- Log user-access and system use and ensure that the system can be audited in line with the system's risk profile.

ISO 27001 identifies four primary controls for managing access rights:

1. User registration,
2. Privilege management,
3. User password/token management, and
4. Review of user access rights.

User registration is about the formal approval and documentation of user access and which type of access is granted in the information systems. Each type of access, view, create, modify, or delete have their own access constraints and their owns risks. For instance, a person may have access to an order to cash process but a specific part of the workflow only in view mode and to another part in modify mode. Side remark, it is called user access for a reason: The user must be identified, generic accounts should be a no-go.

Whatever the layer of the information system, such as application, database, network, operating system, specific user rights, privileged accounts are powerful accounts in the fact they can modify the application or the network behavior for instance. They must be audited especially as with these accounts you can by-pass the controls implemented in the processes.

Passwords remain still commonplace, standard processes for allocating and resetting user passwords should be implemented to reduce unnecessary exposure of temporary or default passwords and minimize the effectiveness of social engineering attacks against security administration staff. Policies that mandate minimal levels of password length and complexity also reduce the effectiveness of common password attacks. However, passwords alone no longer provide a satisfactory solution for critical systems and services. The use of two factor models involving the use of tokens and/or other credentials (e.g. biometrics) also require similar holistic management processes.

To ensure that user registration is performed consistently, the processes for granting and revoking privileges must be formalized and simple. The logging of all the user access rights changes is a by-product of the point above, there is no reason not to have it in place. Changes to user-access rights and the privilege levels of specific individuals must be audited in a timely manner, timely depending on the risks. Changes must match the changes in roles of people, objects, or programs. The organization of a company will vary to support along the time its strategy, structure, assets, and risk tolerance. How these vary will affect the way in which the auditors will analyze the risks. Current trends impacting the audit work and the level of controls required are:

- The external boundaries of networks become more difficult to define as interactions between customers, business partners, and suppliers continue to grow and increase in complexity. Adding the fast increase of what is called the Internet of Things, the external boundaries become more blurred. Access controls are necessary to generate and enforce the divisions of functions and capabilities that these external users can control.
- The coronavirus COVID-19 enforced the trend of having human resources increasingly working in non-conventional environments with flexible arrangements and requiring flexible access to information and systems.
- Services provided externally, cf. the new trend with the cloud, become more broadly accessible, user-access management helps contain the availability of services to only authorized users.
- The need to protect information from unauthorized disclosure increases commensurately with the value of information for the company or the legal implications notwithstanding the bad reputation if somethings goes wrong.

What auditors should do to be pro-active? Auditors need to make their life easier with this time-consuming task. Auditors usually come after an asset is live, accessible to the users. For example, they plan to audit a new application once it is live, the best they might do is coming just before the go-live and audit the accesses set-up. But it's way too late, because they only have time to observe any issue and barely time to assess the actual design, if the design is making sense and applicable whatever the company structure, from a small to a big legal entity for instance.

The missing piece is having the auditors writing down their needs, requirements and have them included in the application design. If auditors don't ask for what they need upfront, for sure they won't have it. The IT experts, business analysts or developers, for instance, are not literate in audit, all the findings since decades is hard evidence of this fact. How these requirements could be designed? With a segregation of duties matrix, SoD matrix. It is a double entry triangular matrix with duties in rows and columns, as shown in Table 7.1.

It is easier to have a matrix per process and then having a matrix between two different processes, duties of one listed in columns and the duties of the other one in rows. Duties here can be automated duties performed by the application, an object or a program or manual duties performed by a physical person.

Table 7.1 Incompatible duties' matrix

		Sub-process A			Sub-process B
Process		*Duty A1*	*Duty A2*	...	...
Sub-process A	Duty A1		1 or X when incompatible		
	Duty A2				
	...				
Sub-process B	...				

This means that generic processes have been defined by the auditors to be able to have these lists of duties, we will see this in Chapter 10 "Risks management." Auditors may face having these requirements implemented as such, for instance, reasons being the software can't be configured to achieve it or some legal entities in a group might not be big enough to allow the implementation. Auditors may move a step forward fine-tuning each incompatible duties in the matrix, by rating the impact High, Medium, Low, and providing management oversight details if it can't be implemented, for example:

1. No management oversight applicable because activity is deemed high risk,
2. Activity has been duplicated/compensated in a report. If yes:
   a. the differentiation between types of assets must be delineated for management oversight to be applicable. The same process user can perform duty 1 and duty 2 granted, it is not for the same data, and
   b. the differentiation between inventory types must be part of the warehouse structure for applicable management oversight. If there is a data segregation, the same process owner can perform duty 1 and duty 2 granted, it is not for the same customer/account/inventory type,
3. Same process user can perform duty 1 and duty 2 granted, it is not for the same customer/account/data,
4. One level up approval. The same process user performing duty 1 and duty 2 for the same data need manager's approval,
5. For changes made by the process user for conduction of duty 1 and duty 2 for the same data, management oversight is needed,
6. Management review of security monitoring logs on a weekly basis. Review is to include reasonableness of the times employees accessed the warehouse/cage. When abnormal activity is noticed it must be researched and resolved, and
7. Independent person performs accounts reconciliation.

Such recommendations allow a project team to be more specific in the design of the system to be flexible enough for the different size of the legal entities in the company. The matrix will look like as shown in Table 7.2.

Table 7.2 SoD matrix with management oversight required

Process	Duty A1	Duty A2	Duty A3
Duty A1		1	2
Duty A2			8
Duty A3			

The cells may be colored Red, Yellow, Green to show the High, Medium, Low risk grading. This work is useful as it helps simplifying what could have been complex audit requirements. Being practical, it does not eliminate the need for physical inspections. What is the point of having well secured access to the applications and having confidential documents left on desks? A tidy desk or even clean desk policy might be necessary to be written and promoted. Depending on the level of risk, it could be a single simple additional question in the audit workplan. Auditors know what to expect for each entity as a basic set of active controls. The project team defines how they are configured, and which additional specific local controls may have been added. As a result, the enterprise as a fully designed consistent control environment reduces the chance of having a user performing an unintentional action impacting the information system, for instance, entering incorrect data or deleting data or clicking on an unsecured link in an email. Even so, some controls might have been forgotten, and the design revised. Nonetheless, it is worth reminding again and again to the end-users how to act safely and the basic security measures to become reflexes. Being proactive helps limit the unintentional acts, what about intentional ones?

7.2 INTENTIONAL ACTS

Intentional acts will chase forgotten and ill-designed controls or rely on human nature. Attackers as ENISA call them can be insiders or outsiders. They will leverage both controls issues and human dispositions. Fraud is a typical example of an intentional action. The difficulty for the courts is to characterize this fraud. Fraud is generally understood as the intentional use of deception, trickery, or some dishonest means to deprive another of his or her money, property, or legal right. The exact definition depends on the legal environment in which the fraud occurs.

The Association of Certified Fraud Examiners (ACFE) has developed a fraud classification model known as the fraud tree. It identifies 49 different individual frauds, grouped into categories and subcategories. The three main categories are:

1. Fraudulent statements,
2. Misappropriation of assets, and
3. Corruption.

Fraudulent statements are usually made by senior management and produce the greatest losses for the organization involved. Asset misappropriations are typically implemented by employees. They have the highest frequency of occurrence and produce the lowest losses. Fraud tends to be insignificant at the individual level and is very difficult for auditors to identify. The PwC's Global Economic Crime and Fraud Survey 2020 reveals that fraud has continued to increase and new ways of operating have been found. One caveat to this increase is that companies are building the capacity to identify acts of fraud. Fraud is evenly split between internal and external fraud, 39% and 37% respectively while the remaining 20% is a collusion between internal and external. External does not equals cybercrime, it can simply be customer, or vendor/supplier.

> More than half of internal perpetrators still come from middle and senior management, but junior managers have also been major contributors to internal fraud in some regions. This indicates a potential weakness in internal controls, where these measures serve as checkbox exercises rather than effective processes embedded in an organization's culture.

In addition to preventing fraud indirectly addressed in the previous chapter, the difficult part is to have facts to resolve, negotiate or go to court. For instance, the Société Générale's complaint against Jérôme Kerviel filed in France in early 2008 is an interesting example of potential internal fraud. At a press conference on January 24, 2008, the president of Société Générale, Daniel Bouton, announced a fraud of 4.82 billion, due to a single market operator (Jérôme Kerviel) who would have created "a company within the company." The afternoon of this same January 24, the bank files a complaint against its broker Jérôme Kerviel for "forgery in bank writing, use of forgery in bank writing and computer hacking."

In this example, regardless of the legal consequences, the bank must prove that these processes are reliable with relevant controls, and that the IT security is state of the art, to infer and attempt to prove the intentional nature of the accused's actions. The ideal situation for the accuser is to demonstrate the reliability of its processes and the extreme ingenuity of the methods used by the accused. Indeed, the less ingenious the processes used by the accused, the more the reliability of the accuser's processes is called into question. The accuser does not want his or her reputation to be tarnished because he or she would be considered incompetent.

This link between process and internal control is strong enough that ACFE and the Committee of Sponsoring Organizations of the Treadway Commission (COSO) published the Fraud Risk Management Guide in late 2016 to help companies better manage their anti-fraud efforts.

All of this may seem complicated to implement after tedious reading of long, highly technical documents, but many of the actions to be implemented can be very simple such as requiring employees to take at least two consecutive weeks off. Having one person taking time off forces the assignment of tasks and associated responsibilities to co-workers. The SEC and the Federal Deposit Insurance Corporation (FDIC-an independent US agency that guarantees bank deposits made in the US up to $250,000) have made statements on this topic through guidelines on vacation planning.

According to ACFE, organizations that implement mandatory vacation or job rotation policies are less likely to be victims of fraud. This is because mandatory vacation rules prevent fraud, which typically requires the fraudster's continued presence to manipulate information and prevent detection. In its 2016 report to the United Nations on workplace fraud and abuse, the ACFE reports that the median amount of loss due to fraud was reduced by 47.6% in cases where organizations had a vacancy or job rotation control and that the duration of fraud was 44.4% shorter when such a control was in place.

Internal fraud can also come from employees who have joined the company with the aim of defrauding it. It is simple to implement, but often with long delays in achieving results. This industrial espionage makes the headlines in our newspapers. But this phenomenon is not recent. At the end of the 18th century, for instance, Lyon's silk industry was put forward by the Louis XV style, which demanded heavy, thick, and highly rambling fabrics for both clothing and real estate. Lyon's manufacturers vied with each other in innovation and invention to meet the demand and filed numerous patents that improved the processes, the manufacturing tools, the looms, and the fabrics. Competitors saw their sales decline and tried to learn about the new manufacturing methods. "Foreign manufacturers were accused of placing their children, even as store boys, with the aim of discovering the secrets of Lyon's industry, and of suborning the skilled workers" (Ruling of the Parliament of March 29, 1715, confirming a consular judgment of March 9, 1714. Ruling of the Council of State of March 7, 1752, which makes the draftsmen justiciable to the Consulate).

If industrial espionage is still a topical issue, information research methods have diversified and are grouped under the expression "technological intelligence." They increasingly call for the retrieval of information available in digital form, which is analyzed with increasingly sophisticated algorithms, even using artificial intelligence or deep learning.

Fraud is also external. The increasing interconnection of company objects with each other, with the internal network and with the outside world creates more opportunities for intrusion. The advantages of digitalization are counterbalanced by a major disadvantage: Computer or cyber-crime. According to PricewaterhouseCoopers, computer crime has rapidly become the second most common type of crime and affects all companies, regardless of industry. Cybercrime starts with the famous social engineering we spoke in Section 1.2 "Regulations, Controls, and Audit" of Chapter 1. More often, in a more insidious way because invisible with IT tools and remotely performed, using defective or incorrectly configured hardware and software. It is a complex world to protect, complex by the quantity of items, as we can see if we sum up the previous figures into Figure 7.3.

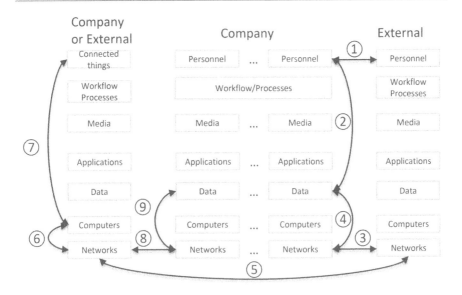

Figure 7.3 A challenging landscape to protect.

In center we have the enterprise, on the left side all the connected objects, and on the right side, contractors, suppliers "you name them." Opening the information system to third parties (companies, people, objects) shows how important auditing information system is critical and how its digitalization is increasing the challenges. Attackers as insiders (29%) is concerning the central part of the figure. We consider employees and non-employee contracted and working within the enterprise, meaning using the tools provided by the enterprise, as part of the insiders. Attackers as outsiders is 37% and it's related to the right side of the figure. The 20% of collusion is the arrow ① at the top right of the figure between "Personnels," personnel being a generic term for a person, an employee of a supplier or a thief. That person will follow the arrow ② to access the data. To do so, the person has access to the data by default as it is part of her/his role. If it is not part of her/his role, the person will try to circumvent the controls in place.

The central part is the main thing we dealt about while speaking about processes, segregation of duties, and access rights. What is concerning is the bottom of the figure and the interconnection between the core network of the enterprise and external networks. Remote cybercrimes start from there and figure out a route to the data, data being initially targeted or accessed by chance. Let's focus on arrows ③, then ⑤ at the bottom of the figure. These arrows are related to the network, arrow ③ groups direct accesses and arrow ⑤ groups indirect access to the information system of the enterprise.

Arrow ③ is about a thief trying to connect directly to a network equipment of the enterprise. Following Yves Lacoste and his book "Geography, it is used, first of all, to make war" (1976), a thief needs to gather information about the network infrastructure, its equipment and so on. To do so, there are two options either he already has information or figure out or guess network hardware and starts from there reaching them, or "ping" them in the IT lingo. With a better understanding of the actual hardware equipment, the software used by the equipment, the thief is able to compare with known vulnerabilities. For some of them, he will have the expertise to exploit them or he may ask for help. If it is too complex or time-consuming or not worth it, he will move to another equipment just like a robber will leave the current front door he was trying to open and focus on a new one. On an audit point of view, a regular scan of vulnerabilities of network equipment is mandatory. An internal policy is not enough.

As soon as the vulnerability has been exploited, the thief will move forward and as an analogy, it's like when we enter a house completely in the dark and we can't see the surroundings. The thief will move forward room by room, equipment by equipment. Each new equipment knowledge provides additional information about its connections. The thief guesses if any new connections is worth moving to, to reach valuable assets. Basically, to protect your house, you can proactively make it more difficult to enter, you may add active monitoring of the security equipment you have implemented, in addition, you can fake a safe-deposit box more or less accessible to fool the thief and add specific equipment such as camera etc., to gather information about your thief, i.e., collating evidences making it easier for you to file a complaint.

Arrow ⑤ is another way for the thief to enter in the enterprise information system. It has gained popularity thanks to all the objects connected through internet to the enterprise network. Unfortunately, all these tools are new and do not benefit of any strong security focus when they have been designed. The thief will test two ways to enter the enterprise network either it is possible to connect directly, arrow ⑧ (similar challenges as of arrow ③), or he has to move up to the operating system of the object, arrow ⑥. As of now it is a time-consuming effort to audit the security of these devices for two reasons, their quantity and quite often the lack of an exhaustive list of all of them. Arrows ⑧ allows the thief to investigate more following arrow ⑨ in the same way he may have done with arrow ③. Depending on the object, arrow ⑥ might be a compulsory choice to either take control of the object and its data or to connect to the targeted information data through arrow ⑧, then ⑨. The challenges for the arrow ⑨ are similar to the ones faced by arrow ④.

The true cost of economic crime is difficult to estimate, especially considering that actual financial losses are often only a small part of the fallout from a serious incident. Collateral damage, including business disruptions, remediation, investigative and preventative responses, regulatory penalties, legal fees, and damage to morale and reputation have a significant impact on long-term business performance. These types of losses, while not always quantifiable, can over time overshadow the relatively short-term impact of financial losses. Basic meaning nonnegotiable points must be put in place, it starts by monitoring user access. Segregation of duties requirements must be defined and fine-tuned to the complexity of the size and geographic implementation of your company. This will limit intentional acts while being the foundation for preventing unintentional ones. The next level is to have in place dedicated cybersecurity policies and tools.

Something worth being remember is that whatever the IT progress, it can be used by the company to protect itself or improve its processes and in the same way by the attackers to attack or improve their process too. The progress made with artificial intelligence is an interesting example. Artificial intelligence becomes more and more powerful and easier to use, more attackers able to use it, we can expect the following:

- Expansion of existing frauds,
- Introduction of new threats, and
- Change in how threats are handled.

The number of existing frauds will raise because of the lower costs to enter the market. Companies which couldn't be targeted could be targeted. In addition, less labor will be required as the software will help automate tasks and improve scalability too. Artificial intelligence will learn and identify new way to attack companies. Remember the scalability achieved for existing frauds, it will apply here too. Attackers may also exploit the artificial intelligence software implemented by a company. Thanks to artificial intelligence software, the two points above induce that attack can be fine-tuned. It is economically worth to attack differently existing targets or to have new ones. For information system auditors, it means that new IT tools must be used whenever they are available. They are to follow and better anticipate the technical trends.

7.3 SECURITY

Security is here a focus on the arrows at the bottom of the previous figure starting with network and moving to the data through hardware and their software, we may call it infrastructure cybersecurity. Coming back to the thief who might enter your house, to secure more you safe-deposit box, you ensure that the room is even more passively and actively protected. However, if these additional protections are too visible or understood as excessive for the thief vs. the ones of the room containing the fake deposit box, the thief will assume that this is the room containing the actual safe-deposit box. In the cybersecurity world, the fake safe-deposit box is called a honey pot.

To facilitate your life and enjoy visitors without all the security burden, you will have a house big enough with rooms dedicated to your visitors. These rooms will have fewer practical constraints while keeping basic security procedures. They are called DMZ short for demilitarized zone. It is a network dedicated space to allowing hosts to connect, proposing a separate and isolated environment between the enterprise managed network and an untrusted external network. That's usually what is implemented having meeting rooms near the entrance of the enterprise building. Visitors are cleared to enter the building but not allowed to move further into the building and pass additional gates.

Let's say your house is in the Versailles castle. The Château now has 2,300 rooms, spread over 63,154 m². Depending on the day, 3,000–10,000 people gather there and form a very heterogeneous and hierarchical society, so a lot of insiders and outsiders in the same building as the royal family. Up to 3,000 people could stay in the castle. In addition, such as in 1682, the building work continued and there were nearly 36,000 workers. As in all royal residences, the king's apartment has the same succession of rooms with well-defined uses: A guard room, two antechambers, the bedroom, and a cabinet. Beyond these rooms, access to which is strictly hierarchical and regulated by etiquette, all the following rooms constitute the private domain of the sovereign to which, in principle, no one can have access unless invited. So, increased level of security leveraging the physical characteristics of a building is not new. If you compare the different pieces of hardware, servers equal rooms, network appliances equal doors, we have some sort of analogy there, helping us understanding what the network architects are trying to achieve. Auditing the security of operational processes is a basic mission of internal or external auditors. The technical infrastructure is more complex than imbricated multiple rooms in a specific order with impressive doors even if some of the rooms have hidden ones. This increasing complexity of the technical environment increases the level of security risks and makes it easier to attack than to defend. There are many reasons for this, but it is mainly the complexity of networked information systems with internet access and the ability of the attacker to choose the time and method of the attack vs. the need for the defender to guard against any type of attack, any meaning known and not yet known by the enterprise.

> Computer security is often advertised in the abstract: "This system is secure." A product vendor might say: "This product makes your network secure." Or: "We secure e-commerce." Inevitably, these claims are naive and simplistic, they look at the security of the product rather than the security of the system.
>
> [BSC]

> Beginning in 2007, "data-centric security" briefly became a buzz phrase full of promise as companies realized that antivirus and firewalls weren't enough to cure their information system.
>
> [AGR]

The importance in an information society is the information, the data in possession of the company are the target of the attackers.

The security of information systems has points in common with security in other contexts, the main ones are:

- Safety is expensive,
- 100% safety is an ideal world,
- Security is both passive and active, and
- The primary motivation for attackers is not technical pride.

Security requires human and technical means that must be adapted to the context. Castles make the best use of geographical constraints and fortifications are preceded by moats or ditches. You have precious objects at home, have you invested in a safe? The safe will usually open with a code, the computer messages will be encrypted too.

Security is rarely perfect because the investment made must be proportional to the level of risk. We have been using signatures for contracts and checks for centuries, but they have always been forgeable. Security is passive and active. What is the point of investing in fortifications if you don't have soldiers? You need soldiers to watch for attacks, to counter them and to defeat the attackers. Attackers are human and their motivations are varied, such as those who want to impress others, take revenge, steal, spy. The attackers are either inside a company site (e.g. employee) or outside a company site. On each of these common points, the security of information systems has particularities that change the way we protect ourselves and manage risks. The first is that the perpetrators of an attack can come from anywhere in the world. The law of the geographic location of the attack is usually powerless and international cooperation, if it exists, is often complex and slow. The second is that attackers often manage to remain anonymous, as does the geographic location from which they operate. The third is that the attacks are easily automated, scaled up to be very large and very fast.

The security of information systems is a matter of concern for businesses and other organizations. France adopted the law for internal security in 2001; since then, many laws on this subject have been adopted, which ultimately lead to the adoption of the internal security code. The law of information systems security is not limited to knowing the techniques of attacks on automated data processing systems. The articles 323-1 and following of the penal code are in fact only the visible part. The company has the obligation to secure its information system. Since the first versions of these articles in 2004, what was only a right has become a real obligation for all companies and more particularly for IT directors, information systems security managers, system or network administrators and all persons involved in the organization and operation of information systems. These general security constraints are complemented by regulatory obligations for information systems in the banking, insurance, health, services, or critical infrastructure sectors. Standards and best practices are proposed by various international organizations such as ISO with the ISO27000 standard, locally in France with the national agency for the security of information systems (Agence Nationale de la Sécurité des Systèmes d'Information) or the national commission for information technology and civil liberties (Commission Nationale Informatique et Libertés), not to mention professional organizations. If it seems necessary to call upon technical specialists in the field of IS security, entrusting them with the legal part of the treatment of these issues is risky or of limited scope.

Security presented the way it is since the beginning of the chapter looks scary, it gives the feeling that only you are being a target, but

> there is an old saw in cybersecurity that being in the field is like being chased by a bear. You don't need to outrun the bear; you just need to outrun the other companies in the field (so that the bear will eat them.)
>
> [RCK]

In the previous chapter, we focused on how an enterprise could be pro-active while designing its internal "business" processes and implementing them. What about all the other software used by the enterprise, such as office tools including video or non-video calls and unintentional acts? We are well aware of the risks brought by emails particularly when they include links or automation. It is mandatory to have employees regularly trained and tests performed. The cybersecurity team simulates diverse types of attacks by emails in order to proactively keep all employees conscious that risks are always there. The tests results in addition of keeping the employees awake, provides data if the trainings are successful, if the tests must be updated or improved, having all employees identifying the fake emails does not prove that awareness is top, it could be that the tests are getting obsolete. The emails threats are and will remain, unfortunately as the technology is improving it becomes possible to impersonate someone by voice or video in addition of text. We pointed already Kevin Mitnick prowess in "social engineering." He was using the tools at his disposal at that time, 30 years ago. Guess what made the news in October? An innovative evolution in social engineering applied to the tools used by Kevin Mitnick, is the addition of the impersonation of the voice of top executives. As summarized by Thomas Brewster in Forbes (October 14, 2021):

> In early 2020, a bank manager in the Hong Kong [office] received a call from a man whose voice he recognized—a director at a company with whom he'd spoken before. The director has good news: His company was about to make an acquisition, so he needed the bank to authorize some transfers to the tune of $35 million. A lawyer named Martin Zelner had been hired to coordinate the procedures and the bank manager could see in his inbox emails from the director and Zelner, confirming what money needed to move where. The bank manager, believing everything appeared legitimate, began making the transfers.

As per the few details provided by the Dubai Public Prosecution Office leading the investigation, it appears that it was an elaborate scheme, involving at least 17 persons. It's the second known case of fraudsters using audio deep fake new technology on top of classical tricks to ensure the success of the fraud. Pretty much everybody is amazed by deep fake related to face swapping in videos, but barely anyone is aware of the increasing availability of deep fake voice software, hard to make compelling news on TV with it. Yes, I know, you've just enrolled in the new voice identification services from your bank letting you access your accounts simply by using your voice. Why a new scheme wouldn't be happening soon? Soon equals as soon as it is worth the effort for the fraudsters. The techniques being is touted as secure and the companies behind these technologies provide numbers and multiple areas being coded to achieve a "0" and "1" file coding + 100 physical and behavioral characteristics unique to you. This is totally different as of now from digital assistants such as Tencent's Xiaowei, Apple's Siri or Amazon's Alexa. Digital assistants, again as of today, focus on what you say (words) and not how you say it. By the way, the term deep is attached to the word fake as in deep learning, to provide the sense that it requires a huge amount of data and processing power for the programs to achieve a result.

This is challenging for auditors. First, auditors must be careful about the quality of the evidences used to assert an opinion. Second, the work-programs, the IT software used must be kept up to date. Third, it is worth when performing the risk analysis, to select the tools relevant to the level of risks.

We are using the word cybersecurity to focus on the digitalized part of security. However, the undigitalized part of it is getting more and more smaller. Think about your pass to enter the building when you go to work. Have you noticed the cameras in all common areas? A few decades ago, you needed keys or a pass-ID, the guard would recognize your car and you. In the building, you would meet and great people taking care of specific rooms, such as an assistant or a librarian. Nowadays, there is no way to have a building without any security system. The security system of a building may be completely not connected—autonomous—or for whatever reason connected to the enterprise intentionally or unintentionally. If the security system is autonomous, i.e., not connected physically or wirelessly to the internet or the enterprise network, there is no cyber-risk at distance. Due to the trend of avoiding friction in information systems and creating recurring cash with subscriptions of services, it is unlikely that such an unconnected security system exists. By the way, as the hardware contains pieces of software, that software is not error prone, for sure some software releases (security patches?) will have to be installed. So here we are as auditors with a link between the information system and the information system related to business applications. Question is for the information auditor "Do I include it in the risks analysis of the information system audit?" Well, the auditor may not but it will have to be justified.

7.4 FORENSIC

We spoke about the "contrat à la grosse" in Section 1.2 "Regulation, Controls, and Audits" of Chapter 1. The "contrat a la grosse" was quite common in Greece many centuries before BC and onward.

> Many investors are likely to engage in the risky but rewarding big adventure loan, with interest rates around 30%, called "maritime profit," as opposed to the land profit, essentially linked to real estate loan, whose rates are closer to 10-15%. To engage in this way, you must be able to judge the quality of the ship, the professional and oral merits of the captain, the dangers of the road, the weather, etc. Thus, once the loan contract is signed, the work of the financier does not stop there. He has to make sure that everything goes well during the crossing and the purchase of the goods... The comfortable Athenians are attracted to it for a very precise reason that Edward Cohen details "it is an unregulated market and totally opaque as to the origin of the committed capital... What is certain, however, is that the fat loan scam is one of the oldest known scams: fraud was part of the risks involved."

> [CCH]

This example shows three typical points to look at when performing an investigation of course but more surely to prevent such things to happen. First, controls must be implemented whatever the business process to avoid having it unregulated and lacking traceability of the data exchanges. Second, a tighter control framework must be designed when the financial risks are higher. Third, to achieve that you must know the business processes and risks related to put in place the right level of controls and the most efficient controls, however that doesn't prevent you from regularly controlling the processes' performance. All things we are already familiar with through the previous chapters. Christian Chavagneux concludes by:

> The swindlers appear as the revelation of the society and the economy from which they come. The modes of formation of the swindle evolve with the dynamics of capitalism.

> [CCH]

Both on an audit or a forensic point of view, opportunities arise when comparing processes design and quality of controls vs. efforts to cheat them. If for the fraudster, the return on investment is not worth the risks and not worth the risks vs. other companies, then the company is for the time being on a safe spot.

Let's follow-up with the example of a case defended by Demosthenes in court dealing with the "contrat a la grosse." So Protos, the merchant, to ensure that the cargo would arrive safely hire a well-known captain and first mate:

> Three days after departure several passengers hear noises in the hold ... and decide to go and see for themselves ... the captain scuttles the ship! To escape his pursuers, the captain ends up throwing himself into the water, forgetting that characteristic that is quite common among sailors: he can't swim. He drowns. The first mate pushes the sailors and passengers to abandon the ship quickly.

In short, it appears that the merchant didn't have the finance and asked a funder. The captain and his first mate respectively find funders too arguing that the wheat is theirs, to obtain credit by pledging cargo. The problem is that they cannot reimburse the credit when arriving safely at destination. The characteristics of maritime contracts is that if anything is happening, such as piracy, bad weather, the ship does not arrive at destination, debtors are free of debt. The merchant's funder, highly experienced, had one of his men on the ship. He promises a bonus to the crew if they save the ship successfully. The story could stop there but no remember, this is on top of a bet on the future prices of wheat at destination. So, there are more legal implications and it is worth reading Demosthenes' plea. This scam is one of the oldest known scams. What has changed since then are the artifacts of digitalization. If the level of controls isn't appropriate, then there are opportunities. But with digitalization, what might be happening as time goes by, are opportunities if the controls' pertinence isn't continuously checked and adapted to the process design changes. This is in addition of the IT risks, seen in the previous chapter.

The importance of the data processed at some point in time may increase or decrease, so the controls might be less relevant. Let's take the example that the financial data going through a process is no more than $50k, so the level of controls has been defined to the associated risk. Due to IT changes to either the applications or the features, the financial data going through can go up to $1M. There is an opportunity there for someone to circumvent the current basic level of controls. If a process has been modified, from the application level down to the network component, the adequacy of the controls must be confirmed. How deep controls must be tested is dependent of the estimated risks and which items were impacted by the changes.

Knowing which items have been impacted is critical to identify which roles or person accesses should be analyzed. For sure, easily it comes to mind that "a person" is an end-user but be sure to think of a "person" as someone accessing your process from any item supporting it from the applications level down to the network level. Let's be specific, a person accessing your information system doesn't equal only to your employees, contractors of third parties, it includes thieves. Hackers being specific IT thieves or thieves with an IT knowledge. The common difficulty we have is to get accustomed to have a broader view and think about all the more or less visible relationship between the various components of the information system. Opportunities may appear independently of any processes change such as when the organization structure changes. For instance, if a team gets smaller, the segregation of duties must be revised, and a new control framework be applied. If two distinct teams with incompatible duties are being merged, at least segregation of duties must be revised. If a technology is getting obsolete against attacks or a vulnerability (nice word to says defenseless in fact) is identified, opportunities arise. Side note, an additional difficulty is that thieves spend all their time, being fully dedicated to find those vulnerabilities and not only using them. This is an important business with the following key activities: They sell their findings, or they exploit these findings, or they sell services based on these findings.

> A major study by Dick Heuer Jr of the CIA Center for the Study of Intelligence, Psychology of Intelligence Analysis concluded: "Major intelligence failures are usually caused by failures of analysis, not failures of collection. Relevant information is discounted, misinterpreted, ignored, rejected, or overlooked because it fails to fit a prevailing mental-model or mind-set."
>
> [CAN]

The auditor must be cautious as a forensic investigator on a scene, not being yet declared as a crime scene. No traces must be left, no changes must be made, because it is a potential crime scene or at it is IT, crime might well be still undergoing. Two types of information must be retrieved the one directly related to the data, i.e., which data have been targeted, and how the data has been accessed. You know when the forensic investigators leave the crime scene once it has been analyzed and then figure out based on the clues who should be interrogated. The target being to retrieve evidences based on the clues to be able to explain what happened. The tricky thing is that IT expertise is required. Moving from clues to evidence is not so easy as it seems.

DNA identification is a good example. DNA contains regions in which short sequences of bases are repeated multiple times. These repeats are found in many spots—or loci—throughout the genome. Because the exact number of repeats at any particular locus varies from person to person, forensic scientists can use these markers, called short tandem repeats (STRs), to identify individuals.

> Forensic science is noisy. We have been trained to think of fingerprint identification as infallible. But fingerprints examiners sometimes differ in deciding whether a print found at a crime scene matches that of a suspect. Not only do experts disagree, but the same experts sometimes make inconsistent decisions when presented with the same print on different occasions. Similar variability has been documented in other forensic science disciplines, even DNA analysis.
>
> [KSS]

When a collection of data is retrieved, the auditor must figure out how to understand the data at disposal. The tools available are the same ones as the ones we spoke about when dealing with data, such as data analysis or artificial intelligence (trained on similar perimeters). Sometimes it is possible that specific mathematical laws apply, such as the Benford law as it is known these days. Tax investigators use this law to select tax fraudsters. The Benford law says that for big amount of data with different order of magnitude, if we group the first digits 1–9 of a measure, it should follow a specific curve, or being evenly distributed with a logarithmic x-axis. Reason is that if a human fraud happened, for instance, having false entry in the ledgers, these numbers should not follow the Benford law. It is a clue and not an evidence, a "should" and not a "would."

When investigating and auditing, data is not only related on specific data such as the ledgers, or sales numbers meaning directly marketable information, but also, data indirectly related to the targeted data. That's where the digitalization of our daily lives and companies' daily life generates a huge amount of indirect data. Reason why, forensic investigators can do without IT expertise, an expertise to be at least as good as the one of the fraudsters.

But let's go further in the next chapter, into the risks induced by the digitalization and increased spread of IT in our daily life and the one of companies.

BIBLIOGRAPHY

AGR: Andy Greenberg, *"This Machine Kills Secret,"* 2012, Dutton, 978-0-75354-801-1
BSC: Bruce Schneier, *"Secrets and Lies. Digital Security in a Networked World,"* 2000, John Wiley & Sons, Ltd., 0-471-25311-1
CAN: Christopher Andrew, *"The Secret World,"* 2018, Allen Lane, 978-0-241-30522-5
CCH: Christian Chavagneux, *"Les plus belles histoires de l'escroquerie,"* 2020, Editions du Seuil, 978-2-002-142550-5
KSS: Daniel Kahneman, Olivier Sibony, and Cass R. Sunstein, *"Noises. A Flaw in Human Judgment,"* 2021, William-Collins, 978-0-008-30899-5
RCK: Richard A. Clarke and Robert K. Knake, *"The Fifth Domain,"* 2019, Penguin Press, 978-0-52556-097-2
SCA: Steve Casner, *"Careful: A User's Guide to Our Injury-Prone Minds,"* 2017, Riverhead Books, 978-0-399-57409-2
SSN: Scott A. Snooke, *"Friendly Fire: The Accidental Shootdown of U.S. Black Hawks over Northern Iraq,"* 2002, Princeton University Press; Revised edition, 978-0691095189

Chapter 8

IT risks

We can open a clock and examine it. Where here is time?

Martin Heidegger, *What is a Thing?*

Technical risks are those risks from raw materials, machinery, hardware, or software used in operational activities in given legal contexts. For the audit of information systems, technical risks are information technology (IT) risks and concern the two elements at the bottom of the diagram below: Computers and networks. These two elements are part of what is called IT infrastructure. They are shown in Figure 8.1.

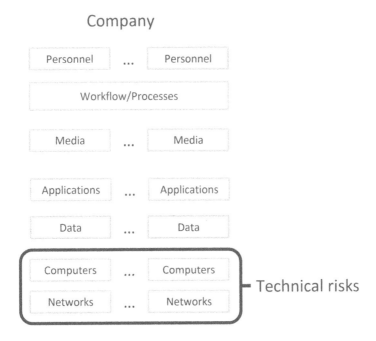

Figure 8.1 Location of the technical risks.

DOI: 10.1201/9781003230137-8

These two elements are part of the physical infrastructure of the information system; they are managed by the IT department. Their position at the bottom of the diagram reflects the risks incurred by the other elements of the information system located above them. It is difficult for the management of a company to figure out the relationships between the risks to the physical infrastructure and the risks to the revenue. Security is a cross-cutting issue for these different elements and is the preferred way to raise management awareness. The reason is that there is an obvious link between security and the risks of fraud, business interruption, loss of reputation, loss of revenue due to loss of trust in the company by suppliers, customers, and even employees.

Of course, IT specialists easily get the budget to increase the network bandwidth and thus facilitate the work of the staff with reduced response times or improved processing times or the access of customers to the sales site. The management easily understands the link between the efficiency of its processes and the investment in computers and networks. They are willing to sacrifice part of their budget for these purchases. Indirectly, scrapping old hardware or applications considerably reduces technical risks. It is also preferable for a company to keep its technical infrastructure up to date because suppliers do not hesitate to stop producing and maintaining equipment that has become technically obsolete.

This is not so simple for an IT department, because management finds it difficult to see a part of its budget being used each year for maintenance actions on elements that are not very visible to them. We presented the example of Equifax in the chapter on legal risks. It would be assumed that the source of Equifax's problems (apart from its processes) is a vulnerability, called CVE-2017-9805, discovered in the freely available (open-source) Apache Struts 2 software. This vulnerability allows someone to run any program on servers that use the Apache Struts 2 software and the popular Representational State Transfer (REST) communication extension (program called plugin).

When you put it that way, you feel as concerned as a CEO listening to his IT manager talk about IT risks. But a vast majority of listed companies use it to deploy web applications written with the Java language. This means that many airline reservation systems used/are using this framework, as well as financial institutions for Internet banking applications. Here you should be more concerned.

However, thanks to accounting depreciation rules and the need to equip staff with all types of computers (desktop, laptop, tablet, or phone), IT managers can get around this difficulty and renew the hardware pool regularly. The IT budget is a wealth of information for an auditor. However, he or she should take care to weigh his or her analysis against the way in which the budget is constituted; it varies so much from one company to another, both in terms of the scope of responsibilities and the equipment covered by the IT purchases.

When the hardware becomes too old, it can no longer be maintained. Bugs or errors are no longer corrected in the absence of new software versions. This is a first risk. Keeping machines that are too old jeopardizes the security of the hardware park, because they are connected with others.

The management of software licenses used in the company is an important concern because of the legal risks. In the same way, the management of the application portfolio is an important activity for the IT department, not only for purchases, but also to identify the machines to be updated when a bug is identified, to know the software installed on each machine. The lack of license management as well as the lack of hardware management are generating risks for the company.

8.1 GEOGRAPHICAL COVERAGE

The term computer here includes any hardware with computing capabilities or processing power and the software that runs that hardware. The risks of the applications that support the different steps of a process have been seen in the operational risks. The machines used in data centers, the computers visible on the desks in your company, the tablets or phones used by sales people, the machines up to the robots on the production lines, the objects connected to the company network are all grouped here under the term computer. This is a lot like a Prevert list, but less poetic. With the progress made in miniaturizing all the components needed for a computer, the most diverse objects are now equipped with processing capabilities. They can retrieve data, process them, store them, and communicate them.

This diversity is an additional argument for managing the hardware portfolio (cf. ISO55000—Asset management). From the point of view of information system auditing, the main risk lies not in the computer as such, but in its connection to the company network, whether in real or delayed time. This connection also has non-technical consequences; for example, it allows the tax authorities to extend the scope of their investigation during an audit of computerized accounting.

We have a vision of these computers that comes from the way we work. Historically, we go to work at our company, we use our badge to enter the premises. We find our desk with the computer on it or we take our laptop out of our bag and connect it to the company network. Or we head to our locker room, drop off our stuff, change and pick up a tablet connected to the wireless network (e.g. Wi-Fi) in the warehouse or factory. By habit, by reflex, we associate computers with work done on the company site. Of course, you know that there is a data center either locally on your site or on another site because some of the applications or some of the data you use are stored in this data center. Our understanding of the IT infrastructure of the information system looks something like Figure 8.2.

This vision is also used to secure a company's information system. We know the company sites we work with; they are represented by a star and they include all the elements of the information system. We use at least a data center, which is represented by a square. It includes the bricks of the information system, computer, and network, plus according to the data and

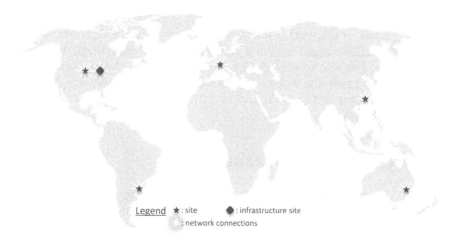

Legend ★ : site   ● : infrastructure site
         ⋮ network connections

Figure 8.2 Basic understanding of a networked information system.

applications choices made. As a user, we also have a vague idea of how these sites are connected to each other.

In fact, these days, the word used to name this is as fuzzy as our under-standing: The cloud. The word cloud avoids questions from non-IT people and reassures them, because cloud is a simple word that we unconsciously associate with a place. It's more reassuring than imagining that our work and processes depend on local, global networks, the Internet, routers, and other communication hardware in addition to communication servers, data, appli-cations and more.

This vision of an information system based on the physical sites of the com-pany would have been correct 30 years ago, but the processing capacities and the availability and bandwidth of the networks are completely changing the reality. For the past few years, we use cell phones as powerful as computers, we go to meet clients or colleagues with our laptop or tablet in our bag. We no longer work only at a company site with the problems that come with crossing a border with your business computer.

We are no longer the only ones working outside the company, machines also work inside and outside the company. That's why in the diagram shown in Figure 8.3, the connected objects are added to the previous figure and it increases the technical risks perimeter. Objects can only be connected to other objects to perform their functions. This is Machine-to-Machine com-munication (M2M communication).

The number of connected objects is estimated to be 30 billion in 2019 and growing steadily. Our company's information system looks more like this in Figure 8.4.

We still have our sites from the previous figure with, in addition, connected objects represented by small dots. The actual possibilities of an object to con-nect to others is not represented as each of them may reach any of them. These

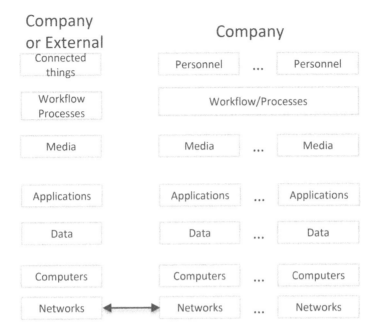

Figure 8.3 Integrating Internet of Things in the information system.

objects are not only what we have grouped under the term computer, but also any physical element that connects to the company network. This representation is a photograph at the moment "t" of the elements that make up the computerized information system. Connected objects are not fixed, when you travel, your tablet travels with you. The risks generated by connected objects

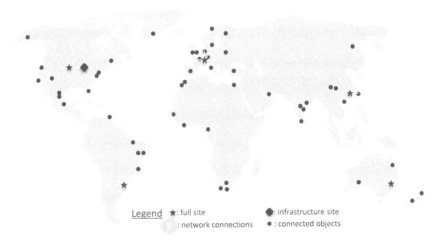

Figure 8.4 More realistic view of an information system.

are twofold: Their quantity and their processing capacities. Many standards are available to help companies implement the appropriate programs and controls to mitigate the risks such as COBIT, the ISO27000 family of standards for implementing an information security management system (ISMS), NIST standards, and to a lesser extent COSO principles 6 through 14.

It is a financial and organizational investment to manage the laptops, desktops, and servers of an IT infrastructure. Adding objects that connect to the network makes the management costs more important and the organization more complex:

- Who buys these objects and with what budget?
- What is the procedure for authorizing the connection of these objects to the network?
- Who updates the software on these objects?
- Who controls the proper functioning of these objects?

So many questions to ask to limit technical risks, so many points to check for an auditor.

The first risk for an auditor as well as for the IT department is to know all the computers that can connect to the company's network. For budgetary reasons, the connected objects purchased may be less secure than objects that would have been recommended by the IT department. For reasons of agility, to deal with the most pressing issues, connected objects are connected by people who do not depend on the IT department, and put the company's IT resources at risk through poor configuration or unauthorized connections. The lack of management of purchased connected objects is detrimental to the proper functioning of the company because of the physical and software obsolescence of the object's processing capabilities, or because a connected object is purchased but not necessarily connected or used as originally intended.

The consequence is that the lack of knowledge about the use of connected objects makes it impossible to control their proper functioning. Do these objects always provide the services for which they were purchased and connected? The risks linked to this lack of knowledge increase with the increase in data mobility and the autonomy of connected objects.

8.2 DATA MOBILITY

Data can be mobile because the data is mobile or because the physical medium on which it is stored is mobile.

Strava is the creator of a fitness tracking app and has ambitions to become the social network for athletes. Their app uses the GPS in connected objects to track when and where a user exercises. Drew Robb, personal infra/data engineer at Strava, explains in a medium.com article the progress their Strava app has made to deliver a global heat map in September 2017 with six times more data than the one released in 2015. It shows "5% of all land on Earth covered in tiles" thanks to people using their app worldwide.

> The realization that the data posted by Strava contained sensitive information was made by chance by an Australian undergraduate student, Nathan Ruser, who used the company's publicly available map to identify the perimeters of US military bases in places such as northeast Syria.
>
> (write Liz Sly, Dan Lamothe, and Craig Timberg in the
Washington Post, on 29th of January 2018)

Nathan Ruser is a student of international security at the Australian National University and a member of the Institute for United Conflict Analysts (IUCA). The map allowed him to find out regular routes (assumed jogging routes) for military personnel. It establishes reliable "pattern of life" information that is not supposed to be divulged to the rest of the world. He tweets on the 27th of January 2018:

> If soldiers use the app like normal people do, by turning it on tracking when they go to do exercise, it could be especially dangerous. This particular track looks like it logs a regular jogging route. I shouldn't be able to establish any pattern of life info from this far away.

To be part of Strava's social network, you don't need to own the latest 1000+ euro cell phone, any GPS wristband or sports watch will do. A single wristband does not contain much computer data. But the regular transfer of the same trips by the same person at different times or by the different wristbands of different people were consolidated and allowed the Strava map (10 terabytes of raw input data) to be created and analyzed to identify trends.

The loss of a bracelet or its theft is detrimental and eventually allows to find its owner by cross-checking with information available internally (cf. social networks). If all the soldiers of the same base lost their wristbands, this would make it possible to identify global trends for all the movements of the base (locations, times, estimated number of people). That all soldiers would have their bracelets stolen is a very implausible hypothesis. One would have to enter the base, find all the bracelets without being noticed and then exit discreetly with them. It's quite complicated. What's the point since the map at hand provides the same information? The bracelets did not move from the base, but the data did.

A computer network is nothing more than the means for data to travel from one place to another, with the particularity that the data that travels is a copy of the data present in the object of departure. This journey is risky, and not peaceful, because the data must overcome all the technical difficulties to reach its destination and not be intercepted by criminals.

It is easy and quite realistic to draw parallels between the routes of the commercial caravans in ancient times and the risks of these journeys with the routes of the data and the risks incurred. The journey of the caravans is marked out by many stages, they cross various countries and use different means of transport, by land and by sea. Nowadays, objects are also transported by air. Between two stages, the risks of loss, destruction or theft of goods are very important. This is one of the reasons why traders use more or less the same routes, for their knowledge of the route, for the quality of the ground (the more people pass through, the flatter the ground), and for the infrastructures on the way, in particular the caravanserais, the villages which are exchange markets.

The merchants also want to be able to deal better with thieves. They grouped together to form increasingly large and well-protected caravans. It is wrong to think that different traders all gathered at one starting town and all went to the same destination. The caravans were not formed at a starting point and for destination the same city. The journeys were slow, and it was necessary to plan stages along the way. The stages, often caravanserais, are places where merchants leave a caravan to join another or sell objects that will leave with another caravan.

For reasons of ease of security, travel, and preferred stopping places, merchants prefer to minimize risks as much as possible, while improving the simplicity of the journey. The more a route is used, the more thieves are aware of their attacks and the less they make them. The more a route is used, the more it is sized to the needs of the caravans. The more politically stable the country through which the route passes, the less risk there is. The larger the caravanserai, the more trade is possible. All the caravanserais are not of the same size, considering the technical constraints, either the fatigue of the men or the animals, they are distributed at practical distances from each other according to the difficulty of the terrain.

The defense against looting and theft is taken care of by the caravan itself. It has its own guards, which also increases the cost for the traders. The more stable the country, the more important the institutional means of security, such as Chinese garrisons and watchtowers beyond the Great Wall or caravanserais. Few people have traveled the entire Silk Road, for example. Goods are transported by different routes and different guides. The idea is to subcontract to local people who are familiar with the terrain, politics, and bandits of their own region, which reduces the risks.

But the easiest way is to choose the least risky routes even if it means travelers and traders have to pay taxes. In China, the Middle East and Europe, states, confederations, and regional powers promote trade and diplomacy. They invest in communication and economic infrastructure: Safe roads, water deposits, inns, reliable coins, standard weights, and measures. Despite the taxes, merchants prefer to pay the controlling authorities for safe passage than to risk encounters with bandits.

The example of the Seljuk Turks is significant for the efforts to secure trade, as was the establishment of maritime insurance in the Middle Ages. Over time, the Muslim powers controlled large parts of the Silk Road. They invested in caravanserais that housed and protected people and beasts of burden. The caravanserais housed more or less large military troops on the same principle established by the Chinese on the eastern part of the Silk Road. The Turkish authorities, whether the unified Sultanate Seljuk or the independent emirs, also built fortified caravanserais separated by a day's journey, about 20–40 km depending on the difficulties of the terrain, all along the main trade routes. This is a distance that now seems very short, but it is classic with the means of transport of the time. Moreover, in France, an edict of 1623 only required the entrepreneurs of public carriages (e.g. diligences) to travel 8 or 9 leagues per day, approximately 32–36 km. (To better realize the difficulties and the duration of the journeys, the site of the University of Stanford visualizes the possible journeys according to various parameters like the season orbis.stanford.edu.)

The Seljuk Sultanate of Anatolia, which controlled the western part of the Silk Road, even offered an additional guarantee to merchants. It created a public insurance guaranteed by the public treasury to manage the risks of land and sea traders whose goods were damaged or stolen by bandits, pirates, or attacks from neighboring states. Contracts are signed between caravanners and traders to guarantee the quantity of goods and reduce transport costs in case of delays; a bit like the transport contracts used by today's logistics companies. All this implies the obligation to list exhaustively the transported goods with the details of the type of goods, the weight, and the volume. For volumes, standardized containers were created, such as amphorae of different sizes (the tonnage of ships is frequently estimated in amphorae). This standardization was a key element in the commercial development around the Mediterranean in antiquity and is still a key element in today's world trade with the standardization of maritime containers.

What happens to the data? The same principles that apply to the transportation of goods apply to data. It travels through cables or through the air. These sets of cables and air links constitute more or less important networks like the trade routes over the centuries, which can be local, regional, or continental, to become global after the discovery of the Americas by the Europeans. A computer network is a set of equipment connected to each other to manage data exchanges. Computer networks are usually grouped into local or global networks or distinguished according to the techniques used. From a technical risk point of view, we will separate computer networks not according to a technique, but according to who manages them. The risks are different between networks where the company manages the equipment and networks where they manage only some of the equipment or none of it.

As for the safety of caravans, if the company invests in equipment, it can better invest in safety and reliability. The technical risks lie in the level of mastery of the infrastructure, i.e., the equipment, cables and airwaves used by the company. This equipment is regularly progressing with new protocols and new techniques. Some risks will appear with these advances and others will disappear. The management of technical risks is a continuous and precise work because it is necessary to manage its park with the necessary information to identify the versions of the software used by this equipment and to maintain this information up to date.

Another technical risk is the inadequacy of the technical infrastructure to the company's needs. It is due to an IT strategy that is not adapted to the company's strategy. Of course, this can lead to delays in projects (operational risks), but inconsistent technical choices or too little technical investment are very common.

An additional feature of technical risks is the dependence of companies on equipment and network providers. A company is already obliged to use software packages for its projects, such as databases or ERP, and possible solutions are to use so-called open-source software and adapt it to its needs, such as databases or Unix-based operating systems. But in the case of infrastructure equipment and networks outside its sites, the company is obliged to use suppliers.

One or more pieces of equipment form the interface between the world that the company controls and the external environment. These hardware interfaces are at risk, just like the software interfaces. It is around this equipment that security strategies are structured. As there are different sizes of caravanserai, more or less fortified and more or less protected by soldiers, several pieces of equipment can be set up in such a way that the data necessarily transit through these pieces of equipment in a certain order to reach the environment that the company masters. In this spirit, all the military techniques and even the military vocabulary are used to distinguish the different possible technical configurations.

Software that analyzes data traffic is equivalent of watchtowers beyond the Great Wall. Some software will try to identify risky data according to various criteria while others will try to smooth the traffic. The complexity is both the control of the level of risk and the flexibility for the users. That's the significance of Citrix's 2018 acquisition of Cedexis. Cedexis designs software that directs data on the paths that move data fastest through the environment outside the enterprise. Citrix had previously been developing equivalent solutions, but in the enterprise environment.

This notion of protecting a network environment is reflected in the efforts made by states to control Internet access. Bruce Schneier (atlantic.com) summarizes his concerns about technical risks:

> Increasingly, everything is a computer: not just your laptop and phone, but your car, your appliances, your medical devices, and global infrastructure. These computers are and always will be vulnerable, but Spectre and Meltdown represent a new class of vulnerability. Un-patchable vulnerabilities in the deepest recesses of the world's computer hardware is the new normal. It's going to leave us all much more vulnerable in the future.

Spectre and Meltdown are two vulnerabilities found in 2017 in Intel microprocessors.

The point that Schneier indirectly raises and addresses in the Strava example is that data also travels because the medium on which it is stored also travels. Just think about the different strategies you use for security checks when you arrive at an airport. Is it wise to travel to countries your company considers risky with your usual laptop or cell phone? What legal rules on data protection apply? We look now at the legal risks involved in moving objects.

8.3 MEDIA MOBILITY

Data carriers are no longer mobile only because they move with us, but because they become autonomous. They are grouped under the term of connected objects and are part of what is called the Internet of Things. They acquire this autonomy thanks to an autonomy of treatment or an autonomy of movement.

An object is equipped with functionalities to reach a more or less complete autonomy. We usually imagine this complete autonomy in the form of humanoid robots. Car manufacturers are also thinking about it. They define 6 levels of autonomy from 0 to 5, which go from the need to have a driver (level 0—no assistance) to the car that does not need a driver (level 5—complete automation).

Autonomy is achieved by:

- Retrieving more and more data,
- The increase of the computing capacities, and
- Communication with even more objects.

Retrieving more and more data is essential to improve decision-making. For example, Apple Inc. is evolving the iPhone® connected object and improving the security of the object by moving from a passcode (risk of 1 in 10,000 thanks to a 4-digit code) to Touch ID® (risk of 1 in 50,000) and then to Face ID® (risk of 1 in 1,000,000 thanks to 30,000 checkpoints).

The need for data for a car to go from one level of autonomy to the next is exponential and the need for computing capacity must follow. Originally simple sensors, objects are now equipped with more and more powerful microprocessors and increasingly important data storage. The technical improvement of these three functions facilitates the implementation of more and more powerful programs, up to what is called artificial intelligence.

This autonomy increases the risks and questions arise:

- Legal questions,
- Questions about the validation of this autonomy,
- Does the software integrated in the object do what it is sold for?
- Does the software integrated in the object not do something other than what it is sold for?

Legal questions related to the responsibility of the connected object, to the point of asking the legitimate question of the creation of the right of the robot as there are the rights of the physical person and the rights of the moral person. Questions about the validation of the proper functioning of the connected object, their autonomy. Let's take the example of what happens with medication. A drug in the hands of a patient is totally autonomous and the patient, also autonomous, is capable of not following the administration method. The marketing of a health product, such as a drug, is a defined procedure with mandatory milestones, regardless of the main countries in the world.

In all cases, a laboratory wishing to market a drug must apply for Marketing Authorization (MA) to a drug agency, such as the European Medicines Agency in Europe or National Medical Products Administration in China. It is based on an evaluation file drawn up based on preclinical and clinical data from previous development phases. The evaluation of the dossier takes at least one year. Even once a drug is on the market, it is monitored. Monitoring is mandatory and is carried out through pharmacovigilance and pharmaco-epidemiology, carried out by the pharmaceutical companies themselves or by research organizations such as the French National Institute of Health and Medical Research (INSERM). As soon as the slightest risk is identified, MA is withdrawn. Medicines act on their environment and must pass many tests before being put on the market. The more autonomy the object has, the more it acts on its environment, to what extent are the suppliers' testing techniques sufficient, credible, and opposable to third parties in case of a problem?

In the case of autonomous cars or trucks, what are the procedures used to authorize the marketing of autonomous cars or any other autonomous product? The development of a new molecule takes about 15 years. The efforts made by the various manufacturers of autonomous objects are necessary, but are they sufficient? What is the risk for a company to use products that are not validated after an official process? These numerous technical risks must be compensated by contracts validated by the company's legal department.

Does the software functionality only do what is stated in the contract and item documentation? In 2014, the International Council on Clean Transportation (ICCT) reported significant discrepancies between the exhaust rates reported by diesel vehicle manufacturers and the actual rates. In 2018, the European Commission is budgeting €1.6 million to subsidize independent testing. Concerns are equivalent to the previous point.

Along the same lines, does the software embedded in connected objects have additional functionality to that stated in the contract and documentation? Cell phone applications have been in the news because they collect data other than what users consent to. Some of these applications retrieve your data even if you have not given your consent.

Don't be surprised, there is no reason why what happens on your computer should not happen on connected objects in general. Facebook, for example, was condemned by the Belgian justice in 2015, because through its sharing and recommendation tools present on more and more web pages, Facebook can record a lot of information about the sites consulted by Internet users. For the same reasons, Facebook was condemned in 2017 by the CNIL in France. Other procedures are underway in 2018 for these same facts, from several national data protection authorities in Germany, the Netherlands, and Spain.

This autonomy is produced thanks to the progress made with artificial intelligence, neural networks, and machine learning. These different techniques can be found in avatars, voice assistants, bots that are more or less talented, more or less autonomous. The most famous example is HAL9000 from the novel "2001: A Space Odyssey." It is part of the series of short stories "Space Odyssey" written by Arthur C. Clarke.

Each of these techniques has its advantages, disadvantages, and limitations. Each one has specific risks in addition to those mentioned above. But the risk whose importance increases with the evolution of the complexity of computer techniques is the provision of proof. That is to say, being able to retrace and redo the sequence of lines of code that led to an action, a decision taken by the bot/robot.

To retrieve data, the object must communicate with its environment. Even a sports bracelet without a screen must "interrogate" your arm to know your pulse, for example. The object is created and more or less limited in its interaction possibilities. Each of these interaction possibilities is the subject of communication protocols that deliver more or fewer services. The protocols of local communications are not stabilized. We have, for example, an active competition between the different companies that produce connected objects for the home.

This communication also generates many questions:

- Who does the connected object communicate with?
- Is the person with whom the object communicates the one it claims to be?
- What is the content of the conversation between these interlocutors?
- Are these conversations preserved? By comparison, do they "talk" to each other or do they "write" to each other?
- Will the object's interlocutor not repeat the conversation to third parties not known to the connected object and therefore to its owner?
- And so on, with all the issues related to security and trust in communications.

The connected object lives its life and interferes with us at more or less opportune moments. It modifies our vision of the world and our relationship with other humans in both the real and electronic worlds. It interferes with our decision-making, as when some people blindly follow the indications of their GPS while the real world provides contradictory information. Connected objects are becoming more and more powerful and never get tired (depending on the battery). They communicate and interact even in your absence, as often and as fast as they want.

The legal risks are there, but they are misunderstood or poorly considered by professionals and individuals. When will we see in car sales contracts paragraphs on the processing of data collected by the connected car? Analysis are notably undertaken by the independent French administrative regulatory body, Commission Nationale de l'Informatique et des Libertés, (CNIL) on this subject, moreover, with the publication on October 17, 2017, of a compliance pack for connected vehicles.

The digitalization of current objects implies a new risk, being that we don't really own the hardware we buy. In a connected world, firmware updates—software providing the low-level control of hardware—can often eliminate features proposed when the hardware has been bought, for instance Sony PlayStation 3. Tesla motors website mentions, "Our cars regularly receive over-the-air software updates that add new features and enhance existing ones over Wi-Fi." It can get even worse, with more and more objects now relying on Internet-connectivity, companies can often give up on supporting devices entirely, often leaving users with very expensive paperweight as when Google acquired Revolv, then restructured its line of business and closed the Revolv one:

> The Revolv app and hub don't work anymore, but we are offering a refund for your Revolv hub. To get your refund, please contact Nest support.
>
> Thank you for your support and believing in us. We're sad for the end of Revolv, but this isn't the end of the connected home. This is the beginning.

(Revolv.com website)

How much dependent or reliant is an information system on such products? Which processes are the more at risks? Enhancing an information system having it more digitalized is not only hardware as we have seen, it is also time and money. In the continuous changing IT landscape, there is also a risk which may brick other devices used by an enterprise:

> Peloton and Flywheel have agreed to settle their legal disputes over claims that Flywheel copied Peloton's patented technology, according to a Texas court filing dated February 3, 2020. The case launched back in September 2018 when Peloton argued that Flywheel's version of the at-home stationary bike that streams on-demand classes infringes on its patented technology, down to the way workout metrics are displayed and can be used to compete against other live riders in the class.
>
> In the world of the Internet of Broken Things (IoBT), there is nothing more impressive to me than the fact that these things actually sell as well as they do. The risks associated with Internet-connected devices seem insurmountable, save for the fact that we are all cattle being marched along to the slaughterhouse, our faces as serene as could be. Between companies simply deciding that supporting these products isn't worth it any longer and reducing functionality, firing off firmware updates that simply kill off selling-point features, or leaving security holes wide enough to drive a malicious creepster through, it seems that very little thought goes

into the fact that customers are, you know, buying these things. Once that purchase is made, how long that purchase is functional and secure appears to be an afterthought.

But the risks apparently don't end there. Let's say you bought an IoBT device. Let's say you enjoyed using it for months or years. And then let's say that the company you bought it from suddenly got sued for patent infringement, settled with the plaintiff, and part of that settlement is, oops, your shit doesn't work any longer? Well, in that case, you're an owner of a Flywheel home exercise bike, which settled for patent infringement with never mind-you-already-know-who.

(Natt Garun—The Verge, February 5, 2020)

8.4 ARE IT INDUCED RISKS NEW?

We will avoid any suspense; the answer is they're not new. We are so impregnated by the language of computer scientists that we believe that more and more new things are invented or that innovations appear regularly following an increasing trend. As a non-IT auditor, and even for IT auditors, it is possible to get caught up by such a rhetoric, forgetting our needs and constraints as auditors.

> When we are told about technology from on high, we are made to think about novelty and the future. For many decades now the term "technology" has been closely linked with invention (the creation of a new idea) and innovation (the first use of a new idea).
>
> [DED]

George Orwell noted in May 12, 1944:

> Reading recently a batch of rather shallowly optimistic "progressive" books, I was struck by the automatic way people go on repeating certain phrases which were fashionable before 1914. Two great favourites are the "abolition of distance" and the "disappearance of frontiers." I do not know how often I have met with statements that "the aeroplane and the radio have abolished distance" and "all parts of the world are now interdependent."
>
> [GOR]

Yes, as auditors we notice that hardware is more powerful, software coded with new programming languages praised as being more efficient, but the concepts are quite often decades old and classical IT risks remain, such as the quality of what is programmed. With the digitalization, there are more and more programs, so the same risks but with a wider number of programs.

These programs are more and more interdependent, creating opportunities for a risk to have a bigger impact on the workflow and as such a bigger financial impact.

With the new development methods around the agile manifesto, some IT people even goes touting "The Art of Agile Development: No Bugs." As auditors, we know it's false. The only way to achieve that is by using mathematical proof of the algorithm. The IT specialists are creative enough to propose new methods or ideas to produce software, to name a few since the 60s the waterfall idea (not a documented method as such), the V model, the W model, the iterative models, and the time-boxed models. This list is in chronological order. Each new method promotes advantages against the initial waterfall idea and not vs. similar methods or previous methods, such as between agile methods or between an agile method and iterative methods. As auditors a basic approach would be to use a model and track the outcomes and theirs costs whatever the way programs are developed. The easiest one is to use the accounting structure Design, Build, Deploy. Any work before the design of what will be deploy, and after it has been deployed, remains operational expenditures. What can be capitalized if approved will be the Design, Build, and Deploy workload and associated investments. They are new names for work performed before the Design work, such as Intake, Ideation and so on. Unless the auditor's objective is to evaluate the efficiency of an IT department, it is not mandatory to look at these costs before and after Design, Build, and Deploy. It is nevertheless an extremely interesting audit to be performed and it helps better understand the IT processes.

So, why is it important for an auditor to use Design, Build, and Deploy or its own structure? Because the IT departments may use different models and it is easier to audit using cross-references between Design, Build, Deploy and the model used, and it is faster to compare risks against that standard audit structure. The auditor may add additional risks brought by the models used to develop. As an auditor the main risk is the quality of what is delivered. It can have been built the way the enterprise wants; a bug free software reduces operating costs after the go-live and helps avoiding successful intentional acts from attackers.

Whatever the IT new tools and the new technical advancements such as bitcoin, data analysis or artificial intelligence there are bugs. How are they tracked? How are they reduced? Figure 8.5 shows the sequence.

Ideal because any outcome is tested progressively, meaning that when the User Acceptance Tests are designed, they are designed leveraging the Design documentation. So, the Design documentation is being formally reviewed due to tests design. It improves the quality of the Design and provides a confirmation that both the Design documentation and the User Acceptance Tests are consistent. The most common current malpractice is to design and perform the tests after something has been developed as shown in Figure 8.6.

If this is the case in a development process, then as auditors we should investigate more this topic. Before seeing what is specific to these new tools,

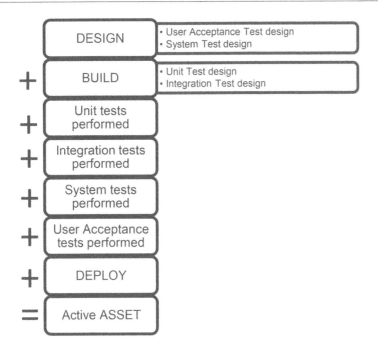

Figure 8.5 Ideal steps' sequence.

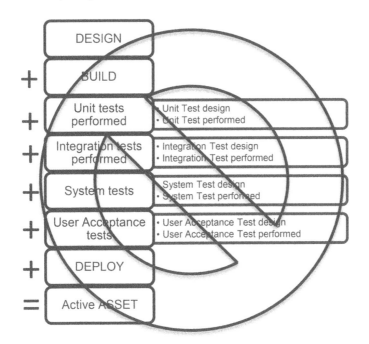

Figure 8.6 The most current malpractice.

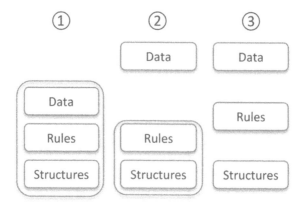

Figure 8.7 Basic set of bricks: Data, rules, and structures.

let's summarize the issues we are already facing with the current ones and not yet resolved: The tests. For this, let's say that to automate a process we use the following basic elements to play with: Data, rules, and structures. Data is the information structured, grouped the enterprise wants to act on. Rules is the knowledge structured, summarized by the enterprise. Structures is the context and how the rules and the data will interact. The three of them may be grouped on the same support, such as on the left ① of Figure 8.7. The quantity of data is getting bigger and it is practical to use another support for the data, middle of the figure ②. Then when rules are becoming more complex or being modified quite often or when they are not yet actually when defined, they are separated too on another support, ③.

Moving from ① to ③ increases the importance for an auditor of understanding the quality of the data, the pertinence of the rules and the constraints of the structure. What's happening now is that the rules are not fully known, the data are incomplete to better understand the rules or both of these issues. Let's leverage Jill Leporre's book "If Then. How the Simulmatics Corporation Invented the Future" to explain it. It is quite refreshing and useful for us to step back and think about the current context when thinking of artificial intelligence. Simulmatics Corporation was created in 1959, its name stands for simulation and automatics. The Dartmouth summer research project on artificial intelligence took place a few years before in 1956. Its objective is an *attempt* "to find how to make machines use language, form abstractions and concepts, solve kinds of problems now reserved for human, and improve themselves." Its agenda was (in italic, extracts of the explanations in the proposal for that research project):

- Automatic Computers,
    - "If a machine can do a job, then an automatic calculator can be programmed to simulate the machine;"

- How Can a Computer be Programmed to Use a Language?
  - "It may be speculated that a large part of human thought consists of manipulating words according to rules of reasoning and rules of conjecture. From this point of view, forming a generalization consists in admitting a new word and some rules whereby sentences containing it imply and are implied by others;"
- Neuron Nets,
  - "How can a set of (hypothetical) neurons be arranged so as to form concepts;"
- Theory of the Size of a Calculation,
  - "If we are given a well-defined problem (one of which it is possible to test mechanically whether or not a proposed answer is a valid answer) one way of solving it is to try all possible answers in order. This method is inefficient, and to exclude it one must have some criterion for efficiency of calculation;"
- Self-Improvement,
  - "Probably a truly intelligent machine will carry out activities which may best be described as self-improvement;"
- Abstractions,
  - "A number of types of "abstraction" can be distinctly defined and several others less distinctly. A direct attempt to classify these and to describe machine methods of forming abstractions from sensory and other data would seem worthwhile;"
- Randomness and Creativity,
  - "A fairly attractive and yet clearly incomplete conjecture is that the difference between creative thinking and unimaginative competent thinking lies in the injection of some randomness."

The words "artificial intelligence" was then used for the first time to make the distinction from what the computers were used to do. To perform new things, with an initial focus on predicting elections results, scientists were hired by Simulmatics Corporation.

"The scientists of the Simulmatics Corporation acted on the proposition that if they could collect enough data about enough people and feed it into a machine, everything, one day, might be predictable, and everyone, every human mind, simulated, each act anticipated, automatically, and even driven and directed, by targeted messages as unerring as missiles." Here we go with data. To achieve that in the 50's, "They wrote in a new language, FORTRAN, using an expression known as an IF/THEN statement to instruct a computer to simulate possible actions and calculate their consequences, under different conditions, again and again and again. IF this, THEN that. IF this, THEN that. IF this, THEN that, an infinity of outcomes."

Here we are with rules and structures.

The August 31, 1955, Dartmouth proposal describes what the attendees would like to study.

M. L. Minsky explains his proposal for research by:

> The machine is provided with input and output channels and an internal means of providing varied output responses to inputs in such a way that the machine may be "trained" by a "trial and error" "goal-seeking" behavior... The important result that would be looked for would be that the machine would tend to build up within itself and abstract model of the environment in which it is placed.

Doesn't that look familiar to you?

> Machine learning (ML) is the study of computer algorithms that can improve automatically through experience and by the use of data.

> (Wikipedia)

N. Rochester is interested in another topic:

> In writing a program for an automatic calculator, one ordinarily provides the machine with a set of rules to cover each contingency which may arise and confront the machine. One expects the machine to follow this set of rules slavishly and to exhibit no originality or common sense. Furthermore, one is annoyed only at himself when the machine gets confused because the rules, he has provided for the machine are slightly contradictory. Finally, in writing programs for machines, one sometimes must go at problems in a very laborious manner whereas, if the machine had just a little intuition or could make reasonable guesses, the solution of the problem could be quite direct.

Doesn't that sound a little bit scary for an auditor? Yes, it is, and it hasn't changed a lot since.

In the 2020s, how the programs are developed, and the capacity and calculation power of computers changed. The main changes relate to how data is being gathered as even in 1956, it was already acknowledged that considerable amounts of data were needed and how IF/THEN has been replaced. The IF/THEN programming has been replaced by programs defining themselves the rules, "rules of reasoning and rules of conjectures." Data and rules have been split from the structure being now *motor abstractions*," as called in 1955 wording or an engine nowadays.

Data is critical in today's testing process of the rules. The rules are defined, refined by the system while going through all the data set. So how pertinent is the data set? Does it represent the full perimeter on which the system is supposed to show its analyzing prowess when in production? The data pertinence is something you already heard about many times in the news, in a bad way as it impacts people life. Jill Leporre summarizes this for the Simulmatics Corporation efforts:

> By "human behavior," they meant the behavior of men; by "artificial intelligence," they meant their own intelligence—a fantasy of their own intelligence—which they intended to graft onto a machine. They did not consider the intelligence of women to be intelligence; they did not consider a female understanding of human behavior to be knowledge.

And the more artificial intelligence system are deployed the more bias will appear/be known or being visible/showing up due a data set never tested before the system going live. It happens also that you can't collect a data sample representative of all the perimeter. Some companies are investigating creating revenue by providing synthetic data. Synthetic meaning created by computers. As an auditor seeing again the word computers raised concerns, such as how good is the synthetic data set? The concern is similar on auditing the Disaster Recovery Plan of a company, if it relies on third parties, further investigations must be performed, or on auditing a network each time a new connection is made to external or not owned components, the scope of the audit must take them into account.

> Artificial Intelligence (AI) is influencing people's everyday lives and playing a key role in digital transformation through its automated decision-making capabilities. The benefits of this emerging technology are significant, but so are the concerns. The EU Agency for Cybersecurity warns that AI may open new avenues in manipulation and attack methods, as well as new privacy and data protection challenges.
>
> [ENISA]

ENISA is concerned by the fact that artificial intelligence is influencing people, and it does. But one of the reasons why artificial intelligence is interesting is to avoid the risks due to people reasoning being widely influenceable. The 2021 book "Noise. A Flow in Human Judgment" from Daniel Kahneman, Olivier Sibony, and Cass R. Sunstein is consolidating both things we already know and key new studies [KSS]. The improvements on artificial intelligence techniques are targeting avoiding bias in their programming.

> Very large data sets are essential for sophisticated analyses, and the increasing availability of such data sets is one of the main causes of rapid progress of Artificial Intelligence in the recent years. For example, large data sets make it possible to deal mechanically with broken-leg exceptions.
>
> [KSS]

Having better data sets is a target of deep learning. The objective is to be able to include extremely rare event occurrences of data enabling the programming improving its analysis.

This is what concerns us as auditors, how the artificial intelligence programming has been developed, this concern is not new. Based on how artificial intelligence systems are developed, there is a convergence in the audit requirements for the design and implementation of an artificial intelligence system, such as:

- Reliability, safety, and robustness over time,
- Transparency,
- Privacy protection,
- Fairness, non-discriminatory treatment, and respect for the fundamental values of dignity, and
- Compliance with laws and regulations, from design and along its life usage.

With a legal perspective, the main concern is about transparency or the difficulty of identifying responsibilities due to the non-accountability of the different actors due to the diffuse aspect of artificial intelligence systems and so the dilution of responsibilities. Transparency for what? Well, various items:

- The non-traceability of actions,
- The non-traceability of results to the sources,
- The difficulty to bring all the evidences, and
- The difficulty to assign the responsibility to an individual in case of action contrary to the rules and the law.

In this context, there is a question mark over the place of the human being in the decision-making process and therefore in the attribution of responsibilities. Indeed, the decision-making process itself depends greatly on the responsibility that this decision requires. But, even in the case where predictive AIs would only be decision aids and the human would keep the final control on all decisions, what would on all decisions, what about the responsibility of the human in the case where these predictive AIs would take into account the latest medical techniques and would not base his care on their conclusions, conclusions of which she/he would not have a perfect control because of a conclusions of which she/he would not have a perfect control because of a certain opacity in its functioning. Could the person be held responsible for a loss of chance for the patient to be cured? Some propose to give a legal status to some AI that have a physical interaction (e.g. robots, autonomous car) to address these liability issues. But would these entities have the free will? Would it be wise?

Are they similar concerns with the blockchain? Blockchain is now well-known thanks to cryptocurrencies, particularly since 2008 by the bitcoin.

Even if Wozniak told Brian Sozzi and Julie Hyman in an interview with Yahoo Finance on October 29, 2021:

> Bitcoin is mathematics, mathematical purity. There can never be another Bitcoin created,

there are risks anyway using the blockchain technology. The first challenge is that different technologies are used and ways to program and implement a blockchain, so the risks will be different. Some of them are related to its usage, such as whenever there will be the need to delete data, for instance the publication of false information, of copyrighted materials, of illicit content, or the need to have a contract broken by a judicial decision. In short, the blockchain does not help on the content but on its potential alteration: It does not help verifying the validity of information, and only allows to prove that the information circulating has not been altered.

The technology can be touted as mathematically pure and it's ok, but what about its implementation? We've seen that in Chapter 2 "Information System" and in Chapter 7 "Human Uncertainties," each time a new technique is used to protect, each time efforts are spent to circumvent that new technique. For information system audit it means two things, current procedures and controls must be audited as usual and particularly how the current procedures and controls are kept pertinent vis-à-vis the changes, the enterprise organizational changes, the enterprise environment changes and the IT changes. Nevertheless, the blockchain started being recognized worldwide as evidence before the courts. The "Hangzhou Internet Court" in China in June 2018 considered evidence authenticated by blockchain technology to be legally admissible. However, the court considers that in this specific case, the use of a reliable third-party blockchain platform without any conflict of interest allowed the legal basis for the evidence of intellectual property rights infringement.

Let's put blockchain in context by leveraging a post from Google on December 7, 2021, called "New action to combat cyber-crime":

> Today, we took action to disrupt Glupteba, a sophisticated botnet which targets Windows machines and protects itself using blockchain technology ... A botnet is a network of devices connected to the internet that have been infected with a type of malware that places them under the control of bad actors ... After a thorough investigation, we determined that the Glupteba botnet currently involves approximately one million compromised Windows devices worldwide, and at times, grows at a rate of thousands of new devices per day ... Unfortunately, Glupteba's use of blockchain technology as a resiliency mechanism is notable here and is becoming a more common practice among cyber-crime organizations. The decentralized nature of blockchain allows the botnet to recover more quickly from disruptions, making them that much harder to shutdown.

To summarize, auditors face the same challenges plus new ones. Same challenges such as how programs are developed, tested, and maintained. New challenges such as programs are developed, tested, and maintained. Yes, it looks similar, but the technologies are different. It relates as always to confidence on the information provided and available. Auditors must be careful as they have to refrain their end-user reflex saying that if the computer provides an information it's true, it's all about confidence.

When describing the empire of cotton as the world's most important manufacturing industry from 1000 to 1900 CE, Sven Beckett summarize how a global worldwide empire functions:

> The global cotton trade, as we have seen, rested on credit. Credit rested on trust. Trust, in a global market extended well beyond the kin of any family or tribe, rested on information.

[SBE]

Rachel Botsman defines trust as "a confident relationship with the unknown" [RBO] and describes trust as a way to deal with risks and unknown when dealing with partners, and therefore uncertainty. Confidence in this book is as a way to be confident in the future based on trust.

Confidence is built on facts and information, how much confidence and for how long confidence is pertinent are the topics of our next chapter.

BIBLIOGRAPHY

DED: David Edgerton, *"The Shock of the Old. Technology and Global History Since 1900,"* 2006, Profiles Book Ltd, 978-1-86197-306-1

GOR: George Orwell, *"George Orwell: 'As I Please',"* 1943, first published, Tribune

KSS: Daniel Kahneman, Olivier Sibony, and Cass R. Sunstein, *"Noises. A Flaw in Human Judgment,"* 2021, William-Collins, 978-0-008-30899-5

RBO: Rachel Botsman, *"Who Can You Trust?,"* 2017, Hachette Book Group, 978-1-5417-7367-7

SBE: Sven Beckert, *"Empire of Cotton: A New History of Global Capitalism,"* 1986, Penguin Random House UK, 978-0-141-97997-7

Chapter 9

Confidence

When there is no trust, the common people will have nothing to stand on.

Lun Yu, *The Analects of Confucius*

The first chapters summarize the evolution of auditing needs for investors, directors, and third parties of companies. It is both necessary to know the history and necessary to learn from the experience:

Learning from past experience in intelligence, as in most other fields, is, of course, easier said than done.

[CAN]

The following chapters describe the different legal, operational, and technical risks and their interrelationships. It is time to present the possible options to have confidence in the proper functioning of an organization. As a result, you may have the feeling that the overall picture is rather gloomy to audit information systems. Let's stay positive and say that companies' environment has changed. It is highly digitalized. The digitalization impacts the pertinence of the evidences gathered when auditing, the speed auditors adapt their audit strategy, and further down their work programs. This chapter is about how to be confident. The following chapters, Chapters 10–12, are about how auditors can be "agile," and I rather say flexible, adaptable as agile is a misused and overused word.

But why using the word confidence instead of the word thrust? First of all, as auditors we are gathering clue some of them can be directly used as proof but quite often are indirectly used as proof. Second, because both notions refer to hopes that can turn into disappointments. Trust establishes confidence as trust is the mean by which someone achieves confidence in something. The other way to achieve confidence is through control. Trust between companies and investors has always been based on human relations. The borrower proves his good faith, his good intentions, by providing evidence of his good management, the results of his business strategy and the soundness of his projects. This evidence is directly or indirectly linked to profits, as investors lend money over a certain period.

DOI: 10.1201/9781003230137-9

Trust is also vital within the company, between the hierarchy and the employees, between the members of a team. It contributes to the flexibility, reactivity, and quality of the company's services and products. The information exchanged is then reliable over time and correctly reflects reality.

To guarantee the reliability of information, controls avoid and identify malfunctions or errors, whether intentional or not. They ensure that the company's processes function reliably and more or less permanently.

Trust and especially the implementation of elements that contribute to building and maintaining this trust is essential to the survival of the company. The main elements are controls, the level of control and the associated processes, or internal control. A control must be defined, implemented, and maintained under the responsibility of the company. The term "internal control" refers primarily to the internal control process and by extension to the controls implemented, i.e., the audit, and the associated actions based on the audit result.

Controls, such as testing, provide assurance that the process works as intended and that the services or products developed are compliant. As such, they do not add value to the process. They minimize the consequences of possible malfunctions. They should not disrupt the company's processes or have a very low impact, like taking measurements on physical or chemical phenomena.

The process is here a chronological sequence of actions that leads to a service or a product. Controls can be placed before, during or after a step, an action in a process. Let's take an example that we live every day, we go in and out of our house regularly hoping to always have the keys on us. To find yourself outside your home without your keys is a very unpleasant situation. Let's assume that we occupy an apartment with a landing door without an outside handle. The context already indicates that a control is placed because there is no external handle. This allows you to control access to your apartment. Even if the entry/exit process is little changed in its duration, it completely changes the way we operate. It adds an additional risk: The risk of not being able to return home.

To limit this risk, we decide to make a habit, which we will call an operational control. Do you check if you have your keys before or after you slam the door? In this example, a check during is ineffective except to see the problem coming: We see the door closing and we don't have our keys in our hand, like when a gust of wind slams the door.

If you check afterward, the control is a posteriori control. It allows us to notice the problem more or less quickly. It does not allow us to anticipate or solve the problem. If you check that you have your keys before slamming the door, it is an a priori control. It helps you to avoid a problem, but there is still a risk if you have not checked properly. Indeed, you may have the wrong key. A check is put in place to track one risk, but not all risks. In this case, and in the event of subsequent checks, it is wise to have a plan "B" i.e., a compensatory solution. We can decide to leave a set of keys with a trusted person.

Usually, for convenience, we leave a spare with a neighbor, the building super-intendent, or a friend. Of course, we could imagine more or less complex variants to correct more quickly or at lower cost the risk managed by the control. We may be concerned by nature and decide to put in place several controls, in this case, complementary, and several compensatory solutions. The combination of these controls and solutions provides a certain control level. The auditor relies on the controls and the level of control to form an opinion and have reasonable assurance on the proper functioning of the processes. The level of control is assessed by the auditors as sufficient or not, in relation to the risks incurred by the company. To have the right level of control, we must use a structured approach and adapt the controls used to the level of confidence we want to have, but also the length of time we need to have this level of confidence.

The level of trust is inversely proportional to the risks we can bear, to our appetite for risk. The duration of confidence is proportional to the duration for which the level of risk, which you can bear, does not increase. It must be simple and coherent, i.e., easy to implement and adapted to the organizational context. Neither the number of controls nor their complexity guarantees a reduction in the level of risk. If salespeople leave confidential documents on their desks during or at the end of the day, information technology (IT) controls over business applications are of little value.

In 2009, Arnold Kling wrote an essay "The Chess Game of Financial Regulation." He argues about the need of simplicity vs. the push on more complex regulations after the 2008 financial crisis:

> Instead of trying to make the regulatory system harder to break, we might think in terms of making it easier to fix. Ideas such as functional regulation or regulatory consolidation might make our financial system harder to break, but they also could make it harder to fix.

And added:

> We tend to think of the task of regulation as one of making systems hard to break. An alternative to consider is making systems easy to fix. Think of a computer. You can try to use firewalls and anti-virus software to make your computer hard to break. But it still pays to back up your data to make it easy to fix.

We must consider the context in which the risk is assessed. If you have not been vaccinated against the flu, you are at risk of catching it. This depends on the geographical area in which you are living, the health precautions you are following, and your physical condition associated with your age. You want to avoid getting the flu this winter or limit the consequences if you catch a cold. Whatever your "operational" objective, you modify your behavior in a more or less radical way with the firm intention of getting through the winter without getting sick. You modify your behavior and eventually you get vaccinated for this year's winter. The solutions chosen gives a level of confidence associated with a duration and for a certain investment. The investment in vaccination is all the more relevant as we modify our behavior to avoid putting ourselves at risk.

This chapter shows the links between the various controls and how to combine them to obtain a level of confidence for a given period. Annual financial reporting provides a mandatory legal framework around which we distinguish:

- Short-term confidence,
- Medium-term confidence, and
- Long-term confidence.

The duration of these three types of confidence depends on the company and its context. How may we distinguish the durations? Short-term confidence is around 3–6 months, medium-term confidence is between 6 and 12 months approximately and long-term trust is no more than 18 months.

This term of confidence, which looks to the future, should not be confused with the reasonable assurance of the external auditors who observe past performance. This term of confidence does not concern the difficulty of obtaining the same opinion by different auditors based on identical facts. This point was excluded from our analysis in the introduction.

9.1 SHORT-TERM CONFIDENCE

What are the means to be implemented and what are the controls to be in place to support short-term confidence? Under what conditions can we say that we are confident in the company's operations over the next following months? Short-term confidence is about obtaining reasonable assurance that is reliable over the next 3- to 6-month period. The duration of the audit to obtain this confidence must be fast, ideally within a week or two of work. It may cover legal, operational or IT risks with different depths of analysis depending on the scope of the audit. So, either the work is limited in scope or the investigation is limited. The audit work to obtain reasonable assurance in the short term is not work on the cheap. A company often needs to have a good understanding of the risks in the case of a company takeover, to modify a strategy, to assess an active project or to seize opportunities. It is necessary to specify what is within the scope of the investigation and, above all, what is not, for what reasons or what constraints. The auditor then selects the risks and the work that must be carried out to provide an opinion quickly.

The need to obtain an opinion quickly is found in all work related to the legal evolution of a company such as mergers/acquisitions and restructurings. These audits can be carried out in a short period of time. They address a selection of the balance sheet and income statement items considered important by third parties, or assess legal, tax or IT risks, or projects critical to the future sustainability of the turnover, such as a new "digital transformation program"—quite trendy these days as ERP implementation projects decades ago. In the case of a company acquisition, the buyer may only be interested in intangible assets such as patents, trademarks, internet domain names. The work is simple because it is based on factual elements. The results are based only on elements that are stable over time. If the buyer is interested in geographical locations or personnel, these elements, although operational, are also perennial in time. If, on the other hand, the buyer is interested in technical expertise, the analysis becomes riskier. It is necessary to choose the indicators to apprehend the risk of losing this expertise such as the current attrition rate and possible future attrition rate. In the extreme case of the scarcity of a technical expertise, the financial valuation of the company is based more on its talents, its technical expertise than on the products designed.

We can take the classic example of the "New United Motor Company" plant set up by Toyota in 1984 as a joint venture with General Motors. This production plant was closed by General Motors two years earlier, in 1982.

> GM provided the plant. Toyota provided the production methodology. The ownership was 50:50, but Toyota was in charge of day-to-day operations... we agreed to hire back people who had been laid off from the plant.
>
> [KSH]

Almost all professionals considered Toyota's strategy, if not doomed to failure, at least extremely risky, since the former employees were stakeholders in the reputation of this plant, which was considered the least efficient in the United States for General Motors. But Toyota was confident in its ability to implement lean management and had negotiated agreements with the United Automobile Workers Union to facilitate the implementation of this new culture. The risks identified about resources give rise to another type of highly targeted audit, the social audit. They address the legal risks of social legislation. All aspects of the company can benefit from this type of intervention which have a limited scope. If, regardless of the size of the scope of analysis, the amount of data is significant, specific techniques are of interest to limit the duration of the work by either reducing with proxies the amount of data to be analyzed or automating the analysis work while ensuring reasonable assurance for the auditor. To form an opinion, the International Standards on Auditing require the auditor to obtain reasonable assurance that the financial statements, taken as a whole, are free of material misstatement, whether due to fraud or error. Reasonable assurance is a high level of assurance. This level of assurance is obtained when the auditor has obtained sufficient appropriate audit evidence to reduce the audit risk to an acceptably low level (audit risk is the risk that the auditor expresses an inappropriate opinion when the financial statements are materially misstated.) However, reasonable assurance is not an absolute level of assurance. There are inherent limitations in an audit that result from the fact that most of the audit evidences on which the auditor reaches conclusions and bases his or her opinion leads more to presumptions than to certainties. So how do we quickly form an opinion? An auditor can rarely be certain (not thinking here about a man-and-dad business) of the validity of the financial statements. However, the auditor must obtain sufficient relevant and reliable audit evidence to form a reasonable basis for the opinion. Please we assume nevertheless here that the auditor is able to call a bank and ask for the validity of the amounts recorded in the ledgers (cf. Wirecard fraud).

There are two complementary approaches. The first is to ensure the consistency of the quantity, location, and selection of controls, and the second is to ensure that the controls are properly functioning. Auditors frequently intervene on processes that are more or less well documented, without any hindsight other than their previous experience. They will notice that the documentation is perfectible or incomplete. They will select a sample to identify the quality of the functioning of one or several control points. They very rarely come up with pragmatic requirements on the expected controls to compare with the processes and constraints of the audited entity (e.g. the size of the staff, the complexity of the business processes or the turnover). Auditors are barely if not at all involved in process redesign projects or in the development of new processes. They cannot correct the design of new processes or integrate their needs into the design. They may be rarely involved in auditing the project management prior to production/delivery.

There are two possibilities for the auditor to perform the work. The first is to reduce the scope to provide a limited but detailed opinion. The second is to keep a broad scope to assess generic risks globally. A broad scope, such as numerous information system risks, and a detailed risk analysis are incompatible with a quick audit. Of course, audit firms use this service to prove that they have met their obligations regarding the IT environment, particularly for small entities. This intermediate approach is useful for auditing companies with low turnover, simple operational processes or whose information system is not very digitalized. An additional benefit is to help sell related services because it identifies potentially risky subjects. To have an opinion on the short term is therefore only possible if the risk to be evaluated is sufficiently precise. If it is broad, the opinion is less pertinent because only a part of the controls will have been analyzed. So how to specify the risk?

The risk is either legal, operational, or technical in nature. The legal risk must be the most specific of the three because otherwise it is impossible to limit the regulatory documentation on which to rely on. Operational risk adds complexity, either because the environment in which the company operates is large and varied or because many different techniques are used. Multinationals face a complex and growing thicket of overlapping rules, laws, and cultural expectations for the same operational processes. In emerging markets, they're often unclear. The increasing automation of all operational processes is increasing the technical complexity of the processes needed to meet these requirements. Just look at the organizational impact of the Foreign Legal Use of Data Clarification Act (Cloud Act) introduced in Congress on February 6, 2018:

> A provider of electronic communication service or remote computing service shall comply with the obligations of this chapter to preserve, backup, or disclose the contents of a wire or electronic communication and any record or other information pertaining to a customer or subscriber within such provider's possession, custody, or control, regardless of whether such communication, record, or other information is located within or outside of the United States.
>
> (https://www.congress.gov/bill/115th-congress/house-bill/4943/text)

General IT process controls must in this context be fully compliant with best practices and provide what is legally required. Operational risk is easily defined in a generic way when a single process is analyzed. It often refers to the reliability of a business process as a whole, which in itself is time-consuming to audit and not feasible in a few days. In the 21st century, business processes exist only exceptionally without computer support such as complex automated machines. How can you have a reasonable assurance without considering the applications and data and the whole underlying technical infrastructure? Not taking this technical environment into account limits the scope of the opinion. Taking the example of a cash collection or invoicing process, it is possible to print or export reports and analyze them. The analysis may confirm the absence of malfunctions. But this absence of malfunctions is only valid at the time of the audit. Indeed, a bad configuration or a bad attribution of access rights, or the deployment of an application update can from one day to the next invalid the opinion. Choices must be made to carry out the work over a limited period by explicitly documenting the limitations.

Another example is the audit of the turnover of an Internet publisher. We can audit the company's financial processes and make sure they are working well. We can see if there is any growth in revenue and make guesses about the future. Part of the revenue comes from the prices of advertising spaces on their websites, prices calculated according to the traffic on the site. But:

- *As much as 50 percent of publisher traffic is bot activity—fake clicks from automated computing programs.*
- *Bots account for 11 percent of display-ad views and 23 percent of video-ad views.*
- *Digital advertising will take in $43.8 billion in 2017, $6.3 billion of which will be based on fraudulent activity.*
- *So why brands are willing to spend $6.3 billion advertising to bots? The first reason is that the current "ad tech" business is like the Wild West during the Gold Rush—filled with scammers [JTA].*

Technical risk is very difficult to study over a limited period if the scope is not reduced. One must be wary because the technical environment includes many operational processes, each of which requires time to analyze, as is the case for IT processes. Technical general controls must be deployed to ensure that automated controls function properly when they are first developed and implemented. They also help information systems function properly after they are implemented. Automated reconciliation controls will only work properly if the technical general controls are designed, implemented, and operated to ensure that the correct files are used in the reconciliation process and that they are complete and accurate. In addition, proper security limits access to the system to only those who need it, thereby reducing the possibility of unauthorized changes to the files. Activities to control any changes to the technology help ensure that the system continues to function as intended.

To form an opinion quickly, the scope of the audit must be limited and the audit criteria precise. An experienced auditor will be able to put the results into perspective both in relation to the entity's sector of activity and in relation to what has been put outside the audit scope. A recurring difficulty in auditing is when one is unable, due to lack of time or third-party validation, to test the entire population and must rely on a sample to form an opinion. The professional reference literature until recently and current practice until now has confirmed this method and opinion: "A rational basis can be obtained using either non-statistical sampling or statistical sampling, in both cases it is correctly performed." The reason it is still used quite often despite this bias is that it favors experience. Judgmental sampling is used when an auditor uses experience and prior knowledge to calculate the number of sample units and specific items to study in the population.

We are forced to move away from "truths of fact" as the philosopher Hannah Arendt calls it. Given the amount of data manipulated in the processes and the lack of reproducibility of the results, a non-statistical selection of a sample is counterproductive in several ways. Non-statistical sampling analysis uses results without a clear sequence of logical steps. There is no reference for understanding the procedures used. Without a clear understanding of how evidence and analysis are related, it is not possible to improve judgments or change procedures. It is the status quo with no reference to evolve, adapt to change, or defend the analysis, for example in court in response to a legal action.

Because non-statistical sampling analysis has no formal notion of improvement or optimization in the amount of evidence collected or in the way it is interpreted, it inevitably leads to poor instructions being given or resources being misallocated—some areas will be over-audited, and others under-audited. It will not be possible to identify whether this is the case, or even to suspect it.

Non-statistical sampling analysis alone provides no conceptual framework for teaching and communicating risk judgments. In large organizations, these are important needs. On the other hand, statistical sampling has several advantages, including a framework for understanding the processes involved, studying the analyses, and clarifying thinking. Statistical sampling improves risk analyses and provides stronger evidentiary support, as evidence is evaluated in a logically defensible manner. The formal framework facilitates not only training and education, but also the communication of analysis. They avoid the risk of unconsciously selecting a sample that will support the auditor's intuition. Therefore, it can reveal situations that may conflict with the auditor's intuition and daily common sense. This will result in hours of additional analysis.

Recent studies have demonstrated and contradicted the generally accepted view of the origin of the supporters of Nazism in Germany in the 20th century before World War II:

> Contrary to the old claims that it was the party of the countryside, or of the north, or of the middle class, the NSDAP attracted support right across Germany and right across the social spectrum. Analysis at the level of the main electoral districts misses this point and exaggerates the differences between regions. More recent research based on the smallest electoral unit (the Kreis) has revealed the extraordinary breadth of the Nazi vote.

> [NFE]

If it is not always possible to test 100% of a population, how can we define and reduce the size of the sample to be tested? By statistical sampling. A reduced sample size not only reduces the duration of the tests, but also reduces the audit costs, justifies the work method, and manages the risks more efficiently. Data analysis is an option to be able to provide better assurance in a short period of time. To ensure that this is feasible, it's better to add on top of it, artificial intelligence. Artificial intelligence should be used to provide guidance and not definite feedback. The auditor must stay in charge. Using data analysis and artificial intelligence requires the basic steps we spoke about being followed:

- Specific definition of the scope in terms of data and what is looked at,
- The collection of the data for a sufficient period of time, and
- Validated proxies to analyze the data, i.e., proxies or KPIs already in use for similar businesses. No new proxies should be used to infer conclusion. They must have been tested thoroughly before to use them live.

When leveraging artificial intelligence, the program should have been thoroughly tested and conditions of use clearly defined and shared. To achieve short term confidence, best practices, experience, and trustworthy tools must be used. In fact, this is a way to provide new services already developed, tested, and used to lead to medium- or long-term confidence. So, let's move on how to achieve medium-term confidence in the next chapter.

9.2 MEDIUM-TERM CONFIDENCE

Audit work for medium-term confidence is the cornerstone of the majority of the audits performed. That's when IT processes or tools are audited. Here auditors have to answer not highly specific questions such as for short term audits and must provide a better understanding of the overall context. What means overall context? We agree that digitalization is progressively permeating all business processes, making these processes highly dependent on the quality of information technologies in place and highly reliant on the quality of the data shared by one process to another. For a reason, audit companies started in the 80s to promote the audit of information technology general controls (ITGC). Since then, what is called ITGC nowadays as largely evolved from then to include additional topics still related to IT matters. They are still apart as different type of controls, when in fact due to the digitalization they must be part of the tools to use to audit the company's information system.

The challenge to achieve medium-term confidence is to first be happy on what is in scope is fine and second, be comfortable that it will remain as such. The first point is our legacy work-programs dealing to audit business processes to which IT controls have been added, the controls we spoke about previously such as are the processes documented, who can perform what, is the software set-up according to the design documents, such as are the management rules configured according to the specifications? Once we're happy with that, is all what the auditors have seen will remain as such or will it be maintained in a sustainable way? This second point must be looked at in two folds: Who has admin rights enabling them to bypass what the auditor is happy with for instance and are the IT processes used to enhance or update the applications correctly defined, followed and so on? Let's position all this in Figure 9.1.

The first point, "Am I happy?" is about looking at the current status, i.e., what has been surrounded in the middle of the figure. Doing so one may have a clue on how it worked looking at data. A clue only as a rule may have changed 2 or 3 months ago. All what the auditor sees is the latest implemented rule, data based on the previous rule setup may still be there in the database. The second point is about will it remain as such moving forward. The confidence can be achieved auditing what has been surrounded with dashes on the left side of the figure. Auditing the IT department processes provides understanding on how they are applied, and they can be investigated. A way to test them is to compare historical changes approved to go-live and check the data at that time, before and after being "pushed in production" as IT persons say.

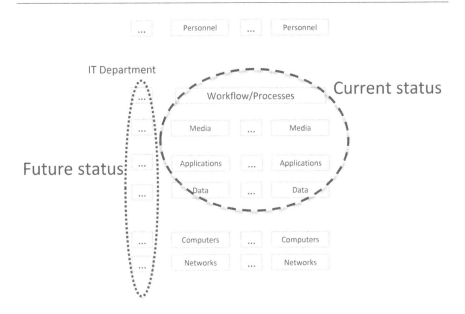

Figure 9.1 Auditing current and future status.

Auditing a business process is business as usual for auditors, and IT as we know now has added additional layers underneath what we see on screens or what is printed. With the huge amount of data available to the auditors it is mandatory to have a plan, i.e., knowing what you want to look at, to better leverage IT tools. In the 20th century, we used to select a data sample then, thanks to new tools, we started gathering all the data and used some data analysis software facilitating our life as they were keeping track on how the analysis was performed. It is worth remembering us of the different methods used at that time before checking what is happening with full data extracts.

Statistics were and are the only sustainable and reliable solution to help the auditor obtain a relevant sample, to measure the sufficiency of the evidence obtained and to evaluate the results. Relevance is related to the design and size of the sample. Statistical sampling allows auditors to measure sampling risk and therefore design sample sizes to provide sufficient evidence. When the population is large, the size of the population has a very small impact on the required sample size. Tables are available for small population sizes. They provide appropriate smaller sample sizes. The results of statistical sampling are objective and subject to the laws of probability. Therefore, the sampling risk can be quantified and controlled, and the desired degree of reliability, the confidence level, can be specified.

Sampling risk is the risk that the selected sample is not representative of the population.

The statistical sampling has the following characteristics:

- Random selection of a sample, and
- The use of probability theory to analyze the results.

There are different methods of randomly selecting a sample, such as:

- Random sampling,
- Systematic sampling, or
- Stratified sampling.

In random sampling, the assumption is that there is an equal probability of selecting each sample unit and that all possible combinations of sample units have the same probability of being included in the sample. The auditor must ensure that the selected sample is representative of the population from which it is drawn because the assumption is not verified.

Systematic sampling consists of sequencing all elements of the population. The sampling units are arranged, for example, alphabetically or numerically. The auditor divides the population into "n" equal-sized intervals based on the required sample size. A sample unit is then selected from each of the derived intervals. The selection interval is determined by dividing the population size by the required sample size.

To use stratified sampling, the auditor separates the population into homogeneous subgroups based on a common characteristic. The auditor then samples each stratum. The results of the sample must be evaluated separately and combined to provide an overall estimate of the characteristics of the population.

On what criteria should the elements of the population be identified? Three possibilities:

- Attribute sampling,
- Discovery sampling and
- Variable sampling.

Attribute sampling selects a characteristic that a component of the population has or does not have. It tests binary, yes/no, or error/no error questions. In attribute sampling, an estimate is made of the proportion of the population that contains a particular characteristic. It is based on a binomial distribution and is usually applied in compliance testing.

Discovery sampling is used in the search for critical deviations such as fraud or irregularities. It can be used when the auditor wants to determine if an acceptable rate of irregularity in the population has been exceeded.

Variable sampling applies to dollar values or other quantities, as opposed to the binary proposition tested by attribute sampling. It is used for substantive tests, which attempt to provide evidence that an account balance is materially wrong. Variable sampling consists of a family of three statistical techniques (unit-mean approach, difference sampling, and ratio sampling) that use normal distribution theory and is an approach to predicting the value of a particular variable in the population.

These methods can be leveraged in complementary ways if it is possible to have a larger sample size and more sophisticated evaluation formulas than simple or stratified sampling methods. To use them the auditor must have the mathematical basis and be trained to use them in the professional context, otherwise it leads to many errors explained in Catherine O'Neil's book "Weapons of Math Destruction," like this one:

> In statistics, this phenomenon is known as Simpson's paradox: when a whole body of data displays one trend yet when broken in sub-groups, the opposite trend comes into view for each of those subgroups.
>
> [CNE]

The automation of analysis methods in the 21st century does not guarantee the quality of its use. Therefore, the analysis of 100% of the population is still relevant. The evolution of computer processing capabilities is giving a new lease of life to this approach. What is an historical example of a 100% population audit? The annual or fixed date inventory. A practice that has existed for centuries, for valuable items:

> From the early tenth century, the Benedictines at Cluny Abbey in southeast France appointed an armarius to be in charge of the books—the armarius being responsible for the armarium, or cupboard, where the books were kept. It was his job to oversee the annual book distribution at Lent, when the monastery's collection was spread out on a carpet and each book checked against a list to ensure that nothing had gone missing over the previous twelve months.
>
> [JFL]

Time-limited inventory mobilizes many resources, usually staff with support from outside resources, over a period of a few days with extended hours. Two options are to implement a perpetual inventory or a rotating inventory. Continuous inventory is the counting of the quantities available in stock immediately after each good receipt and each good issue. The rotating inventory indicates which item is to be counted in or out of stock. The rotating inventory is the periodic and planned counting of the stocks over the year. In practice, it is a better alternative to permanent and annual inventories. With a rotating inventory, lists of classified items are provided at well-defined periods and the count of available quantities for each list is done several times during the year.

An intermediate technique between the analysis of a part and of the whole population is the carve out. Information systems produce an enormous amount of data, both through their operations and about their operations. The progressive end-to-end digitalization of all processes generates even more data such as with the deployment of connected objects. This huge amount of data exceeds the analysis capacities of paper and pencil, computer spreadsheets and dedicated tools are needed.

These data are of increasingly varied types with different characteristics, traditional data in text or digital format have been added to the so-called unstructured data such as sound, video, images and semi-structured as XML or RSS feeds. Considering this data produced rapidly in large quantities and in various forms has become a theme in its own right: Big Data. The main data analysis methods used include A/B testing, association rule learning, machine learning, and many others. As much as the company uses these techniques to generate value, the audit uses them to identify trends or outliers. Advances in data processing, particularly the evolution of the speed of data processing, will eventually make it possible to abandon sampling methods in favor of exhaustive control with the help of artificial intelligence performing deep analysis. Artificial intelligence is already used in different activities and we are indirectly subject to it. The companies leveraging these technologies will have to be compliant with new legal rules to come. In April 2021, the European Community proposed new rules, guidance, and actions for trustworthy artificial intelligence. Margaret Vestager, Executive Vice-President for a Europe fit for the Digital Age said:

> On Artificial Intelligence, trust is a must, not a nice to have.

They do so by introducing a new "Regulation of the European Parliament and of the Council on machinery products." It is a technology neutral regulation and so applies to artificial intelligence. It tries to address different current known and future risks when dealing with the digitalization of machines and subsequentially with the interaction between machines and human.

> There are a number of requirements on traditional technologies not related to new technologies that were identified either as not clear or safe enough, as too prescriptive and potentially hindering innovation.
>
> [European Commission—COM (2021) 202 final]

In the same way the General Data Protection Regulation (GDPR) was proactively governing the processing of personal data in Europe, this new regulation on artificial intelligence will impact how the companies leverage this technology to make business. It already split the usage of artificial intelligence in four areas:

- Unacceptable risk: Artificial intelligence considered a clear threat to the safety, livelihoods, and rights of people will be banned.

- High risk: Artificial intelligence used in eight specific domains:
  - Critical infrastructures,
  - Educational or vocational training,
  - Safety components of products,
  - Employment, workers management, and access to self-employment,
  - Essential private and public services,
  - Law enforcement,
  - Migration, asylum, and border control management, and
  - Administration of justice and democratic processes.
- Limited risk, and
- Minimal risk.

The EU is considering strict obligations for artificial intelligence systems before being put on the market for "high risk" related domains and highly suggest that they should be leveraged by companies for artificial intelligence systems targeting "limited risk" areas. Does it mean that auditors will need to totally rewrite their work programs? Well, which are these obligations?

- *Adequate risk assessment and mitigations systems,*
- *High quality of the datasets feeding the system to minimize risks and discriminatory outcomes,*
- *Logging of activity to ensure traceability of results,*
- *Detailed documentation providing all information necessary on the system and its purpose for authorities to assess its compliance,*
- *Clear and adequate information to the user,*
- *Appropriate human oversight measures to minimize risks, and*
- *High level of robustness, security and accuracy.*

It seems auditors will have to be careful not to overlook artificial intelligence systems on an IT point of view. The IT related obligations above are either standard IT controls or points of attention we spoke about in the previous chapters, including this one emphasizing the risk related to how the system has been tested and traceability on how it works. It's a confirmation that artificial intelligence systems are systems as others for auditors. They have to comply with the classic IT audit controls.

For the management of the company as for auditors, medium-term confidence is critical. It essentially concerns the operational and human aspects of the company's processes, considering internal control and operational risks. This work provides confidence over the next 6–12 months. In an ideal world, controls have been chosen upfront to cover the risks (cf. next Chapter 10 "Risks management"). In addition, procedures have been drawn up to ensure that the controls are working properly and that they are applied. Each control implemented in the operational processes or not allows to cover more than one risk, such as the legal and compliance risk, the operational risk, and the technical and IT risk. The work program should take that in scope.

9.3 LONG-TERM CONFIDENCE

Where lies the difference for auditors between medium-term confidence and long-term confidence? Medium-term confidence is highly related to the internal control efficiency. Internal control is a system defined and implemented by the company under its responsibility. As we saw, it comprises a set of resources, procedures, and actions specific to each company to:

- Support the control of its activities, the effectiveness of its operations and the efficient use of its resources, and
- Take appropriate account of significant operational, financial, and compliance risks.

More specifically, it aims to ensure that the company:

- Is compliant with laws and regulations,
- Internal instructions and communications, particularly from top management, are followed by the employees and third parties
- The business processes are applied and not circumvented, and
- Financial information is reliable.

As a result, what auditors call internal control is therefore not limited to accounting and financial processes alone.

What it does not cover, is all initiatives taken by the governing bodies or management, such as defining the company's strategy, setting objectives, making management decisions, dealing with risks, or monitoring performance. Being confident about the long term is something investors are highly interested in. They like to have medium term confidence of course (cf. the quarterly investors meetings) but are actually extremely worried about how a company will sustain its turnover or growth or be resilient to the technology changes. A Gen-Z manager won't know about Blackberry Limited smartphones. It will even be hard to find a Gen-Y manager who remember them.

> $500 fully subsidized with a plan! I said that is the most expensive phone in the world and it doesn't appeal to business customers because it doesn't have a keyboard, which makes it not a very good email machine ... I like our strategy. I like it a lot ...
>
> (Steve Ballmer speaking about the first iPhone™,
> Microsoft CEO, 17 January 2007)

This was only 14 years ago. Who remembers that smartphones used to have a tiny keyboard? Two risks that concern all companies are either to remain on the same operating modes or to think that the environment, the Business to Business relations will not evolve. This last point is precisely described by Jonathan Taplin who explains how digital technology has changed the economic environment of music. More particularly, how the discourse held by entrepreneurs did not correspond to what happened:

> The techno-utopians like Alexis Ohanian told us that the Internet would kill all the gatekeepers. But what's really happened is that a new set of gatekeepers-Google and Facebook-has replaced the old.
>
> [JTA]

Also, investors always wonder about the durability of a company when the founder, nicknamed the charismatic leader, decides to sell, or leave his company. Everyone then makes assumptions and projections based only on the people who could eventually replace him, as during the succession of Steve Jobs at the head of Apple Inc. While this is of interest for investor, it is difficult to audit that for auditors even if they have to identify risks impacting the future of the company such as a contract not correctly written or financial engagements reducing the capacity of the company to handle unexpected market conditions (resiliency)—think about Evergrande current challenges in 2020 and 2021 for instance. Long-term confidence is necessary not only for the company's management and third parties, but also for the employees. It concerns not only the operational and human aspects of the company's processes, but also the technical aspects. This work provides confidence over the next 12–18 months at most. Confidence is necessary for business, but above all for its continuity. Long before the Dutch East India Company took over the monopoly of trade in India, Lisbon set up the House of India in the 16th century to manage its trade with India. Philip II left it the monopoly after the annexation of Portugal to the Kingdom of Spain. To prevent other nations from learning about the lucrative nature of this trade, the House of India avoided publishing anything about what was happening in India, both financially and organizationally.

Portugal installed a viceroy to head the local government in India. He managed both civil and military affairs. His powers were limited, which limited the risks, and he reported in detail to Europe upon his return, which allowed for precise control of the management of trade. But even with these controls or constraints, the position of governor was very interesting. So much so that when Afonso de Albuquerque came to replace Francisco de Almeida as Viceroy of the Indies, he was imprisoned by the latter, who refused to return to his office. Three months later, a fleet from Portugal freed Albuquerque. Upon his death on December 16, 1515, the king, concerned about the dangers and temptations in a rich and very remote region, decided to change viceroys every three years. He therefore added another control to the office.

The long-term trust of the king was based on three key elements, detailed accounts provided by the viceroy, limited powers, and a shortened term of office. The shortened term was instituted because the king could no longer have the same confidence in the new viceroys. They appointed them for a period of three years with processes that remained unchanged, as they had always allowed him to be assured of the proper functioning of local government through detailed accounts.

How successful were these new arrangements? Null and even counterproductive, they facilitated the takeover of trade by the Dutch East India Company. The viceroys had only three years to build up their personal fortunes. They modified or took advantage of the local functioning (processes) to become rich at the expense of a long-term management that would not have penalized the management of military affairs. Incorrect solutions to problems can easily put at risk the company. What looks like an obvious decision is not and what does not look like can be effective.

> Successful crime reduction can come in a variety of forms. In 1980, for example, West Germany made it mandatory for motorcyclists to wear helmets. Over the next six years, motorcycle thefts fell by two thirds. The reason was simple: inconvenience. Thieves could no longer decide to steal a motorcycle on the spur of the moment. Instead, they'd have to plan ahead and carry a helmet around. A few years earlier, the Netherlands and Great Britain had introduced similar helmet laws. Both had also seen a massive drop in thefts, showing how social norms can influence crime rates.
>
> [AKU]

This difference between short- and long-term management is also present in the management of companies according to the distribution and types of shareholders or whether the capital is listed on the stock exchange or not. Long-term confidence, at most 18 months, is very difficult to obtain. Not only must robust and reliable business processes be put in place, but also the probability of imponderables must be considered. A company lives and changes over time, such as the increase in its turnover, the extension of its market to new geographical areas, the purchase of companies, the resale of sites. But it is always necessary to monitor the evolution of the company and the competition.

Physical components (e.g. infrastructure) and intangible elements such as business strategy, controls, or process speed changes become outdated or obsolete. The obsolescence here has less to do with the deterioration or state of disrepair due to time than with the inadequacy of the means used due to the evolution of technologies. For example, how credible are the speeches made by CEOs and their right-hand men at shareholders' meetings? The CEO will claim that the company he manages has a strong innovation strategy that facilitates the creation of new products or services. But is the technical infrastructure able to support this strategy? Is it possible that the applications used are so poorly managed or poorly interfaced that the company's operations and processes get stuck or that the numbers accumulated in the accounts are far from reality?

Increasing the production of a product impacts the processes. It is not always physically possible to expand a site or increase production; climate change and the impact of the terrain also have an impact. We are in the first quarter of the 21st century, but distance is still a strong management constraint for an international company. The means of communication solve only a part of the constraints, those linked to the quasi-instantaneousness of information transport. The possibility of printing in 3 dimensions should make it possible to limit this geographical constraint.

Should 19th-century infrastructures (e.g. roads) be maintained, modernized (e.g. sea lanes with tankers) or supplemented with new infrastructures (drones)? The increasing digitalization and the availability of information on all business processes completely change our relationship to reality. Don't key indicators or dashboards condition us to react and analyze automatically as time goes by, while the context, the world around the company has changed? The execution of the company's strategy and, more prosaically, of its processes, production, and invoicing, depends on the employees and the environment in which they operate. The possibility of going on strike is a more or less important risk depending on the country where the company's sites are located. The more or less strong rules of law or international relations reduce the relevance of financial forecasts.

In an ideal world, an effective system of internal control provides management and the board of directors with reasonable assurance regarding achievement of an entity's objectives. The term "reasonable assurance" rather than "absolute assurance" acknowledges that limitations exist in all systems of internal control, and that uncertainties and risks may exist, which no one can confidently predict with precision. Absolute assurance is not possible. Long-term confidence can't be achieved if medium-term confidence is not. That's the reason why COSO considers that the control environment concerns the involvement of the organization as a whole, from the involvement of the board of directors to the accountability of individuals. If the board of directors is actually involved, they should be careful on what they think the solutions to be to improve business turn-over or avoid operational challenges.

We hear frequently the word agile (we look at this word and its impact on auditing in Chapter 11 "Information system audit strategy"), if it should be used, it should be used to gain long-term confidence. Why? Because of the fact that 21st-century information systems are highly digitalized. Following information technologies progress and their use, has been a sine qua non-condition for any company wanting to follow the trend and leverage IT as soon as possible. Along that trend, new words became new buzzwords with the intention to deliver fast. The risk to follow fast when designing a business process is that other criteria might be forgotten such as security. Of course, the faster a process is and the more secure its internal control, the more beneficial it is in terms of maximizing the use of capital and the relevance of the solutions implemented. Trends permeate the organization and create risks the auditors should be conscious of while reading the quarterly company documents shared with the investors.

When Charles Perrow wrote his book "Normal accidents" [CPE] in 1984, he took as examples for his analysis complex technological systems such as nuclear plants, chemical plants, aircraft, airways, and marine accidents. He identifies three common characteristics that make a system likely to be susceptible to what he calls "Normal Accidents":

- The system is complex,
- The system is tightly coupled, and
- The system has catastrophic potential.

Don't you think that these three conditions apply to information systems? The information system is complex and the bigger and international the company is the more complex it is. Information systems are already and will be more coupled than not. More coupled or linked internally as digitalization doesn't leave any space without information technologies but also more coupled externally with third parties for instance, just look at the trend for things "as a service" or cloud-based services or all the tiny pieces of information technologies with every trivial piece of hardware, having them connected to the company's network. The information systems have catastrophic potential, this one is for us pretty obvious now. Catastrophic potential for instance because of business processes blocked due to piracy or because of the potential impact on the community, such as automated health management systems. To assess these three characteristics, the auditor must be provided with high-level documents of the information systems supporting architecture at levels as summarized in Figure 9.2.

On the right side of the figure from bottom to top, we have two basic documents, one describing the architecture of the infrastructure and the second one listing the applications portfolio. The architecture of the infrastructure and the applications portfolio are rather used or understood as static documents, some color must be added, for the infrastructure landscape, having a map with some additional man-made infrastructure information such as the roads, the railways tracks or the sizes of the cities. For the applications landscape, adding the services provided by an application, such as who's in charge, with what it communicates with, the costs associated with it. So, this is mandatory for a Chief Information Officer to have, not having it, would be like a Chief Executive Officer without accounting documents. But all this doesn't explain how the resources are used, how critical each of them is for the company. The purpose of the document called "urbanization" is an analogy

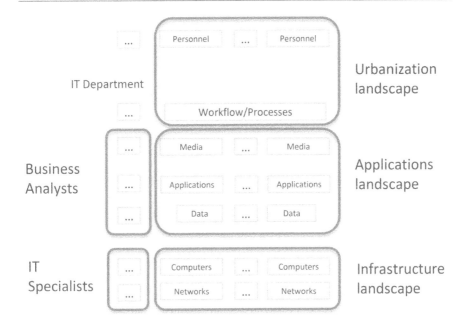

Figure 9.2 High level information system documents.

of the additional information required by an official to perform her/his duties, from the mayor to the president of the state. It shows how the resources are used by the employees and which ones are part of the most profitable revenue streams. It is highly practical for auditors also to have these documents. Of course, they must be maintained in a timely manner. In a snapshot, discrepancies or inadequacies are easily identified such as are the applications' items being part of the most profitable workflow supported by a low-risk infrastructure? But it is quite interesting also to match the applications and the infrastructure information with the persons maintaining them. Are they internal, external, third parties? If internal, are the IT specialists well trained and are the applications and infrastructure items well documented? (remember the Configuration Management database [CMDB]).

Easy then to compare the business strategy with the IT strategy and identify gaps or areas of concern for the auditor. Next step is to leverage all this information with the risk's analysis (Chapter 10) and then to detail the audit strategy where it is more helpful (Chapter 11).

BIBLIOGRAPHY

AKU: Adam Kucharski, *"The Rules of Contagion,"* 2020, Profile Books Ltd, 978-1-7881-6019-3

CAN: Christopher Andrew, *"The Secret World,"* 2018, Allen Lane, 978-0-553-41881-1

CNE: Cathy O'Neil, *"Weapons of Math Destruction,"* 2016, Crown, 978-0-553-41881-1

CPE: Charles Perrow, *"Normal Accidents: Living with High-Risk Technologies,"* 1999, Princeton University Press; Revised edition, 978-0691004129

JFL: Judith Flanders, *"A Place for Everything,"* 2020, Picador, 978-1-5098-8159-8

JTA: Jonathan Taplin, *"Move Fast and Break Things,"* 2017, Hachette Book Group Inc., 978-0-316-27574-3

KSH: Koichi Shimokawa, *"The Birth of Lean,"* 2009, Koichi Shimokawa and Takahiro Fujimoto, 978-1-934-10922-9

NFE: Niall Ferguson, *"The Square and the Tower,"* 2017, Penguin Random House UK, ISBN 978-0-141-98482-7

Chapter 10

Risks management

> Risk: A dollar amount which tells how bad it could be if everything fails.
>
> Paul A. Strassmann, *The Politics of Information Management*

The company defines the perimeter of activities for which the employer pools profits and risks and for which it is responsible in this respect. The unity and continuity of this perimeter were first seen in accounting, but the standardization of accounts, from the second half of the 20th century onward, has changed this. Accounting now favors the splitting up of the company, the uncoupling of profits and risks. The first form of this fragmentation is spatial. The perimeter of the firm is disappearing as a place of mutualization, to make way for a collection of units placed in competition with one another in a growing permeability between the inside and the outside.

The second form of this fragmentation, perhaps even more serious in its consequences, is played out in time. Until then, accounting aimed to inscribe the disposition of goods in a genealogical order, because through the way in which each generation works, it is society as a whole that plays out its existence and the conditions of its possible recommencement. Accounting thus inscribed the activity of the company in time, or more precisely in a plurality of interlocking and interrelated times. This function is undermined by the adoption of the principle of independence of accounting periods when this independence is considered as a reality and no longer as a fiction. This slicing up of the life of the company into units of equal and autonomous duration now leads to the disassociation of short and long time periods.

Risks do not follow any dedicated calendar. Risks comes in and out of scope depending on the environment and the different decisions, choices made by the top management to the employees throughout time. Risks must be managed on a regularly basis. Risk management consists of

> coordinated activities to direct and control an organization with regard to risk.

> [ISO 31000:2018]

DOI: 10.1201/9781003230137-10

All the activities are described in the ISO 31000 standard and it is not worth describing, paraphrasing its content but saying that

> the purpose of the risk management framework is to assist the organization in integrating risk management into significant activities and functions. The effectiveness of risk management will depend on its integration into the governance of the organization, including decision-making. This requires support from stakeholders, particularly top management.

> [ISO 31000:2018]

This chapter is about risks management and the information system. Out of scope, but highly influential in the risks analysis is the legal structure and organization of the company. Here is an example from the 15th century provided by Katherine Pistor:

> The Medici business included textile manufacturing, with far-flung operations that crisscrossed Europe ... Each line of business and each local was organized as a separate partnership with its own books and accounts. The senior partnership in Florence entered into separate agreements with junior partners who managed the operations... Every partnership had to send its profit back to the parent partnership in Florence ... and it had to close it books at least once a year and send them to Florence for auditing... A purchaser of textiles from the London offshoot of the Medici empire brought a case against the partnership in Bruges for breach of contract in 1453... claiming that the entire business empire of the Medici was in fact "one company and had the same master." The court dismissed the argument, stating that the merchant had contracted with the junior partnership in London, which therefore was first in line to account for the merchant's losses.

> [KPI]

Risks were used in the previous chapters as example to show what can happen if controls or processes are not in place. This is the time now to focus on the risks and the way we grouped them in Chapter 3, in Figure 3.5, and updated it in the Figure 10.1.

There are the four intersections demanding in-depth analysis:

1. Legal risks impacting operations and reverse operational risks impacting legal ones,
2. Legal risks impacting information technology (IT) and reverse IT risks impacting legal ones,
3. Operational risks impacting IT and reverse IT risks impacting operational ones, and
4. The most complex part: Legal risks impacting both operations and IT, Operational risks impacting legal and IT, IT risks impacting legal and operations.

Figure 10.1 Risks interdependencies updated.

It expresses a different message than the previous figure, having legal risks impacting operations and IT (①,②, and ④), then the operational risks vs. the IT risks induced by the structure of the layers (③). For the scope of this book, we have an information system point of view and are more interested by the intersections ②, ③, and ④. These are the reasons why we start with risks at the company level and follow with the risks at the operations and IT levels. A common characteristic of all the risks is that their perception by the top management and the employees varies along the time, and it does so because of the current company's ecosystem and its context. We may use an analogy saying that the information system is an ecosystem, there are internal interactions between the different actors but also with the company's environment:

• Handling the environment changes is being proactively part of all the regulatory bodies such what the main audit companies do, and
• Creating environment changes is having a company applying the "break things and move fast" idea reflecting what's happening instead of how the motto is usually presented "move fast and break things."

We may also leverage the overall structure we used previously from personnel "down" to networks adding the three groups of risks, as shown in Figure 10.2.

10.1 ENTERPRISE RISKS

An enterprise is characterized by its legal structure, its organization, the products, and services sold and other key information. The enterprise's strategy defines how with this information, it will achieve new financial results.

At the strategic level, an enterprise can decide to grow externally. A company grows also by expanding its geographic coverage, starting business in countries for which the C and B level management doesn't have experience and the business processes might not have been designed with them in mind. Consider the example of Avon Products Inc. The SEC found it guilty of violations of U.S. federal law after an investigation that began in 2011.

Figure 10.2 Another way to represent risks interdependencies.

Avon Products, Inc. is listed on the New York Stock Exchange. The violations occurred in China in 2004 and 2005. The internal auditors found that there were malfunctions at the end of 2005. It was not until 2008 that Avon investigated allegations made by a whistleblower to its CEO. Avon Products, Inc. is charged with failing to maintain its financial statements in sufficient detail to fairly reflect transactions and failing to implement sufficient internal controls to provide reasonable assurance and prepare a balance sheet and income statement in accordance with generally accepted accounting principles. Internal audit is found guilty in 2008. Avon must pay $300 million in legal and other costs, including $135 million, for paying bribes and offering gifts to Chinese officials. Avon had already spent tens of millions of dollars on its own international investigations. Three executives were terminated in May 2011, including the region's CFO. The CFO leaves his position in November 2011. The CEO resigns from her position in early 2012. This is a typical business case we all aware of when dealing with third parties. External growth looks also familiar because it is focused on the synergies between companies and potential benefits or costs reductions. We are familiar also because

the record levels of deal-making, both in terms of deal volumes and values, continued from late 2020 into the first six months of 2021.

[PwC]

Buying a company is a priori not related to an IT risk. Unfortunately, even if initially, due diligences were performed successfully and even if operationally, all goes fine and the merger or an acquisition looks successful, it might be not. Marriott International announced on November 30, 2018:

> On September 8, 2018, Marriott received information that an alert from an internal security tool was related to an attempt to access the Starwood guest reservation database. Marriott quickly engaged leading security experts to help determine what occurred. Marriott learned during the investigation that there had been unauthorized access to the Starwood network since 2014. Marriott recently discovered that an unauthorized party had copied and encrypted information and took steps towards removing it. On November 19, 2018, Marriott was able to decrypt the information and determined that the contents were from the Starwood guest reservation database.

Marriott International, on November 15, 2015, had signed a merger agreement with Starwood. The following two years a project took place to retire Starwood reservation system and move all into Marriott's reservation system. During the investigations, experts mandated by Marriott found that, there were evidences of an unauthorized party on the Starwood network since July 2014, and that, in 2015 and 2016, an attacker had likely created a copy of two tables, which the attacker later deleted.

This example shows two key things, a simple one and an obvious one, both overlooked. A company decision must be reviewed against information system implications. It is consistent with the fact that every business is reliant on IT and the more the information system is digitalized, the more IT risks increase. A company business depends on IT meaning that due diligences should not only include IT general controls to audit but also key information system risks to investigate. If it can't be done before the signature of the agreement it should be performed shortly after when all information is accessible.

One of the reasons proposed by Cordelia Fine is:

> Risk researchers have also found that both knowledge and familiarity in a particular domain reduces perceptions of risk.

[CFI]

As the poet Wallace Stevens wrote:

> You must become an ignorant man again.
> And see the sun again with an ignorant eye
> And see it clearly in the idea of it.

[WST]

At the company level it is worth having a Chief Risk Officer overseeing risks management and reporting to the top management and not the audit committee.

Three main reasons for that, the Chief Risk Officer is a CEO adviser, she/he is a supplier of information to the audit team such as for the overall risks analysis and actions plans to monitor them, and the Internal Audit is independent from the CEO and reports to the Audit Committee. The bigger the company is, the bigger the amount of work for the Chief Risk Officer. Therefore, the risk analysis could be done locally and then compiled. For the compilation, the risks must be grouped together in the proposed three categories (legal, operations, technical) and the impact of a risk on a site (the simplest entity within the company) must be evaluated in relation to the group.

> From the standpoint of an institution, the existence of a risk manager has less to do with actual risk reduction than it has to do with the impression of risk reduction. Philosophers since Hume and modern psychologists have been studying the concept of epiphenomenalism, or when one has the illusion of cause-and-effect. Does the compass move the boat? By "watching" your risks, are you effectively reducing them or are you giving yourself the feeling that you are doing your duty?
>
> [NNT]

Auditors used to assess financial risks when understanding the business model and the current economic environment. Then while preparing the audit plan, areas of concerns or risks were identified particularly for the main operations. Then IT risks were added to the scope, thanks to the digitalization cybersecurity became an area of concern. So, if the company has a Chief Risk Officer what he delivers should be tested. First to ensure that the top management is not misguided with incorrect risks management policies and second for the auditors to leverage the deliverables as input when working on the audit strategy (more in the next chapter). There is another way, an indirect one, to have a better understanding of the enterprise risks. A well-known consequence of enterprise risks is the insurance costs and the insurance coverage, costs depending on history and the type of activity for instance and coverage because some enterprise risks can't be insured or at an expensive cost. Insurance companies have their own constraints of course but it is interesting for the auditors to compare the risk heatmap provided by the Chief Risk Officer with the feedback from the contracted insurance companies. It is wise to leverage all the information available to assess the risks, starting with the Chief Risk Officer and the Insurance information. Depending on the duties of the Chief Risk Officer not all the scope required to prepare Information System Audit Strategy might not be there. In regards of the insurance companies, if a selection has been made between different companies, all the results are valuable not only the ones from the contracted companies. All these companies may have different point of view about the risks faced by the company and their criticality, plus some actions plans to reduce these risks. The risks for which the company has contracted an insurance will help decrease the criticality of a risk. All this is represented in Figure 10.3.

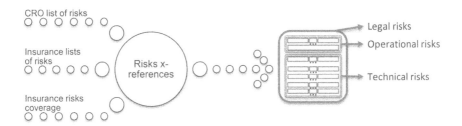

Figure 10.3 Leveraging risks' information.

On the left all the input available regarding risks, then some work to be done to group and compare the risks to achieve, at the left side, with a matrix of risks split between legal, operational, and technical risks. Of course, links between risks should be mentioned too. Even if the result at the end of the exercise looks pretty nice, it is worth interviewing the top management to have their opinion on what they consider as risks and being at risks. This will provide additional context to the result. This is common practice for auditors as it is for other companies in different fields:

> ArTactic, a London-based art-market research and advisory company founded in 2001, does not claim to predict but digests and analyses publicly available information about particular artists and their work, including auction results, as well as exhibition histories and important collections. They produce "risk ratings" and publish a "Heatmap" based on a survey of two hundred collectors, advisors, dealers, and auction-house experts (sounds familiar?), who are asked to rate their "feelings" about the markets for specific artists as either positive, neutral, or negative.
>
> [MFI]

As our scope is information systems, how cyber risks are managed is of great importance and should be checked by auditors. Great importance because it is a huge business for insurance companies, and it is critical to companies turn-over.

> It is forecast that the European cyber insurance market will grow exponentially between 2020 and 2030, doubling in size between 2020 and 2025. On average, growth rates between each year are said to be around 20 percent. These high growth rates are not due to the ever-increasing reliance on data and technology in business operations, but also reflect the less-mature nature of the European market compared to the United States. Generally, cyber insurance is designed to protect businesses from risks arising from the use of data and technology in business operations.
>
> [Statista Research Department—2020]

Furthermore, investments by businesses in their own cyber security may also lead to more demand for cyber insurance, as potential clients become more aware of the cyber risks involved, while a certain level of cyber maturity would facilitate the process of obtaining residual cyber insurance coverage (as it reduces potential moral hazard and information asymmetries between the insurer and the client).

[EIO]

In 2018, the Financial Stability Board published a cyber lexicon for the national financial authorities and international standard-setting bodies, for them to share a common understanding of cyber terms. It has been developed based on the various bodies dealing with risks. Let's leverage three definitions:

Cyber security:

- *Preservation of confidentiality, integrity, and availability of information and/or information systems through the cyber medium. In addition, other properties, such as authenticity, accountability, non-repudiation, and reliability can also be involved.*
  Source: Adapted from ISO/IEC 27032:2012.

Cyber risk:

- *The combination of the probability of cyber incidents occurring and their impact.*
  Source: Adapted from CPMI-IOSCO, ISACA Fundamentals (definition of "Risk") and ISACA Full Glossary (definition of "Risk").

Cyber incident:

- *A cyber event that:*
  - *jeopardizes the cyber security of an information system or the information the system processes, stores or transmits, or*
  - *violates the security policies, security procedures or acceptable use policies, whether resulting from malicious activity or not.*
  Source: Adapted from NIST (definition of "Incident").

The definition of cyber security encompasses information and information systems. Information equals data in this book and information systems all the digitalized information system of a company. The funny thing is that if any object (cyber medium) is used to protect whatever asset of the company such as a warehouse, an agency, as soon as it is connected to the internet or the company network it will de facto be part of the digitalized information systems of the company and will have to be monitored, therefore audited.

To make it short cyber risks are part of the high level or companywide enterprise risks analysis. They could have been moved to the technical risks, but their impact is not limited to local assets, they can disrupt the all company business. You have already read a lot of such impacts in the news. They rank for the first time in the yearly Allianz survey

> as the top peril for companies globally in the 2020 Allianz Risk Barometer for the first time after receiving 39% of responses from more than 2,700 risk management experts in over 100 countries and territories—the largest number of respondents ever. Seven years ago, cyber risk ranked only 15th with just 6% of responses.
>
> [ALZ]

The usual coverage proposed by insurance companies are:

- Data restoration,
- Cyber theft,
- Third party loss,
- System clean-up costs,
- Electronic data incident,
- Cyber extorsions,
- Administrative investigation and penalties,
- Network interruption,
- First responses, and
- Extra expenses.

As cyber risks are critical, prevention is key to avoid cyber incidents and be prepared to act as soon as it is taking place:

- First actions must be the right ones including the traceability of what has been done before and after the incident,
- Knowing actual company's geographical exposure is key as it implies many regulators and many cultures, and
- Company's data is growing fast and could be growing faster than company's ability to handle it. Processes around data management, their location, and their accessibility in particular should be well defined.

We usually read these actions with the company in mind. Let's look at them from the hacker seat:

- The more the preparation of the theft is taking time, the more a hacker should avoid traceability,
- Geographical implementation of the company must be leveraged by a hacker, by selecting an easy target on a technical point of view but also starting the theft from a state not legally bound with the state of the headquarters of the company and ideally also as a hacker be located in a state not bound either of none of them, and

- The geographical spread of IT enhanced objects is an opportunity as they may not be designed to handle the data growth either transmitting or storing it.

So, knowing where the vulnerabilities of the company are and managing the risks involved are mandatory. All this requires planification, time and actual investigations, analysis, and assessment—of accounts, people, communication, events, data—all governed by complex, technical and ever-changing rules across multiple jurisdictions. The information system auditor should check upfront if it is done. If not, it is a lack of management oversight and the auditors will have to build by themselves such a risks heatmap. Legal risks can also have a big impact on the company, from the overall company down to the technical elements of the information system. At the company level, legal risks look more like constraints to be aware of. There are two main areas of interest, compliance with regulations and contractual agreements related to technologies leveraged by the information system, such as a contract with a "cloud" provider. The contracts must ensure that the company's duties in regards of compliance with regulations and IT best practices are explicitly taken care of by the supplier when outsourced.

To summarize a yearly risks analysis at the company level should be performed. It provides an overall map of the risks used when looking at operations and technical risks. Two types of risks requiring not only a significant amount of work but also a relevant risk analysis with the reasons why some risks are audited, and others are not.

10.2 OPERATIONAL RISKS

We presented operational risks already at a high level in Chapter 5 and further in Chapter 7.1 with regards to unintentional acts. They are either directly related to the digitalization of the processes or indirectly related to how operational processes are monitored. An example of indirectly related ones is when some metrics used to monitor a process become indicators, good enough proxies to revenues. We took the example of the "fake clicks" indicator being used to increase ad-revenues, but this is not new at all:

> With the potential dollar value of television' attention harvest becoming so obvious, any pretenses to a higher purpose that broadcasting once had were ending quickly. Now it was clear, as an economist put it, that "programs are scheduled interruptions of marketing bulletins." The trend was exacerbated by another increased quantification. The networks began to consider audience attention their "inventory," which was sold using metrics like "gross rating points or GRP," a formula that estimated the likelihood of people seeing the advertising at least once (the cumulative audience), and the frequency with which the advertising played.

[TWU]

Therefore, auditors shouldn't be shy asking questions being afraid not to understand the answers because of the current technical verbiage that might be used. By the way too much verbiage should be considered as a sign of something being hidden. Again, IT is what it is, and new buzzwords will be used but they are only masquerading old requirements or intentions. It is key for auditors to ensure that the indicators used to generate revenues are valid or making sense, and also check if the indicators are not misled.

Another example from Netflix announcing on October 19, 2021:

> Later in the year, we will shift to reporting on hours viewed for our titles rather than the number of accounts that choose to watch them. There is some difference in rankings, as you see below, but we think engagement as measured by hours viewed is a slightly better indicator of the overall success of our titles and member satisfaction. It also matches how outside services measure TV viewing and gives proper credit to rewatching.

When you are a young startup, it is better to communicate on the number of accounts—who watched for 2 minutes minimum a title—instead of number of hours per title.

The main impact on operational processes by the digitalization is that managing operational risks requires more rigor and preparation. We have noticed that when emphasizing the importance of workflow design documentation to manage segregation of duties risks. It was a good start, let's go deeper in this topic. There are two main types of operational risks to be managed, the user access management and the business rules management. Other operational risks should have a legal or technical root cause-quite often mainly technical are dealt with in the respective chapters.

In regards of user access management, core principles should be guiding all the efforts:

- "Categorization" and "classification"—clearly categorize and value all data and processing resources and enable the status of each resource to be correctly "labeled."
- "Least privilege"—provide the least amount of access necessary for a given user to complete their business role.
- "Need to know"—provide access to systems and information only where there is a need for the recipient of such access to have it.
- "Controlled access"—define procedures to monitor, enable and disable access methods, and enforce security policy at all access points.

Once guiding principles have been defined for a company, the next step is to define the processes needed for user access management, key processes are

- User provisioning—requesting, establishing, and issuing user accounts,
- User de-provisioning—closing user accounts,

- Access change management—adding or removing access from an existing user account,
- User-access audit and review, and
- Access-breach detection—processes to support the identification of access breaches.

Before focusing on user, we should also make the distinction between current or common accesses and privileged accesses. Common accesses are the ones we think of when not being an IT person and privileged accesses are the ones granted to IT people. Privileged access is any access where the user can bypass established system controls. This would include, but is not limited to, database administrator (DBA), network and system administrators and default ("root") operating system administrator accounts. Synthetized in Figure 10.4 are the usual ways to look at common and privileged accesses.

So, what should be done at least for user access management, either common or privileged accesses?

User provisioning is a critical process, quite often people have a huge tendency trying to bypass it for simple reasons such as the requester is late starting the process or the process requiring more time than expected by the requester—the process could be actually wrongly designed. A formal user registration process should incorporate the following:

- The HR department should initiate the process for all employees and at least in validation of the user access for any other end-users.

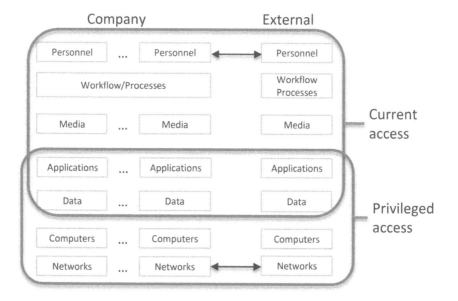

Figure 10.4 Common and privileged access.

- Authorization of access by the relevant system owners via a formalized and documented process,
- Acknowledgement by users of their understanding and acceptance of the conditions of their access to the relevant information and systems,

A user access form is valid if approved/signed by:

- The HR department,
- The user's manager,
- The system owners, and
- The IT department.

It looks complex, but it is not—well, it depends how it has been implemented. Common situations are that frequently, the HR department considers that it does not have to be involved in the requests for consultants who work on a regular basis. Also, standard "login/password" requests are directly move to the end-user computing department, and it provides access on the faith that it has been asked. These are two operational risks to be checked by auditors. HR should know who's working for the company either be directly (employees) or indirectly involved (contractors, third parties). The different types of persons working for the company should be defined as the workflow for the request approval. The user access management provisioning always involves two parties, the department requesting and the IT department providing actual access to the information system. There is de facto a transfer of responsibility from the user' department to the IT department. The IT department should only provide access to a person based on a valid request, one which has been through all along the user provisioning process. The consecutive process to be designed is the user de-provisioning. A formal user de-registration process should incorporate the following:

- De-authorization of access by the relevant system owners via a formalized and documented process,
- The HR department should initiate the process for all employees and at least be in copy if not the initiator for all other end-users, and
- A user access form is valid if approved/signed by:
  - The HR department,
  - The user's manager,
  - The system owners, and
  - The IT department.

The third user access management process to be designed is the user access change process. When staff change roles within the organization, or the nature of their involvement changes (e.g. from a contractor to an employee), there is a need to automatically review their authorization and access capabilities across the organization.

User access change management is about:

- Adding or removing access from an existing user account, and
- Reviewing access rights to update/revoke before a user changes job roles or leaves the organization.

User access management and accounts should be regularly audited and reviewed to detect incorrect access privileges. All user-access profiles should be subject to the following reviews, coordinated by the Information Security Manager:

- Review of all user-access rights by the system owners on a periodic basis,
- Review of all privileged (e.g. administrative) access rights by the system owners on a periodic basis, and
- Regular monitoring by the system administrators of access activity to identify and remove inactive or redundant accounts.

The periodic basis is something to be defined along with best practices and the evolution of the technology used, common durations go from three to six months, being long shots in regards of risks. What should be added to these processes to tackle privileged accesses? The following additional requirements are:

- The creation of privileged user access should require authorization of both the relevant system owners and also the information security manager,
- Privileged access rights are to be assigned to different user accounts from those used for day-to-day activities—i.e., staff should not use privileged accounts for their primary job role, and
- All changes to privileged accounts should be logged and auditable.

All this is necessary but does not include the specificities of the company, nor the constraints of the applications or the workflows complexity. To ensure consistency and better visibility on why user access management is implemented one way or another at an entity, it is wise to define standards first, then specify the organization's roles and cross-reference processes with roles. Once this is done, the constraints of the different types of entities implementation should be applied, in parallel, applications constraints should be considered, as application may not have the features to configure part or all the global requirements, as described in Figure 10.5.

These efforts are to enhance the segregation of duties matrix introduced in Section 7.1 "Unintentional Acts" of Chapter 7 All the processes must be identified, then they must be broken into steps. These breakdowns provide the standard structures for each process in the company. For each process a list is created between each step and all the other ones to tag incompatible duties. Each incompatible duty must have an explanation and management

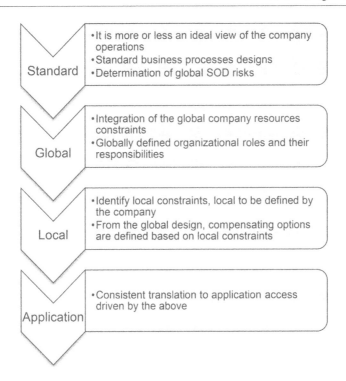

Figure 10.5 Managing SOD risks.

oversight. Management oversight includes for instance, business managers, forensic manager and provides the impact and the likelihood for each incompatible duties, using a ranking from low to high. It could be related to:

1. No management oversight applicable because activity is deemed high risk (asset misappropriation or fraudulent financial reporting).
2. Activity has been duplicated in the report. If yes:
   a. The differentiation between types of assets must be delineated for management oversight to be applicable. For example, the same process owner can initiate the purchase of sprinklers, but not the disposal of sprinklers. Then the same process owner can perform duty 1 and duty 2 granted, it is not for the same data (customer/account/ same asset/same liability).
   b. The differentiator between inventory types must be part of the warehouse structure for applicable management oversight. For example, the same process owner can authorize inventory related to fire equipment and maintain inventory for sprinklers. Therefore, if there is a data segregation, the same process owner can perform duty 1 and duty 2 granted, it is not for the same customer/account/ inventory type.

3. Same process owner can perform duty 1 and duty 2 granted, it is not for the same customer/account/data.
4. One level up approval. The same process owner performing duty 1 and duty 2 for the same data/customer/vendor need manager's approval.
5. For changes made by the process owner for conduction duty 1 and duty for the same data/customer/vendor, management review of Master Change Report can be used as a management oversight.
6. Management review of security monitoring logs on a weekly basis. Review is to include reasonableness of the times employees accessed the warehouse/cage. When abnormal activity is noticed it must be researched and resolved.

The fact that by default a duty is manual, automated or bot should be mentioned. As a result, the list of incompatibles duties for a business looks like that for the Order Management (OM) process in Figure 10.6.

The exercise can be done between the duties of two different business processes and sum up in a high-level matrix of incompatible duties between different business processes as shown in Figure 10.7.

The likelihood and impact of the risks for incompatibles duties provided by the management can for instance be averaged to create a heatmap between processes and within each process as shown in Figure 10.8.

This provides enough information to fine-tune the access rights to the global roles to eventually split it in non-compatible duties, to finalize a companywide list of roles. The next step is to add the application used to perform a duty in the lists. You remember that the ideal world on the left in the figure below looks in reality more like what's on the right of Figure 10.9.

Some applications don't allow to single out specific duties, therefore plan Bs must be developed to manage the risks. Some applications don't allow to

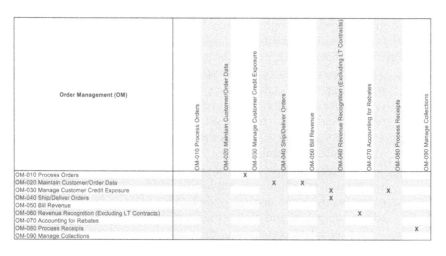

Figure 10.6 Example of OM incompatible duties.

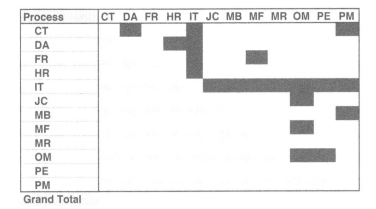

Figure 10.7 Example of incompatible duties between business processes.

create roles in the way they have been designed. Again, plan Bs must be developed. How the incompatible duties are managed must be explained. These documents will then be used in many occasions, such as by the admin when providing or updating access rights for a user, by a project team when designing the new business processes or of course by the internal audit team.

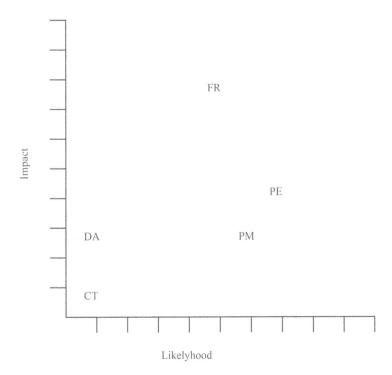

Figure 10.8 Heatmap.

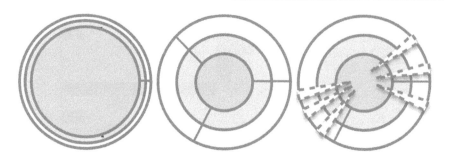

Figure 10.9 Urbanization of the information system vs. risks.

10.3 TECHNICAL RISKS

Operational risks management is mainly focused on user access rights, and the set-up of the applications supporting business processes. But risks management must deal also with another perimeter, the technical risks perimeter, and it is quite a big one. Figure 10.10 helps us visualize from where technical risks are coming from. They relate to the technical layer data, computers (processing power) and networks, where human and programs requires access to maintain up and running the information system. That's all what is at the bottom of the figure. Then thanks to the digitalization of a huge number of objects, all the items identified on the left part of the figure are included. It is not related to human having access to the information system, but non-human items connected to the company's information system and behaving based on their set-up.

At the bottom, there are privileged accesses provided to IT specialists. There are also programs developed and configured to automate recurring

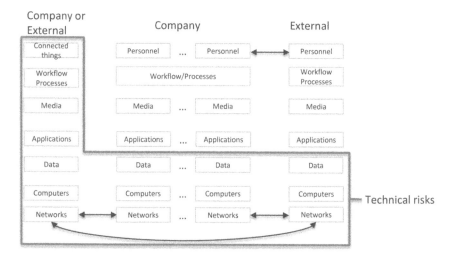

Figure 10.10 Technical risks.

tasks and requiring access rights. They too should be particularly monitored and included in a heatmap both IT specialists and programs, such as what is done for application for user access rights risks management. In addition, the matrix should take care of the objects, they should be identified along with their access rights. Identifying connected objects could by itself be time consuming. A reason is that these purchases could be made locally without the risk manager or the infrastructure manager being aware of them. Therefore, non-monitored objects with access to the information system would be there in the wild available for hackers. It reminds us that security prevention is an ongoing task and a compensating control is to regularly have a software scanning the network.

While all the hardware is listed it is worth also noting the software and its release running on this hardware. Hardware includes at least all the network equipment, the machines providing processing power. That's were additional technical risks are coming from, what is called vulnerabilities. A vulnerability is a weakness that could be exploited by an attacker. A weakness is a nice word to say that there is an error in the design or a bug in its implementation. The worst-case scenario is that a single vulnerability could be leveraged to enter the information system and either acting directly to perform an exploit or wait for an opportunity to arise to perform an exploit, or step by step having each exploit providing more rights, or moving closer to the target, the data or simply blocking the information system stopping the business as an easier shot and requesting a ransom.

An attacker is either interested by data or if too complex to retrieve it by blocking the operations, in both case a ransom can be asked or for the data simply sold, depending on how the information system security is designed and how vulnerabilities are corrected (patched) in a timely manner. For user access management, to avoid a fits all solution, different constraints were considered. The same approach applicable to data too. Data are subject to legal constraints, depending on where it is located and who must access it. Data are subject to confidentiality constraints such as the ones dealing with company's operations and turnover. To invest in the same way on the whole information system becomes prohibitive. It is then necessary to limit the costs to rely on the criticality of the data and protect it accordingly. The list with the hardware and software is completed with the data, its location, its criticality plus the database management software used. Therefore, data makes the link between the segregation of duties matrix and the technical risks matrix. There is then a full map of the data and how it can be accessed top-down, through the business applications, or bottom-up, through the network. Side remark, the privileged access to the database management software is de facto critical. For operational risks management, a causal link is usually made between the turnover and the security enforcement cost. This relation is not relevant for technical risks management when it concerns cyber security. Indeed, cyber security is not sites' specific but the whole company, more precisely the company's information system. An attacker, located everywhere in the world, may enter the information system using any items connected to it and located everywhere worldwide. (An option is to segregate the company's network to limit the spread and the impact of an exploit.)

So, this raises two points. The first one, it is not economically possible to apply the same cybersecurity measures to the entire information system. For an auditor it means that the cyber security tools, policies, and procedures have been designed in the same way the segregation of duties have been taken care of. The end result is an infrastructure heatmap, infrastructure including data, computers, and network equipment. The more critical the data is the more secure the access to it must be. The infrastructure architect with the help of the security specialist fine tune the infrastructure design adding the security equipment and software. The software is configured to monitor the different sub-domains of the architecture. The second one is about the legal environment in which the equipment is located. It may provide more or less legal protection, when bringing a case to trial. This information should ideally be listed too.

The information system heatmap is also key to analyze the impact of correcting new discovered vulnerabilities. Vulnerabilities management is like the Sisyphean or the Danaids myth with a little twist, actions are repetitive but the object changes, it is new type of water or a different boulder. Let say that at some point in time, there are 100 vulnerabilities, sorted per criticality. The team is scheduled for one month to solve them by upgrading the software. If an average of 25 new vulnerabilities are discovered per week. It is an ongoing operating expense all year long. But to be sure we have it right the adjective new is not about new vulnerabilities missed and recently identified but actually new vulnerabilities identified by security specialists and not known until now. The management of vulnerabilities is quite complex to organize. The processes and how vulnerabilities are tackled is of importance to the auditors. All this looks fine but what about equipment, or objects not directly managed by the company such as for a joint venture. Does the company allow this? The auditor should have the information available if an equipment is not configured and monitored by the company. The management of technical risks requires constant efforts and investments.

Another typical technical risk is the out of support hardware or software. One trivial reason for the out of support for the hardware of software is contractual agreements not renewed. Well, the increase of hardware and software assets connected to and being part therefore of the information system makes contract management a riskier process. IT specialists working day in and day out to maintain the information system up and running may forget about the contractual details if they are not automatically made aware of them. Auditors should check if this is managed. An additional reason is that the update of software could be automated, and it is not done when the support contract ended. Something looking practical when it has been signed, should nevertheless been tracked on a contractual point of view. Well, speaking about contract, does their perimeter and services provided still making sense? Let's say that the hours for support are daytime hours. Let's add that this contract is for the network. It still looks good, you may event think right now why not, no issue there. Well, this contract is for your core datacenter delivering services 24/7. It is less likely that you would be happy with it. In the same way, an information system is modified with more or less components, the organization and the physical sites of the company may change, meaning that new sites are added and closed, or their business importance changes. Your core data center will be less and less relevant if applications, one after the other, are moved without a well identified overall program part of an IT strategy.

A not so unusual reason is the supplier has gone bankrupt or has been acquired and no longer provides the services or products. Sometimes it is possible to anticipate when you know that you are the only left client of the suppliers. On an audit point of view, such things are part of the IT managers duties, and an urbanization plan might even be available. This may happen when new technologies, from start-ups for instance, are used by the company. There is actually a risk when the technology supports critical business processes or data. The number of different technologies used in the information system must be not too much or not too few. It goes with the constraints of management, defining standards and selecting few hardware providers has internal benefits. Knowledge management is easier to keep, the resources can resolve issues or implement new hardware or software faster. The correction of vulnerabilities is performed faster, as soon as a solution is found, the fix can be pushed faster, however the impact of a vulnerability might be bigger. The matching between the knowledge required and the knowledge available within the IT team is critical. Keeping an old technology up and running induces indirect operating costs and constraints to have knowledgeable resources available. A quick answer would be let's move to the cloud—it's the new motto having everything externalized. On an audit point of view if the management of something is externalized, the contract should be checked, how the services are provided should be audited and also the supplier compliance to best practices or standards. An obvious example is cyber-security, being sure that the duties we spoke about are taken care of by the third parties.

We have listed all along this chapter ending with the cyber-security risks impacting the all company, its operations and you name them. So, it is wise for a company to have a Disaster Recovery Plan in place and the auditor should check if one is available. There is an on-going chicken-egg discussion between proponent of Business Continuity Planning and Disaster Recovery Planning. The most common shared understanding of these two expressions is that the Business Continuity Planning is a top-down analysis from the business processes to their resiliencies and the Disaster Recovery Planning is more about resiliency of operations and IT resources being available fast in the case an event is happening impacting the information system supporting the operations. As already seen, there is no way that you can find a business operation not supported by IT resources. Do you remember the last time you went in a hurry to the computer store next door to get some family photos back from your hard drive? Tons of memories that are no longer accessible because the hard drive is no longer working. You were reassured when the technician told you that he was able to recover all the photos and videos (happy ending for once). So much for the bill, you got your memories back. All this because you didn't take the time to duplicate the files on another physical medium, and ideally on at least two, it's still family memories that you won't be able to relive (may be reading this example, you've just realized that you haven't performed any backup, it is still time to correct that). Well, apply the reasoning to the company, it requires more preparation and organization. It is not only the data but the programs and any other files to transfer to another hardware and have operation running on it plus afterward create the new development, tests, and quality environments. Digitalization makes the content of the Disaster Recovery Plan more and more identical to the business continuity plan. There are plenty of literature on these two topics. Well of course as usual for an auditor, we have to check if it has been tested, a document only is worthless.

BIBLIOGRAPHY

ALZ: Allianz Global Corporate & Specialty SE, *"Allianz Risk Barometer 2020: Identifying the Major Business Risks for 2020"*

CFI: Cordelia Fine, *"Testoterone Rex, Myths of Sex, Science and Society,"* 2018, Norton, 978-0-393-08208-1

EIO: European Insurance and Occupational Pensions and Authority, *"Cyber Risk for Insurers – Challenges and Opportunities,"* 2019, Publications Office of the European Union, 978-92-9473-213-2

KPI: Katherine Pistor, *"The Code of Capital: How the Law Creates Wealth and Inequality,"* 2019, Princeton University Press, 978-0-691-20860-2

MFI: Michael Findlay, *"The Value of Art: Money, Power, Beauty,"* 2014, Prestel Verlag, 978-3-641-08342-7

NNT: Nassim Nicholas Taleb, *"Fooled by Randomness,"* 2007, 2nd edition, Penguin Books, 978-0-141-93023-7

PwC: PriceWaterhouseCoopers, Brian Levy, Global Deals Industries Leader, Partner, PwC; CEO Magazine North America, July 25, 2021

TWU: Tim Wu, *"The Attention Merchants,"* 2017, Atlantic Books, 978-1-7823-9485-3

WST: Wallace Stevens, *"Notes Toward a Supreme Fiction,"* 1942, Cummington Press

Chapter 11

Information system audit strategy

> Since these mysteries are beyond us, let us pretend to be their organizers.
>
> Cocteau, *Les Mariés de la Tour Eiffel*

In the finance audit world, the word strategy is used for an audit work. The term strategy here refers to the actions taken by the audit committee or the head of the internal audit team or the partner in charge of an external audit company, to define the main lines of analysis for the following quarters. While doing so, the information audit strategy is for auditors about keeping the right balance between staying independent while avoiding unnecessary costs. Staying independent is key for two main reasons. The first one is that the auditors must have a high-level view on the information system and the risks, going into details would be at risk losing the big picture and less value added. As we noticed, the information system is composed of a huge number of items highly interrelated; it is easy to be lost into details. The high-level view helps identify the main trends and the items concerned. The second reason is they cannot be judge and jury. Nevertheless, the global vision allows them to identify areas for improvement. As an example, take our discussion on the robustness of business processes, the audit team has finalized a global template for the segregation of duties. Why not sharing it with the project team implementing a new ERP for instance? The audit team is only sharing the requirements and not saying how the system should be configured to avoid them. The requirements are not related to particular activities but to all.

So, what could be the risk of sharing requirements? We know the two basic principles of management and regulation:

- You know what you are measuring, and
- What is measured will be diverted.

We can adapt them to have two basic principles of the audit strategy by:

- We know what we audit, and
- What is audited will be circumvented.

DOI: 10.1201/9781003230137-11

We have an opinion on what we monitor, but only on what we monitor. There is no guarantee that we will get more reliable figures or other things that we would like to improve, just because the effectiveness of a control would be monitored regularly.

If a control penalizes the fluidity of the work, its simplicity of realization, it will be irremediably bypassed. It will be all the less effective if a department or individuals within a department have put forward numerous arguments to prevent its implementation. This indirectly justifies the involvement of internal audit as early as possible in information technology (IT) projects.

By necessity or by deliberate choice, companies are trying to take advantage of digital technology. Since computers have been available, their hold has been expanding from research centers, the military, and large companies able to afford mainframe computers before the 1980s. In the 1980's with the mini-computers, the medium-sized companies are affected. The 90s start to put paper to shame with laptops. At the same time, the first Internet shopping sites compete with physical stores ("brick and mortar").

Currently, the digital economy is increasingly replacing the economy based on historical networks, so much so that it is difficult to imagine a company being created without a digital presence. This digital presence must be, at the very least, a domain name, a site with even a single page and a contact point. If not a commercial presence, it is in any case a marketing presence that already codifies the first relationships with interlocutors.

Of course, companies are still planning new projects, managing them, and generating new revenue or reducing operational expenditures as a result. But they are doing so with almost all information digitalized and business processes that are moving at the pace of digital speed.

The audit strategy must also be adapted for both external and internal auditors. The external auditors used to audit once a year on an ad hoc basis at the end of the fiscal year. A first adaptation was to split the audit work and to spread it over the fiscal year, generally, a first part of planning work, a second of intermediate work and a third of final work.

But publicly traded companies have an annual earnings release obligation, and typically have quarterly investors meetings. The audit strategy is evolving, as management needs to be assured that plans are being carried out safely and that they are being monitored. Internal auditors help achieve this. They are present in the company throughout the year, know the resources and have a detailed knowledge of the company's activities. They can therefore implement all available audit techniques and tools and adapt them as they go along, distinguishing between risk management, the development of an audit plan and the implementation of the audit plan.

Risks change, appear or disappear on the one hand because of the company's activities and on the other hand because of the activities of the economic environment. Even if they have already been analyzed, they must be re-evaluated as soon as a new fact appears or during regular meetings with the business executives.

A 15-month shifting window for the audit strategy is the most flexible and manageable framework. 15 months is a fiscal year plus a quarter. It is possible to manage risks without an artificial break as when the audit plan is based on the fiscal year. The risk management dynamic is maintained and facilitates the planning and execution of audits. These 15 months must be looked as a 15-months sliding window updated on a quarterly basis.

11.1 BACK TO BASICS ON AUDIT STRATEGY

Let's start with an indirect impact of digitalization: The word agile. It shows the influence of IT in everyday business verbiage. This is the magic word that started spreading out at the beginning of the 21st century. It is a word promoted by a group of 17 IT developers. In February 2001, they issue a common statement called the Manifesto for Agile Software:

> We are uncovering better ways of developing software by doing it and helping others do it. We value:
>
> • Individuals and interactions over processes and tools.
> • Working software over comprehensive documentation.
> • Customer collaboration over contract negotiation.
>
> Responding to change over following a plan.

Since then agile became the trendiest word in business. It got rid of its IT legacy to be used by everyone. The good thing is it is not trademarked. This created a lot of opportunities. The word agile was connoted to simple development processes, having a lot of efforts made to add some meat to the bone, i.e., adding methods for all things not mentioned either in the 42 words of the manifesto or its 12 principles. Being able to propose agile to bigger endeavors, it was needed to scale it to support all the duties of an IT department, then extend its scope to other areas than the IT department. This has been done with the word scale. It is reflected in Figure 11.1 in the increase of trademarks related to services in the years following 2012.

By 2010, the trend extends to all departments of the company including finance and auditors, when its usage has been scaled to the all company. In the same way as in computing, advantages are put forward. These compensate for bad auditing practices according to these articles. It is an interesting opportunity for consultants to generate turnover or for a new manager to justify changes by criticizing old habits.

It is needed for an audit team to be flexible, internal audit teams have always had to be aligned with business changes and be pro-active, so this not a new need. External auditors have also had to be flexible, it is done thanks to the relationship between a partner and its client, so the partner is informed of business changes and can update the audit strategy for that client or change

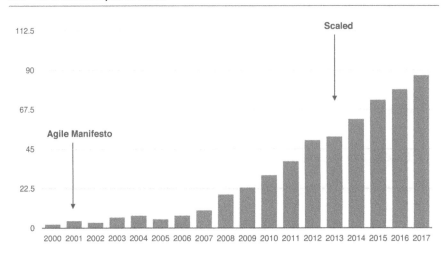

Figure 11.1 Agile-related trademarks' trend.

audit objectives to correspond to new risks or new likelihoods. Adding agile to the word audit is not enough to improving the quality of information system audit work or the added value of the information system audit report to the stakeholders. The audit strategy must not be seen as a one-shot exercise, performed in Q4 each year for the year after. The 15-month audit strategy should be updated on a quarterly basis. Let's see the shift from a financial to an operations point of view of the company in the figure below. Operations encompasses all company's activities supported by the digitalized information system, activities being current operations and projects endeavors. On the left side, there is a basic P&L structure, both revenues and expenses are due to current operations and projects. If we look through the lens of the information system, operations and projects create both revenues and expenses within a certain period of time. The faster the project delivers the better it is, of course. The risks we listed up to now and more specifically in Chapter 10, impact operations and projects are linked indirectly to revenues and expenses, such as shown in Figure 11.2.

How is the business strategy linked to the risks' analysis? A company has at least a business strategy, for the company or per line of business or per region for instance. Each strategy is decomposed into initiatives, in the same way goals are into objectives. An initiative can be split further down if needed such as into programs, anyway an initiative is linked to the current operations, current business processes and to new products, new services delivered by projects. Figure 11.2 misses the link with the company's strategy. As a result, risks are related to the strategy in addition of operations and projects, such as in Figure 11.3.

The word initiative is a generic word encompassing business initiatives and programs. A program is split in projects and activities to maintain in working condition the information system and enhance it.

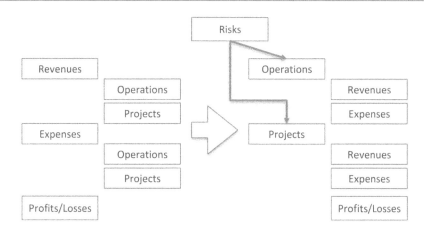

Figure 11.2 From a financial to an operational view.

Enterprise risks are more related to the strategy, operational and technical risks to operations and projects. The input to create or update the information system audit strategy are all the items we looked at, the ones of the information system (Chapter 2), the legal, operational and IT risks (Chapters 4, 5, and 8), the level of confidence required (Chapter 9) and the risks heatmap (Chapter 10). The work done provides the lists of actions ranked per priority. Unfortunately, all cannot be done at once or during the following five quarters, due to resources or budget constraints for instance. Choices must be

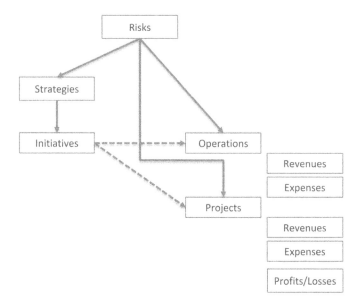

Figure 11.3 Business strategy and risks.

Table 11.1 Top risk areas

	Top 15 other risk areas	Frequency	%
1	No periodic reviews	308	5
2	Accounting	196	3
3	Insufficient user documentation	193	3
4	Inaccurate data	105	2
5	Delegation of authority	99	2
6	Excessive user access rights	91	2
7	Process formalization/documentation	88	2
8	Account reconciliations	87	1
9	Incomplete/inaccurate disclosure to Corporate/HQ functions	86	1
10	Accruals	81	1
11	Transaction processed without approval/review	61	1
12	Contracts	59	1
13	Disbursements	62	1
14	Timely data	59	1
15	Employee	54	1

made and what is helping to make them? All the information is summarized in a table showing the top risks areas such as the example shown in Table 11.1.

Being positive, interesting information is available in the previous years of audit results. They provide a lot of useful data, even if the company has not applied all what we have presented. It is possible to tag each finding against one control. It takes more time to do of course if findings have to be retrofitted to the overall matrices in Section 10.2. Doing so, it shows trends specific to the company. Each finding is tagged at least against the company entity, the line of business, the region, the process, and the sub-process, if it is a repeated incident. As a result, we have a list of all the findings with the same tags. The interesting part is leveraging the trends on where findings were found during the audits in previous years. Let's say that in Table 11.2, the different standard business processes are listed in the top row (e.g. Procure materials and services-PM, Order management-OM, Manage taxes-CT) and in the first column, the years. Each cell contains the number of security related findings against the number of times that process has been in scope.

Table 11.2 Number of security related findings/number of times a process has been in scope

Process Fiscal year	PM	MF	OM	PE	FR	CT	JC	MR	IT	HR	MB	DA	PR
N	0.5	0.2	0.3	0	0.4	0	0	0.5	2.7	0.3	0.2	0	0
N + 1	0.4	0.3	0.3	0	0.4	0	0	0.2	2.3	0.3	0.2	0	0
N + 2	0.5	0.7	1.1	0	1	0	0.2	0.3	7.5	0.7	1.5	0	0

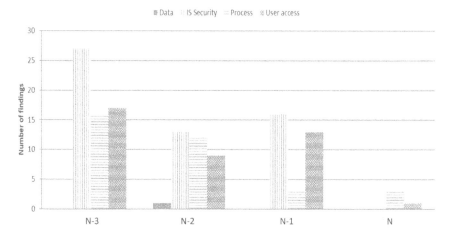

Figure 11.4 Diving in audit results.

Different trends are visible, a stable trend such as for PM, (second column), an increase such as for OM (fourth column) or a decrease such as for CT (seventh column). When the trend is either stable or increasing, it requires further analysis on the root causes and also the context, are the incident clustering per Line of Business, per country or region, or even if the audit team is split per region do they audit in the same manner, i.e., grouped per audit team? As you notice in this example, IT results (tenth column) are really high. It is worth diving in and for example, splitting the findings between Data, Process, user Access and IS Security (DPAS) such as shown in Figure 11.4.

These trends display the remaining risks, i.e., the findings remaining after all the maturity improvement actions have taken place, such as enhancing the level of controls, implementing cyber-security awareness. It is worth integrating these results in the audit strategy.

We have plenty of information to map the risks vs. likelihood and impact but what about risks being "resistant" like antibiotic-resistant bacteria? It is a concern. What is the root cause? Are the actions ineffective and should be changed? Are the controls inappropriate? Did the IT resources change and as a result it is not a repeat as such? Auditing is not only about findings issues but selecting the best actions to resolve them.

11.2 DIGITALIZATION AND AUDIT STRATEGY

Digitalization can help us in two ways, directly improving how we audit and indirectly by analyzing more easily the information system as auditors can leverage audit tools and techniques.

We know that we must organize what must be done during the 15-month sliding window. We identify all the risks. We design guidelines, configure tools whenever there is an opportunity of a return on investment. A return on investment is achieved when multiple audits are dealing with the same information system topics (e.g. segregation of duties) or if it avoids costs such as when control levels are defined and shared as requirements by a project team. Any workload spent to improve a software once implemented for instance will at least generates additional expenses to correct the issues, lack of trust on the project team and time lost for the end-users.

We used a heatmap to identify preeminent issues or risks. But the heatmap is like knowing the main symptoms without knowing the patient body. Let's represent the risks with different sizes, the bigger the size, the bigger the impact is, on the schematic representation of the different elements of the digitalized information system, as shown in Figure 11.5.

Let's assume this figure is the representation of the risks on an application or a business process. It shows how bad the situation is for that business process. If a business process is supported by one application only then the figures are equal. Based on all the audit results there is such a figure for each business process. Like a doctor facing dysfunctions of different organs, you could solve the dysfunctions of each organ. But the body is a complete system with all the organs communicating with each other like a computerized information system. These figures are interesting but not sufficient, what is needed is the same thing but with the representation of the root causes. A patient's condition may be due to a single cause that consecutively impairs the functioning of different organs or that leaves room for other diseases to

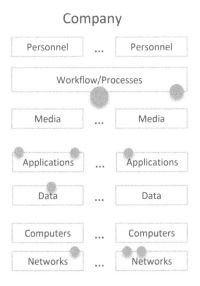

Figure 11.5 Mapping risks.

flourish. Another option is the appearance of concomitant causes. Whatever the reasons, it is necessary to address the causes.

As in medicine, it turns out that the patient could be an unknowing patient. Let's take back the example of Marriott, with an attacker whose objective is to be present without disturbing the operations and just quietly get information on the functioning or particular data. This is the reason why when a patient arrives at the hospital various routine tests are prescribed. This is why the audit strategy must include routine audits that at first glance do not seem to respond to visible symptoms. Their results are essential to confirm that the basic parameters are coherent and if they are not, or if they are at the limits, to plan more specific complementary audits.

This approach is easier to implement by internal auditors than by external auditors who, with given budgets, have to maximize the scene effect and decrease the backstage effect, i.e., audit the main risks first (those with the most important impacts), and complete according to the remaining budget with other risks. For major risks it is important to plan for the 15-month period when audits will be performed. The 15-month period is in today's world quite long, it is wise to revise the planning when the risk analysis and therefore the root causes are usually reviewed at least every six months. Once the causes are identified, it is possible to automate the audits for those for which it is possible, the most important ones first of course. The automation is more or less complete and goes from the extraction of data to the writing of reports through the search for issues. It is possible to analyze the data or the functioning of the management rules. Different vendors offer software solutions outside the applications where it is possible to interface the applications and transfer the data to a database dedicated to the audit (data analytics). The next step is to use artificial intelligence software to prepare a pre-analysis. Pre-analysis that the auditor will review and amend or complete if necessary.

Artificial intelligence is also interesting to automate routine audits. But before using it, it is beneficial to refine the process and the analysis of the results with manual methods. The process and the analysis of the results must be well documented and explained. In addition, it allows to train the novice auditors and once trained to send them to the field. The cost of conducting the audit is minimized and the quality is maintained. These manual methods can be enhanced with data analysis. The undeniable advantage of data analysis is that on the one hand it avoids all the discussions about the relevance of a sample and on the other hand, the whole population at a given time is controlled. These assignments can be done by novice auditors who run the programs. Less time is spent on reporting and more time on analysis if needed. The analysis requires more knowledge of the business, experience, and more hindsight from the auditors. It is this analysis that allows us to refine the programs, to improve them. Once the programs are finalized, i.e., the reports provided are relevant and easily understandable, other programs can be developed to further automate the production of new reports with new parameters or with additional data in scope. The next step is to schedule the

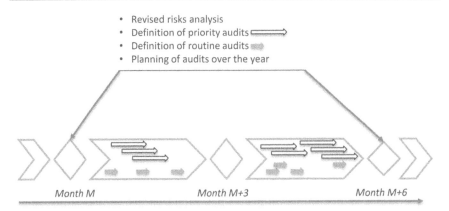

Figure 11.6 Scheduling = dealing with constraints.

audits along the next 15-month window. Priority audits should be scheduled first. Once the planning of these priority audits has been approved by the audit committee, their completion according to plan is critical. These priority audits provide necessary assurance not only for the audit committee but also for institutional communication to investors in particular. The overall view of this planning is shown in Figure 11.6.

It is composed at the bottom by a quarterly schedule with milestones that allow for summary reports and risk analysis reviews. If the risk analysis requires it, the schedule of the audits is modified. The priority audits are the white arrows and the regular audits the grey ones. The initial global schedule is composed of audits whose workloads have been estimated with the most probable values, i.e., considering a typical auditor with average expertise and knowledge for each audit. Of course, this does not reflect the reality, but it allows to focus on the global coherence because the usual challenge is to match the date constraints with both the number of available auditors, their expertise and their knowledge, but first with the number of available auditors. So, it's a question of capacity management.

The first thing is to check if the workload is consistent with the number of auditors in the team. If the workload is for 11 auditors and the team is composed of 10 auditors, it is possible to slightly modify audit dates. If, on the other hand, the workload is for 20 auditors, audits must be rescheduled, with different scenarios proposed to the audit committee. But before going to the audit committee, the second thing to do is to make sure that the auditors' expertise matches the audit needs. Audit management tasks can hardly be assigned to juniors. The third step is to match the knowledge with that required to perform the audits. It is risky to assign an auditor to an IT audit or a financial audit etc. if he/she does not have the skills and the level of mastery of the subject.

What parameters should be used to take all these constraints into account? The main parameters are prioritization, duration, expertise, knowledge, and resources. Eventually, it will be necessary to play with these four parameters at the same time. Prioritization is a choice of the audit committee, a choice made on the expected benefits of each of these audits. It is preferable to go to the audit committee with different solutions obtained by playing on the other parameters. The duration of an audit can be reduced by preparing in advance an automation of the work or by assigning experienced auditors or with a strong knowledge of the subject. Preparing upstream automation of the work mainly concerns the use of automated data analysis. This investment is all the more relevant because once the data analysis on a given domain is finalized and tested, it can be transferred to the audited business managers. They can then regularly check the good functioning of their domain by including this good practice in their weekly reporting. Assigning an experienced auditor instead of a junior auditor reduces the workload and therefore the duration. Where a junior auditor would take 10 days, a senior auditor could take less, e.g. 5 days, if they are 100% assigned to a job this reduces the time by half. The cost may eventually be stable, but it will likely be higher. Expertise on a subject can be more easily well thought-out if it is anticipated. Improving an auditor's subject matter expertise starts with training, then shadow work and finally assignments on increasingly complex audits in that area. All or part of these costs can be allocated to the training plan and not to the audit directly. Knowing that no part of the information system is spared by digitalization, it seems obvious that all auditors have a minimum of computer culture. This provides a common base of understanding that facilitates exchanges and makes the work more fluid. In addition to this common base, it is neces- sary for reasons of efficiency and reputation to have auditors who master, that is to say are comfortable with the tools used, starting with the software packages. This means that this knowledge is not on previous versions that have become unused by the auditees. The speed of execution of the work is facilitated but above all the auditors are not in a situation of inferiority in terms of knowledge with respect to the auditees. The auditors must be able to understand the answers of the auditees, ask additional questions and identify errors if they exist.

If the work of refining the schedule does not yield convincing results, the solution is to negotiate more budget to have more auditors or specialists. The auditors are usually assigned to activities that are not yet filled, thus not changing the overall schedule. This addition of auditors can also modify assignments already made to smooth out the workload. Of course, the exper- tise and knowledge of the auditor can influence the duration of the tasks. Indeed, when a task is unaffected, they were scheduled with the load and duration being the most probable values (cf. beta law approximated by the triangular law). The specialists will support the teams on complex technical subjects that would have required a lot of time for the teams to understand. They can classically intervene in the back office for the simple reason that it is easier to find people who know the techniques than the functioning of the company or the auditees. For example, the automation of data retrieval is a key support work for auditors, the specialist focuses on developing the data retrieval environment and programs that meet the needs of auditors. Auditors who know the company have the freedom to analyze the results. Another example of the implementation of a new ERP of which the auditors have no knowledge. The intervention of an expert is useful to complete the work plan. Let's take the example of a business process that benefits from a needs analysis as mentioned in Section 10.2 "Operational Risks" of Chapter 10, with the four stages "standard/global/local/application." It intervenes to finalize the application step, by specifying how the control can be configured in this new ERP. From a planning point of view, the upgrade of the work plan can be done well in advance. The expert comes back during the audit to help and train the auditors if this has not already been done. This example shows the main difference between a consultant or a specialist of a specific module or features and an auditor, the auditor has a transverse vision, from the beginning to the end of a business process, while a specialist will have a fine understanding of a part of a process.

Thus, each quarter a revision of the schedule has to be made and each semester a possible revision of the global schedule. According to the geographical coverage of the company, the planning includes the foreseeable constraints of the countries of the entities to be audited, such as holidays. The schedule is adapted for specific constraints such as unfavorable weather, or sick leaves.

11.3 INFORMATION SYSTEM RISKS DUE TO ITS COMPLEXITY

The digitalization of the information system indirectly requires from the auditors a better understanding of its structure in addition to the specific technical skills mentioned above. "Information system risks" is a focus on how the complexity of the information system creates practical constraints for planning the audits.

Since the beginning we have presented the computerized information system with elements grouped in different types, such as network, computers, data, or applications. Even without a specific computer culture, we see that the network is composed of very different elements, as for the computers. Computers represent computing power that can be rented. The current trend is to have providers for storage rental and application rental, both of them called "as a service" and not rented. These three types of leasing meet a need for providers to have regular income and for customers to get simplicity. This simplicity is sometimes called agility or flexibility. But agility and flexibility in relation to what?

The automated information system is composed, as we have seen in Chapter 6, of what is used by the company's business and must be maintained in operational condition and what will be used to create new revenues and must be developed. Obviously in both cases, computer scientists are needed. Due to the different technical elements a wide range of technical skills is required. Some will be internalized, and others will be rented to consultants or subcontractors. In addition to this, new IT techniques are regularly on sale, be it development methods such as the agile manifesto, new hardware or new software or new versions of software. The information system is therefore over time a system with an increasing entropy, mainly due to the growing number of components and different techniques. Hence the continuous struggle of IT managers to reduce this increase in entropy. The more entropy increases, the more operating costs increase, and the more risks evolve and grow. So, when there is too much to do, it is necessary to first sort out what is manageable or should be kept in-house and what is not. As soon as a component of the information system is sufficiently industrialized, it can be taken over by a third party. This starts with the components of the data center when they are viewed through the prism of computing power. This can be rented as a service. Another trend is the shift from in-house developed software to software packages by outsourcing the development. The software package is now also offered for rent. To simplify, all means are good to externalize the risks related to the information systems, like outsourcing the maintenance in operational condition of the information system or to externalize the developments or at least to simplify them by reducing them to the configuration of software packages. Risk outsourcing can bring benefits if the outsourcing contracts are properly designed bearing in mind the operational constraints of the company, such as availability at certain times of the day or all or part of the week. Outsourcing adds flexibility to an environment because it is the provider's responsibility to handle workload changes. Outsourcing makes an existing environment agile because it's up to the vendor to deliver solutions quickly.

But whether the work is done internally or externally, it can only be done by competent people who have knowledge of the elements of the information system. This knowledge is often in the minds of people, the older the person is in the company the more important is his knowledge of the information system. On the one hand, he/she knows many more elements of the information system and their functioning on the other hand. To outsource it is necessary that the scope is defined, i.e., that the list of managed elements is available, and that for each of these elements an adequate documentation is available to maintain them. This list and this documentation are part of the prerequisites in a contract, otherwise it is an extra cost for the company because the supplier will take care of the formalization of the knowledge for example. This is exactly what happens when a company outsources its service desk.

The more complex the information system is, the more difficult it is to outsource the management of subsets of it.

The first factor that increases the complexity of the information system is the increasing quantity of elements. The increase in the variety of elements due to digitalization is the second important factor increasing the complexity.

What are the main groups of elements in an information system? We have already discussed them in the previous chapters. If we return to the diagram of the decomposition in sub-layers of the information system, there are two types of elements, those which facilitate the communication (network) and the others which communicate with the other components thanks to the network elements. Since a few decades with the omnipresence of the Internet an information system is no longer a computing power to which users directly access, as in the 20th century, but becomes a network on which computing powers are connected. The other elements use this network infrastructure and change accordingly. What does this mean in practice? Let's take a digitalization example such as the technical choices made by the Tesla Motors company ending with some vehicle owners not getting into their vehicles on November 19, 2021. A classic solution to get into his vehicle is to use a key, until then no problem, you have your key in your hand or not. An option provided by Tesla Motors is to use your cell phone. The phone connects to the Tesla Motors servers which gives the authorization and the door opens. Setting up the network between the user and his car adds a risk and the possibility of malfunctions. In addition, it adds complexity, on the one hand by adding all the phones of the users connected to the servers.

Adding an element means adding a relationship with at least one other element. A link represents for example a network connection, a membership relation, like a cell phone used by a person, or a relation like a connected object present on a site. Thus, we obtain a simple example of the visualization of these relations in Figure 11.7.

Now let's apply this reasoning to the computerized information system. Figure 11.8 shows the structure that we have been using since the beginning, with the addition of a symbolic representation of these links on the left. On the basis of this representation, the elements are grouped from top to bottom by the connected objects, then the process division which itself groups the elements by sub-processes, these same elements are communicated via media, paper prints or screens for the visible elements, below we have the set of applications with their interfaces, these applications have an existence only thanks to the data and the software which manage them, these data are hosted on computers, computers which communicate between them and others which

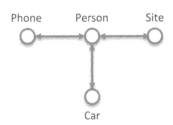

Figure 11.7 Simple example.

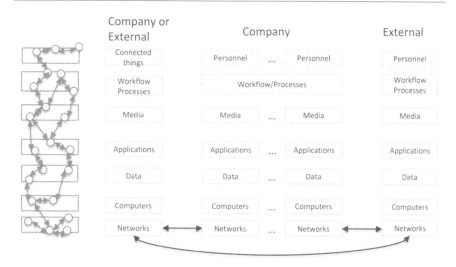

Figure 11.8 The computerized information system.

are not managed directly or indirectly by the company (cf. subcontracting mentioned above).

It is obvious that the more the company has sites or is present in different countries or exercises different trades, the more complex the representation of the elements and their relationships becomes. De facto, a manual management is not possible. All the more so as this representation must correspond to reality, it is all the work of updating by adding, modifying, or deleting elements on the one hand and links on the other hand. The modification of an element happens more often than one might think, the reason is that whatever the hardware it uses programs, which must be updated to solve vulnerabilities, add features. When one of these programs is often used or used by critical elements, this information can become an element in the representation to facilitate analysis or research. The case of the deployment of connected objects is representative, these products have been put forward for the services rendered but without effort on the security of their access to the Internet. When a vulnerability is identified on one of the programs, it is first necessary to know all the connected objects active in the information system and if they use this program that generates vulnerabilities. Such as in April 2021, when cybersecurity researchers at Forescout and JSOF uncovered and detailed the vulnerabilities leading to potential attacks impacting millions of enterprise and consumer devices.

All this concerns the active elements of the information system, but we must also consider the elements that are developed for the needs of the company as software developments. The development of a software is in fine a set of computer programs that will be an integral part of the information system. As such, they must be identified, but as to produce them, they must be designed, the documentation of the design, at least, must also be referenced. Therefore,

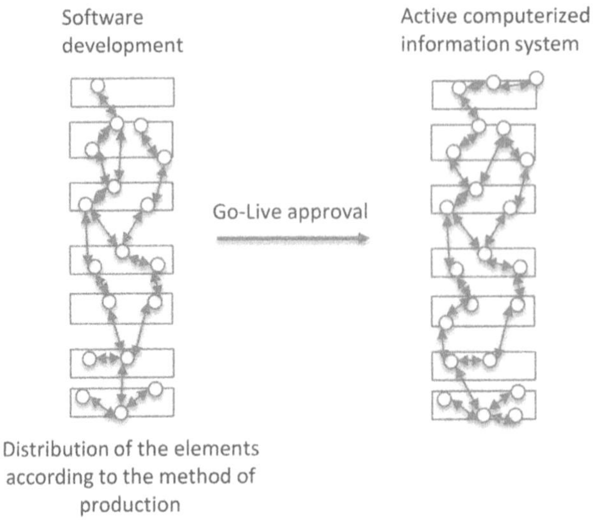

Software
development

Active computerized
information system

Go-Live approval

Distribution of the elements
according to the method of
production

Figure 11.9 **All elements to be managed.**

the identification of these elements and their links must be done during the development. Moreover, without documentation, the costs to produce them cannot be capitalized.

Figure 11.9 summarizes the situation with on the left the elements produced and identified within the framework of the software development, on the right the active elements within the information system, between the two an arrow which represents the transfer into active elements of the information system after the validation of transfer, for example by the steering committee of the project The elements developed within the framework of a project will be grouped according to the method chosen for development, in any case it must be linked in fine to the breakdown of the accounting technique. More generally, the integration of new elements or the modification or deletion of active elements are also subject to validation (change management).

This complexity explains why outsourcing is a recurring topic. For an auditor, it is key to know how this complexity is managed. Without management, the company ends up in situations that are risky for the sustainability of its business, for example because it no longer has the knowledge to maintain a service-critical application and in doing so to improve it or offer new services. The tragic situation, which is not even a caricature because it happens again and again, is the company that maintains the application in an ecosystem that protects it from the evolutions of all other active elements of the information system. Nobody dares to touch this application anymore, hoping that it will not get stuck.

The elements produced by computer scientists have benefited since the 1960s from work called software configuration management. A configuration is a picture of a set of elements at a given time, and this configuration is software because the focus was on computer software development. Since then, this analysis has extended its scope to non-software elements and active elements of the information system, in particular with the notion of component management database (CMDB). The CMDB is necessary to achieve long-term confidence as described in Section 9.3 "Long Term Confidence" of Chapter 9. The knowledge of the elements, therefore having a CMDB or something similar, allows to perform impact analysis and thus to reduce the risks during changes in the active elements of the information system. The information of the CMDB elements can be completed for example with financial information such as purchase, manufacturing or development costs, obsolescence information, or information about incidents or malfunctions with the costs of resolution. The CMDB is a valuable aid to plan more accurate audits by identifying the root causes of risks and to investigate more precisely the root causes of identified issues and propose more relevant action plans. Information about the state of affairs or incidents can be used to identify inconsistencies or risks and to plan routine audits on the management of the information system and even priority audits as important risks are uncovered by the analysis of the information in the CMDB. In summary, how can an auditor consider that the information system is well managed if there is no CMDB or equivalent to a CMDB? What would a financial audit say if the basic financial elements are not available or if the financial reporting is incomplete or incorrect?

Chapter 12

Performing audits

> The future, like everything else: It is no longer what it used to be.
>
> Paul Valéry, *Notre Destin et Les Lettres*

The overall planning reflects a 15-month rolling window and the general constraints of prioritizing the work to be done, the availability of auditors and their skills. A quarterly report is used to analyze the results of the closed audits to update the global planning for the following quarters. The scheme is simplified with audits that are completed before the quarterly closing, in practice the audits take place independently of the quarterly closing as well as the monthly or quarterly accounting closing, such as in Figure 12.1.

What is not present in the figure are audits that are not or not easily planned, such as investigations or an audit performed to analyze a malfunction, such as a cyber security audit after an intrusion. This chapter is about what happens during a "theoretical" quarter with the planning and execution of a standard audit, whether it is routine or not. The activities described are still valid for audits that are requested on an emergency basis, but they are carried out more quickly.

The best practices of financial auditors will be used again, but the financial purpose is replaced by a computerized information system purpose. How does this translate? Let's take the example of auditor training and skills. Historically and schematically, financial auditors with a technical accounting

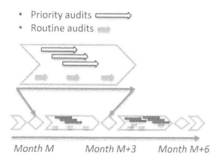

Figure 12.1 From global to detailed planning.

DOI: 10.1201/9781003230137-12

background realize that the increasing use of information technology (IT) resources by companies requires IT skills. The financial auditors generally call upon IT experts with outsourced services. All this happened at the end of the 20th century, it is still common to read in the literature a clear distinction between the financial auditor and the IT auditor and with good reason, because the role of the IT auditor is reduced like that of the financial auditor to their respective technical competences and this is still mentioned in books of the 90s. We have financial auditors on one side and IT auditors on the other, with a blurred area between the two that is found during the performance of audits. This blurred area represents the need for profiles with both business and IT knowledge.

Digitalization is a buzzword defined in various ways, i.e., with complementary points of view. In practice, it has made everyone realize that companies only function thanks to their information systems and not only thanks to their IT in the IT technical sense. The information system of a company and especially its structure and management say a lot about the real ability of a company to implement the strategy described in the annual financial report and the reliability of explanations of quarterly data to investors. This lack of understanding is an explanation for the mistakes of the Internet bubble with companies created with business plans and buzzwords. Professional investors believed that the future would bring profitable companies. Their approach was to bet on the fact that in their investment portfolio, a unicorn (private company worth more than $1 billion) would appear to compensate for the losses of other companies in the portfolio.

12.1 BACK TO BASICS ON AUDIT PLANNING

PCAOB AS 2101 "Audit Planning" standard presents the main steps in planning a financial audit. It describes the responsibilities of the financial auditor to "properly planning the audit" in four chapters:

- Preliminary engagement activities,
- Planning activities,
- Audit strategy, and
- Audit plan.

As it concerns financial audits, two considerations are added:

- Multi-location engagements, and
- Persons with specialized skill or knowledge.

The preliminary engagement activities are about knowing the context in which the audit will take place. In practice, the auditor must know the history of relations with the audited parties and the roadmap provided by the information system audit strategy with the associated schedule. The auditor should ensure the compliance of the audit in particular with regard to auditor independence and ethics.

The second step does not concern the planning of the work as such, but the taking of cognizance. The importance of this understanding varies according to the nature and complexity of the company. The auditor must take into account various points that could affect the financial results of the company and concretely increase the workload and modify the work to be done. The various issues can be grouped into the company's business, its sector of activity, its organization and the way it delivers financial results, then everything that concerns known malfunctions, i.e., identified in previous external or internal audits, and finally everything that concerns the main active risks such as legal disputes and finally the quality of internal control, this last point offers an opportunity to limit the scope of work to be performed if the results of other audits are usable without risk. The complexity of the operations depends on the number of legally autonomous entities and therefore on the methods of financing. There is no causal relationship between the complexity of operations and the complexity of financial audit. If the number of entities is too large for the expected workload, the entities to be audited must be selected, whether for an external or internal auditor. The scope of analysis must be defined, which entities for which audit work? The complexity of the operations depends on the number of legally autonomous entities and thus on how financial statements are achieved. There is no causal relationship between the complexity of operations and the complexity of the financial audit. If the number of entities is too large in relation to the expected workload, the entities to be audited must be selected. The scope of analysis must be defined, which entities for which audit work? It is common to send a letter of intent to the auditees at this stage to notify them and agree on dates when the auditees will be available.

What the standard calls audit strategy is the determination of the scope of the audit, its timing, the risks covered, i.e., the important factors related to these risks, the main activities to analyze them and the required competences. It is therefore to identify all the mandatory elements to actually plan the work, such as constraints, difficulties, dependencies with other results. If the auditees have agreed with the auditors on the timing of the audit, it will be necessary to determine when, how and under what conditions the work can be carried out. An initial sequence of work is the prioritization of tasks according to the importance of the risks they cover. The schedule starts with the work that covers the most important risks and continues with the work that covers the least important risks. If the audit is delayed due to illness of an auditor, there is time to either reschedule the sick auditor or to reschedule the work. Work that covers the least important risks usually takes less time and can be moved more easily. It's a bit like filling a container with pebbles and sand, you put in the pebbles and then the sand and not the other way around. This initial sequence is modified to solve dependency constraints. Some work results are used to start others. It is difficult to have an opinion on the value of stocks in the financial statements if the stock management has not been audited before, so there is an initial sequence of work. Once the list of works is confirmed, it is necessary to estimate the workload for each job and the skills required, and thus to estimate the number of auditors needed, at what time and with what skills. All this covers the strategic audit part of the standard. It may be wise at this stage to maintain contact with the auditees and propose dates for further planning. At this stage, it is possible to know what audits are needed and when. This helps to limit the risk of absence of the interlocutors.

We want to say to ourselves that it is good the work is almost finished, unfortunately it is not the case. The most delicate part begins with what the standard calls "audit plan." The audit plan covers two practical aspects the detailed planning of who does what and with what.

Well, then who does what? It's one thing to have identified skills, but you have to identify the available auditors who will in fact do the work. They don't necessarily have exactly the right skills. Their skills are ideally those required and there is no problem, the detailed planning is identical to the general planning. But more often, it is necessary to check the adequacy of the skills of the auditors assigned to the audit with those required. In case the auditor is more competent, there is little risk on the quality of the results of the work, but in order to stay within the budget, the workload will have to be reduced. Let's take the example of the general planning work that requires five days of work for an assistant, if a senior person does it, it will take three workdays. If the daily cost of an assistant is 100 and that of a senior is 200, the budget is 20% over (100). To stay within the budget, the maximum workload for the senior is two and a half workdays. A complementary solution is to plan in advance training for the assistant to increase his skills, to decrease the workload and improve the quality of the results produced. Usually, the training costs are not charged to the audit budget.

As for the what, we are talking about what is commonly called the work plans. The work plan details a job sufficiently so that an assistant can follow it step by step. It does not guarantee the consistency of the quality of the results, but it reduces their inconsistency, which is already positive. In the case of the audit of the process control settings in a software package, the access requirements must be specified—they will be provided to the auditees in advance not to lose "on-field" preparation time—and the step-by-step commands and expected results listed. If so, the workplan is dependent on the release of the software package. This is part of the information to be asked for at the latest during the audit strategy stage. The work plan and all the tools that can facilitate the work of auditors are beneficial for the consistency of the work and its results. The workload can also be reduced, which is beneficial for the budget and the deadlines. This creates room in the detailed planning to accommodate unforeseen events. Unforeseeable events are essentially the need for additional, i.e., unanticipated, and necessary investigations due to the intermediate results obtained.

Let's take up this important subject of the competence and expertise of the auditors assigned to an audit. It is a critical subject because as much as consulting is primarily a team business, auditing is primarily a trust business. The reputation of the auditors' team depends on their behavior but especially on the added value of the recommendations. The relevance of the recommendations depends on the quality of the work. Work that must be finalized on time according to the schedule shared with the auditees. This competence issue should be anticipated and managed globally by the head of the audit teams, the audit manager if it is internal or by the external auditing company. In the introduction to this chapter, we discussed the historical dichotomy between financial auditors and IT auditors, a dichotomy that is no longer relevant because it no longer corresponds to the reality of business in the 21st century. The reality of companies is digitalization, a word that marks the minds and disturbs the actors of the audit space. The information system does not work in silos, there is not financial technology on one side and computer technology on the other. The two are linked by the information system, it is not possible to have a reasonable assurance if the auditor does not understand the importance of the computerized information system. Let's take Figure 12.2, with the different elements of the information system, we can look at it by schematically placing a horizontal axis for the technical

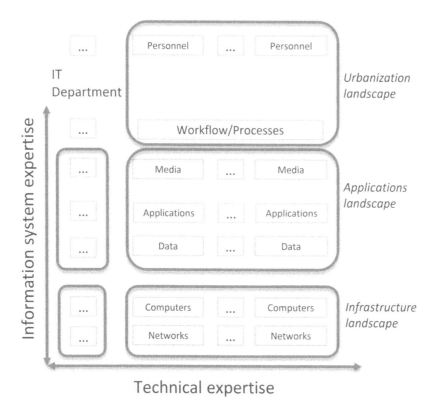

Figure 12.2 Auditors' expertise.

expertise and a vertical axis for the knowledge of the information system. This schematization represents the need for the auditors to have both information system knowledge and technical knowledge.

Technical knowledge is a general term that encompasses different types of expertise in the same field, knowing that expertise is of many levels. Can a tax specialist be assigned without assistance or training to operational audits? Will a tax specialist in Germany be able to help with tax work in India? Can an expert on the Windows operating system be assigned to audit the Unix operating system and its derivatives without assistance or training? The knowledge of information systems is also a general term that covers on the one hand an in-depth understanding of the links between its components and on the other hand a transversal geographical understanding we could say called here landscape. So, are there any information system auditors as such? A priori no because the knowledge of the information system is a necessity for any auditor. So, an auditor in the 21st century is an information system auditor. This implies that other technical knowledge is a specialty in the sense of the PCAOB standard AS 2101. It specifies that "the auditor should shave sufficient knowledge of the subject matter to be addressed by such a person to enable the auditor…to evaluate the results of that person's procedures as they relate to the nature, timing and extent of other planned audit procedures and the effects on the auditor's report."

To summarize, an auditor in the 21st century must, if not already the case, be an information systems auditor with at least one specialization. This helps us to re-read the recommendations of the standard for multi-entity audits with a new vision. The groups are composed of companies spread all over the world and are specialized in different sectors of activity according to the strategy of the group. Each entity has an information system. These information systems are theoretically supposed to implement the group's recommendations such as on security or controls to be implemented in the applications. The applications can be shared, and the computer networks interconnected. This becomes the group's information system as technical evolutions and IT investments are made. The figures in Chapter 5 represent this paradigm shift and the confirmation that in order to control the quality of consolidated financial information and ensure the efficiency of operational processes, the sharing of common best practices (governance and regulations) is mandatory. In this context, the information system is transverse and the notion of audits on multiple entities is not sufficient ("multi-location engagements" in the standard).

12.2 INFORMATION SYSTEM AUDIT PLANNING

The information system ignores the usual limits by adding an extra dimension, or rather multiple connections. Let's take a simple example, a company for reasons of confidentiality has always managed the bonuses of senior executives on a particular workstation that is only accessible locally. The group is growing so much that the work of retrieving the data from the financial system to calculate these bonuses requires more and more time to be finalized, despite the transfer of this information by an IT support. The idea then arises to retrieve this data automatically by creating an interface between this local application and the financial system. The implementation of this interface extends the information system so to speak by integrating two separate sets into one. In fact, the audit of the financial system must extend to this system, which was separate, at least that is how the tax authorities will see it during a tax audit. Since the two systems have become one, it is not even necessary to change the scope of the tax audit.

The more the digitalization of the information system realizes the simplification of the technical and application landscapes, the more the auditors can industrialize their working methods to remain efficient. But let's get rid of the case where, to put it nicely, the information system is not properly managed. It is only a set of technical choices without coherence with non-maintained elements. It is eventually possible to form an opinion on the financial results, but it is difficult to be confident in the sustainability of its turnover or the implementation of digitalization strategies.

We have always made work plans that we improve as we go along with the audits and our experience. These are thematic work plans that are independent from each other. We now have companies that exchange and manipulate data with different but connected tools. How can we make sure that the work plans reflect this change of context?

Figure 12.3 shows an example of the distribution of the use of ERPs in a company. For each region is indicated the turnover and the ERP used. Let's assume that the same business processes are supported by these three ERPs.

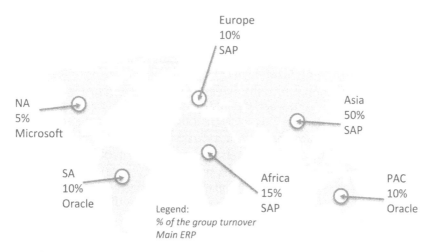

Figure 12.3 Hundred entities using SAP, 30 Oracle, and 5 Microsoft.

Three main ERPs support the company's activities, SAP supports 75% of the company's turnover, Oracle 20%, and Microsoft 5%.

The first thought you have is to say to yourself, is that it would be great if the control requirements would have been specified (see Section 5.1 in Chapter 5 and 10.2 in Chapter 10) because this will greatly simplify the work by having a standard work plan. The second thought you have is to say to yourself, it would be even nicer to have the general work plan completed with the controls specific to the ERP environment that supports the most important turnover, in this example it is SAP. Finally, you say to yourself, the top would be to have the same thing with the other two ERPs, first with Oracle and then with Microsoft. In addition to promoting consistency and a structured view of process implementation, it also reduces production costs.

Let's assume that the workload to audit process A costs 10 hours for one entity. Let's say that the cost of defining the standard controls for this process requires an investment of 20 hours of work with an expectation of 10% reduction on the number of hours to audit process A, and that adding the details of controls etc. for an ERP system costs 40 hours, with an estimation of an additional 30% cost reduction. Let's say that 100 entities use SAP, 30 Oracle, and 5 Microsoft. The basic workload to audit process A for the 100 entities that use SAP is 1000 hours (100×10). The creation of the standard work plan for process A costs 20 hours with an expected gain of 10%, the cost of the audit for one entity is 9 hours, that is to say 900 hours in total (100×9), and thus a gain of 80 hours ($1000 - 900 - 20$). Note that the cost benefits all the audit work on process A, whatever the software used. Adapting the work plan to SAP costs 40 hours with an expected benefit of 30% more per entity, i.e. 6.3 hours ($9 - 2.7$) for one entity, and 630 hours in total ($900 - 270$), and thus a gain of 230 hours ($270 - 40$). The same analysis on Oracle shows a benefit of 229 hours, on Microsoft an extra cost of 21.5 hours, assuming that the 20 hours have been charged to SAP.

Across the board, the investment in the standard controls generates a benefit of 160 hours for all ERPs combined. Another benefit is that the level of expertise required to perform the work is lower, and therefore assistants are assigned to the work. It is obvious that knowledge management is a profitable investment in general and when the information system is computerized even more so. Knowing that we have a detailed list of controls to be tested by an auditor who connects to the ERP and carries out the work plan by testing each control to extract the results. Is it not possible to automate this work which is still very manual? It would be enough to get the information directly from the software, create interfaces between the system and a system to store and analyze this data (this is what many products on the market offer). Of course, not all the tests on the controls can be automated, nevertheless if 50% of the workload can be removed, it is enough to apply the same reasoning as above and compare the investment of this automation with the reduction of the workload. Let's continue our reasoning, let's assume that all this is in place and that the automated tests of the controls are in place and reliable after many uses. These tests can then be part of the routine audits and some of them can be transferred to the respective process owners. This transfer plays two roles, the first is for the auditors to focus on new tests that are more representative of the evolution of the company's business while improving the routine audit's scopes and the second is to bring added value to the managers who can identify malfunctions early on and not wait for an auditor to intervene. The icing on the cake is that when a control is tested it is for the whole population, it is no longer a question of the relevance and validity of a sample. This eliminates auditing difficulties or risks on the one hand, and on the other hand increases the quality of the analysis and proposals of an auditor.

Test automation changes the way audit work is prepared too. Technically, the technical preparation must be planned in advance and the tests performed remotely, the on-site work is reduced, and the travel costs are reduced. All this is not negligible in the current pandemic environment. This also changes the routine audits, since they are becoming more and more automated, and can therefore be conducted on a regular basis, monthly for example. We end up with a structured approach with lower costs from priority audits to continuous auditing, less expertise required, and faster visibility of the results as shown in Figure 12.4.

This approach is only valid if the auditors have a global vision of the information system with three key documents, the information system urbanization, the application portfolio, and the infrastructure architecture. The term urbanization is a notion that IT specialists have taken up in analogy with cities, as in a city the components are of different natures, they communicate with each other and are used in different ways and all this needs to be managed. It is important to have a presentation of the audit strategy and the technical rationalization efforts of the information system. In the above example, how come the company still has Microsoft in its ERP portfolio, which is used by only five entities for 5% of the global turnover? Does the IT director plan to remove this software package in the long run? Has he planned any other changes that may influence the audit strategy? These are all questions that

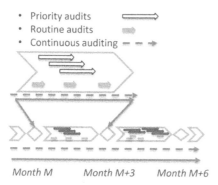

Figure 12.4 Continuous auditing.

should be asked during the semi-annual meeting with the CIO and every quarter to check the progress of the projects according to the plans.

Now let's assume that the ERP is available to all users in the same region or worldwide. The tests can be performed on the whole package in a unique way. It is possible to change some parameters to limit the tests to one entity if necessary. The notion of commitment on several locations becomes purely a financial audit concern. Everything that is shared can be audited at once and remotely. The analysis of the results of the tests, whether financial or operational for example, remains the added value part of the auditor. The rationalization of the definition and relaying of tests highlights the added value of the auditor, which is his ability to analyze the results by considering the company's strategy, its operating context, its current projects, and its operational constraints. Thanks to his knowledge of the company's business, the auditor is known to be able to analyze the tests' results and to propose relevant corrective or improvement actions when dysfunctions are identified. But even without issues, with an understanding of the information system and the current projects knowledge, he can also indicate even if there are no malfunctions identify short- or medium-term potential risks and indicate points of attention to top management. Instead of looking at the past and the present only, he can project himself on the future.

12.3 ACHIEVING REASONABLE ASSURANCE

To project into the future, the information systems auditor must rely on various parameters to obtain reasonable assurance and useful recommendations. First of all, are legal risks considered in both the design and use of the information system? Does the information system used by the company ponder all the foreseeable risks on the one hand and solutions to compensate for malfunctions on the other? Finally, is the technical management of the information system reliable and are the projects managed according to the best practices?

The evolving context of the legal environment must be monitored, but legal risks are external to the company's operations. They must be analyzed essentially when setting up or changing a legal structure, subcontracting, contracting for example. Operational, technical or project audits must integrate these aspects in their scope. The digitalization of business processes makes them dependent on the technical tools used. Operational risks cannot be analyzed without considering technical risks. Figure 12.5 reminds us on the left of the different types of elements of the information system and on the right of the complexity generated by the relationships between these different elements. The arrows are two-way and create a deep vision, so to speak, starting from the workflow to the network elements or inversely from a network element to the elements above.

The complexity is not only induced by these different "layers" but especially because an element of one level can be related to several elements of

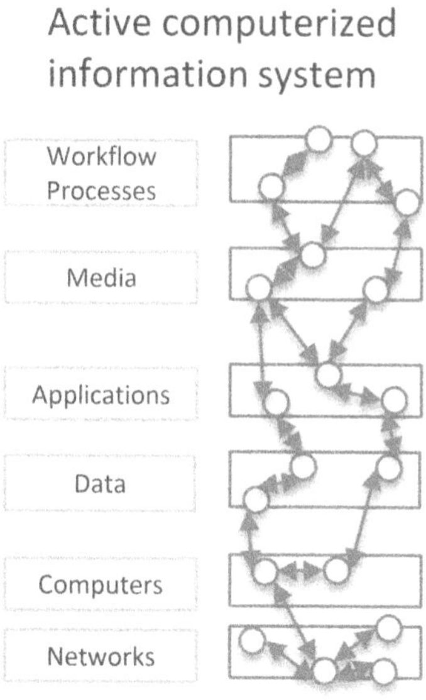

Active computerized
information system

Workflow
Processes

Media

Applications

Data

Computers

Networks

Figure 12.5 Interdependencies of the audits due to the links between the elements.

another level. This means that when looking for the root cause of an error or malfunction, it does not necessarily depend directly on an element related to the one that caused the error. The work of finding a root cause during an operational incident or during an audit is not as quick and obvious as it seems at first sight. Indeed, if the analysis leads the auditor to change "level," she/he needs technical skills for this level. The analysis can lead her/him from the process level to the network level. Side note, now that all the elements are connected by a network, it is common to hear end-users complain and say that it is the network's fault without a reason. Schematically, if an error is found in an application it means that what is displayed is incorrect. The displayed value can be either directly obtained from the database, or calculated in a more or less complex way, such as with only information from the database or from several databases. If the value comes directly from the database, there is a high probability that the application is misconfigured, especially a business rule. If the value is calculated, it is certainly the calculation that is incorrect. So much for the technical reasons. Just as well, it is an unintentional error with this data alone or with others that have been entered incorrectly. Or it could be an intentional error. If it is the case, it can be due to misconfigured or stolen access rights, so we are looking at data towards the top of the schema and it can also be due to vulnerabilities in the network and computer layers that have allowed access to attackers.

December 13, 2021, Lily Hay Newman, senior writer at WIRED titled her article "The Log4J vulnerability will haunt the Internet for years." Log4j is a software logging library from the Apache open source operating system.

It is used by just about every cloud service and enterprise network in the world. Therefore, the vulnerability, publicly disclosed on December 9, 2021, is exposing at least millions of applications and services to attackers. In fact, we don't know exactly the number of applications and services impacted. Evidence suggests that attackers have been exploiting the vulnerability for some time before it has been disclosed. This library is open source and is available to anyone for use when developing a software even within your company. That's why she's is right reminding that it will become a haunting vulnerability. The interesting thing is that this recent event summarizes why we need information system auditors: "The vulnerability allows unauthenticated remote code execution" as explained by Microsoft in December 11, 2021. In short, it is open bar for an attacker. Think about some threat and they will be able to perform it. December 11, 2021, the Cybersecurity and Infrastructure Security Agency (CISA) stated:

> To be clear, this vulnerability poses a severe risk. We will only minimize potential impacts through collaborative efforts between government and the private sector. We urge all organizations to join us in this essential effort and take action.

CISA recommends asset owners take three additional, immediate steps regarding this vulnerability:

1. *Enumerate any external facing devices that have log4j installed.*
2. *Make sure that your security operations center is actioning every single alert on the devices that fall into the category above.*
3. *Install a web application firewall (WAF) with rules that automatically update so that your SOC is able to concentrate on fewer alerts.*

We notice some words while reading this statement. The first is "asset owners," this assumes that one, the assets are known and two, that there is someone in charge. All this is related to the comprehensiveness of the knowledge of all the elements in the information system and among these select those that have log4j installed (CMDB). Then focus the continuous audit on these elements to identify suspicious behavior. And finally, install software that facilitates the sorting of alerts and allows the best use of the analysis time of the cybersecurity and network experts. All this is to save time to install the patch Log4j 2.15.0, published on December 12, 2021. A patch is a correction of the program to get rid of the vulnerability. Action that can only be done properly if the assets that use log4j are known, see action1 of the CISA action plan. Oh, and by the way, December 14, 2021 researchers are reporting that there are at least two vulnerabilities in the patch, since then itself being patched.

In Section 2.3 "IT Impact on Information System" of Chapter 2, we spoke about "the problem of the two texts" from Shoshana Zuboff, the typographic initiative against cyberbullying from TietoEVRY, a Finnish IT software and service company, so let's imagine the result of the following research issued October 30, 2021, applied to shared programs. Nicholas Boucher and Ross Anderson from University of UK

> have presented a new type of attack that enables invisible vulnerabilities to be inserted into source code ... This enables an attacker to craft code that is interpreted one way by compilers and a different way by human reviewers.

But let's come back to our initial example, it is easy to get short-term confidence by auditing the relevant part of the process and analyzing the application level and the data level. To get medium-term trust, you need to do more. Remember that the term "applications" is plural in the diagram; a process can be supported by different applications that communicate through interfaces. These applications can be on the same physical machine or on different machines and therefore use a network, which makes the exchange from top to bottom and from bottom to top go through several layers. The scope of the audit is more important. In doing so, we have only analyzed one of the options mentioned for this example. What about user access rights and privileged access rights, usually called super-user or administrator rights? These rights allow with a perfectly configured software to modify data. These additional tests ensure a better short-term confidence in the operation or malfunction of the process. To get a long-term view, the auditor must be confident in the effectiveness of the routine tests and better in the continuous audit of the network. Routine, but preferably continuous, network audits make it easier to discover unusual network usage. If no routine audit or continuous auditing results can be leveraged, the network must be audited. The same can be done at the application level, Shushana Zuboff's problem of the two texts applied to the Internet also applies to the entire information system of the company. Therefore, it is possible to analyze the traces left by users when they use applications. The auditor may find that the CFO has used the account of an assistant. Indeed, since he/she is on leave, how could he/she have been connected to the system? (see Section 1.2 "Regulation, Controls, and Audit" of Chapter 1). If the risk is important for the company, it is necessary to invest more time to audit a larger perimeter and to obtain a longer-term trust.

But we are still missing an element that can influence this confidence and that has not been considered. It is the management of changes in the information system. An application does not remain in continuous use without being modified. These changes must be prepared, tested, and approved before being applied to the production environment, the one used by the users. These changes, despite the tests, can cause errors in the production environment, which requires either a patch or to remove the changes. This time lapse can create errors that persist and show up in audit results. The auditor will check the configuration of the application but will find that it cannot be the cause of the errors. Discovering the origin of this error is not easy, as many changes may have taken place since then. More simply, it is possible that the error was not seen but as other changes have taken place afterwards, they have unknowingly corrected the malfunction that caused the error. It is an interesting exercise to prove to the tax authorities the financial results obtained at a given moment on the basis of the applied changes. Documentation of the changes, of the tests and the approval process is important.

Obtaining reasonable assurance in audits of companies with highly computerized information systems requires a comprehensive prior analysis during the audit strategy design. This must take into account the automation of work plans. This automation will certainly be progressive because it is not possible to automate everything at once, not only because it costs time and money but also because it requires a good knowledge of the company's business, its functioning and its digital or IT strategy. Being agile and efficient requires anticipation. The realization of a given audit will benefit not only from this automation for the realization of its own work plan but also from the automation brought to other audits in particular with the development of the continuous audit. The available literature on the subject is vast, Section 3.3 "Digitalization" of Chapter 3 has discussed the main techniques to date. The most important change for the audit is that it is part of a set of planned audits to address the risk analysis but also the risks of the complex information system which limits the value of auditing in silos.

This implies on the one hand that the preparation work which was already important is even more important and on the other hand that the duration of the work on site tends to decrease. The preparation work is more important because it is necessary to obtain general information about the information system and to analyze its structure, organization, operations, and cost structure. Its cost structure reflects the value added by those who maintain it (the IT department in the broadest sense) and its overall amount its consistency with the competition in the same business sector. The IT strategy is an interesting audit point for its adequacy with the business strategy and for the ongoing and planned projects. Except for a radical change of teams, the company has no reason to achieve a radical change in its ability to succeed in its projects in the short and medium term. If the projects were historically successful or unsuccessful overall, there is no reason for this to change overnight. On-site work will tend to decrease because most IT solutions do not require an on-site presence to obtain data but only to discuss the results with the auditors. On the other hand, the implementation of these solutions requires preparation efforts, especially during the first implementation. It is necessary to regularly upgrade the solutions as the information system to which they are connected evolves.

Auditing is changing for the better by allowing more time for analysis. The implementation of automated solutions for the auditor's work is already a work of analysis of the company to understand the data, the management rules etc. The work of data collection is simplified because all data are collected, no more time wasted in justifying the size of its representative sample. The analysis work that follows is more relevant because on the whole data, no case will be forgotten. Of course, as the set of data to be studied is vast, the auditor will have to be trained at least in an auditing aid for data analysis and at best to use an artificial intelligence software that will prepare results.

In the end, the auditor's work is valued because more time is spent on action plans, recommendations, and audits.

BIBLIOGRAPHY

NBA: Nicholas Boucher and Ross Anderson, *"Trojan Source: Invisible Vulnerabilities,"* 2021, eprint 2111.00169, arXiv, cs.CR

Index